The Cockpit

The Cockpit
A Flight of Escape and Discovery

Paul M. Gahlinger

sagebrush press

Printed in the U.S.

Library of Congress Cataloguing-in-Publication Data

Gahlinger, Paul M.
    The cockpit : a flight of escape and discovery / Paul
    M. Gahlinger. -- 1st ed.
    p, cm.
    ISBN 0-9703130-0-4

    1. Gahlinger, Paul M.--Journeys. 2. Transatlantic
flights. 3. Transcontinental flights--United States.
4. Air pilots--United States--Biography. 5. Physicians
--United States   I. Title.

TL721.G34A3 2000   629.13'092
                        QBI00-901532

ISBN 0-9703130-0-4

Sagebrush Press
225 10th Avenue
Salt Lake City UT 84103
www.sagebrushpress.com

Love is a power too strong to be overcome by anything but flight.

Cervantes

CONTENTS

PREFACE

In 1992, I set out on a bold, reckless, and poorly planned adventure. I chose to fly, alone, in a small single-engine airplane from California to Africa.

Why? It was a challenge. It was also a desperate attempt to do something meaningful at a time that seemed increasingly meaningless. The possibility that I might lose the airplane or my life did not seem important. I simply felt that there was somewhere I had to go, something I had to find. Flight can be an escape or a venture of discovery. In this story, it is both.

The journey became a metaphor for my life. As I flew east, I felt that I was going back in time. First to the land of my youth, Canada, and then across the Atlantic Ocean in reverse of the emigration of my parents from Switzerland. In Europe, I was drawn back even further in time through the ages of history. From the lonely and distant view of my airplane, I gazed down on the ruins of the ancient civilizations of the Mediterranean. And finally, my journey led me to the very origin of humanity in Africa.

There were more metaphors. The cockpit of the airplane came to stand for life itself. A solitary pilot is so isolated and so remote, especially when flying in clouds or darkness, that the airplane can feel like a space ship, traveling through time and the void. For a while, that cockpit became my whole world. All the instruments spoke to me. We were a platoon of soldiers cowering together in a foxhole, all of us dependent on each other for survival. I came to know each of those instruments in the most personal way. In the end, it was through them, as much as through the many wonderful people that I met, that I was able to understand my journey.

In the dictionary, the usual definition of *cockpit* is given as something like, "the operating space of a pilot in the forward fuselage of an aircraft." It is an odd word for an airplane cabin, but it makes more sense when the earlier meanings are considered. Cockpit first referred to the pit where cockfights were held. These fights are vicious. The high-strung cocks have razors strapped to their spurs. They are coaxed into a blind fury of rage and fear and then unleashed to a terrifying explosion of blood and feathers. Like bullfights and boxing matches, it is all about stuffing a life of bravado into a few minutes of terror. The cockpit became "a place where many battles have been fought, or an arena for struggle." And then the word grew to refer to "an area in a warship where the wounded in battle were brought" —the little room at the front of the ship where life and death commingled, alone and away from the war outside. A place where the only thoughts were how brief, how fragile, how futile a life can be. That little room became the modern cockpit.

Every journey brings the possibility of truly interesting encounters if only the traveler is open to it. I am deeply appreciative of the many kind-hearted people I met, for sharing their homes and thoughts and indulging me in my foolishness. Most of all, I want to thank Lesley Baxter for her editorial support and enthusiastic encouragement. This is my story, but it belongs to everyone.

Paul M. Gahlinger
Johnston Atoll

Chapter 1

COCKPIT

Three o'clock in the morning. The night has cooled, leaving a sheen of dew on the chain link fence at the airfield. I unlock the gate. As my friend Keith and I drive onto the apron, our headlights reveal rows of aircraft standing at rest like so many tethered race horses. At the end of one row is my airplane. A Cessna Cardinal. One hundred and eighty horsepower, single-engine, fixed landing-gear. Not pressurized, not turbocharged or fuel-injected. No oxygen, no autopilot, not even a Global Positioning System. Just a simple, reliable airplane, handmade in 1970 before the economic recession and the liability lawyers made them unaffordable and brought their short production run to an end. Keith helps remove the tie-down ropes and window coverings. He whistles as the open door exposes an interior loaded to the ceiling with charts, survival equipment, spare parts, and other supplies.

"Man! Are you sure you're ready?"

He looks at me with a mix of admiration and sympathy. After months of preparation, he has heard enough about my carefully calculated plans but, as we both know, the journey is just too ambitious to pull off without a tremendous amount of luck. Keith is a reasonable man and this flight, this whole venture, is beyond reason.

I don't know what to say. I don't know if it is going to work. I only know that I have started on a road that I have to follow, whether it ends in success or failure. I also am not sure that I am ready. There is too much uncertainty. My plan is to fly to Africa in this airplane, but I haven't been able to find any record that such a thing has been done before. Everyone I talked to said it was impossible, even suicidal.

"I'm not sure," I answer as I load a cooler of food onto the floor next to the co-pilot seat. "I'm going to try and I guess I'll just see what happens."

Minutes later, I've said goodbye to Keith and climbed into the Cardinal. I've always felt that machines have a kind of life, a sort of consciousness. I sense it the same way that a dog or a horse is conscious. The machine seems to have a peculiar sort of *expectation*—I don't know how else to put it. The rational side of me has put this down as silly thinking; but there is no question, no doubt in my mind after countless experiences, that the man-machine operation is far more than a simple physical interaction.

Now I get a sense from this machine that reflects my own feelings: a slight anxiety, a note of caution and, most of all, a growing thrill of adventure. Yes, we are ready.

Master switch *On*, and the cockpit is instantly flooded in a soft ruby light. A few instruments light up, the numbers take on a phosphorescent glow, and the needles slowly rotate to their positions. Magnetos *On*. Start. The engine cranks once, twice, and then catches into a steady growl. As I scan the panel, the other cockpit instruments jump into place in a low, trembling idle.

Add a bit of power and we ease away from the parking area. The airplane rocks gently as I taxi down the familiar old ramp that leads to the end of the runway. Decades of summer heat have buckled the tarmac and allowed weeds to grow through the cracks. The Cardinal seems to know this airfield and gently slaloms around the bumps. With a tight swivel at the button of the runway, the sweep of my landing light flings a long beam onto the black corridor ahead, framed by tiny red lights. Full power on. My back presses into the seat as the airplane accelerates. The little red lights slide past slowly, then faster and faster, zipping by and then are gone. The corridor falls away to darkness, and I lift off into the night.

I make an announcement into the microphone attached to my headset. A couple of seconds later, the response: "Cessna three zero seven four five, Oakland Center. Squawk two six one four, what heading would you like?"

The air traffic controllers seem unusually relaxed, maybe even happy to have someone to talk to at this early hour. I had filed a flight plan to Reno, skirting the busy central California airports, but they are allowing me a more direct route.

"Oakland Center, seven four five requests direct Reno, heading zero eight zero if available."

"Heading zero eight zero approved. Enjoy your flight."

As I climb, I can see only stars. Beneath me, the great California central valley floor recedes into black. Soon the dark of the ground merges with the depth of the night and the only world is the cockpit.

Two hours pass and the air is calm. I am over the Sierra Nevada mountains of California at thirteen thousand feet, on an easterly heading. Less than two thousand feet below me, ice and rock are dim outlines in the darkness. According to the outside air temperature gauge, it is three degrees below zero. But I am comfortably warm, bathed in a reddish glow from the instrument panel. A thin sheet of aluminum and plexiglass is all that protects me from the frigid environment just inches away. Yesterday I lay under my airplane and scrubbed the streaks of tar and oil off the underbelly of the fuselage. Pressing the aluminum skin, my thumb dimpled the paper-thin metal. Yet here I am, as cosy as a cat in an armchair.

As I look down on the ice, the purr of the engine is comforting and the aircraft feels solid. Smooth. In a few hours, the warmth of day will bring lift to the valley winds and create invisible, growing mountain currents. Like a flooding river, these wind streams will be pushed up the canyons and higher to the ridges and peaks. They will cool as they rise and then fall back into the cirques and couloirs, building, falling and building again until they are a violent, tumbling cascade of air masses. A small aircraft caught in those currents could be hurled onto the rocky slopes. But at this time of night, the air is utterly calm. The cockpit with its warm, rouge luminance encloses me like a womb. The outside world registers only on the instruments. My airplane is like a space ship. An infinitesimal point in endless space. A tiny shell in a sea of infinity and nothingness. The cocoon of the cockpit provides everything. It is a complete world, logical, comforting and nurturing, protecting me from the unknowable universe outside.

⋏

My thoughts drift back to how I started on this journey. The idea first came as a whimsical daydream that I shared with my girlfriend, Amy. We lived in Santa Cruz, California; Amy in a quaint house by the boardwalk and I in an apartment with floor-to-ceiling windows on the cliff overlooking Monterey Bay. Amy was a travel agent. I was a professor of epidemiology and biostatistics at San Jose State University, an hour's drive away in the heart of Silicon Valley. I was not very satisfied with my job, though, nor with the realization that this was probably going to be my work for the rest of my life. Amy listened to my complaints and good-naturedly indulged my fantasy of a new life. Sunday mornings we had brunch at an outdoor cafe and speculated on a very different future.

"I got another letter from Susan in Nairobi," Amy said one day. Susan, Amy's sister, had joined the Peace Corps in the seventies and fallen in love with a fellow volunteer. They married after their return to the United States. But, like so many volunteers, coming home to the fast pace and commercialism of modern America was a big disappointment. They had returned to Kenya and had brought up their children there, Susan teaching school and her husband working for the government.

"She says there would be a lot of opportunities for us. The tourist industry is just booming and you could easily get a job at the university if the airline doesn't work out."

That was my fantasy. We would give up our jobs, move to Kenya and start a science and adventure charter airline. I had all the pieces figured out. Amy knew the travel industry well and had a good handle on the growing, high-end, adventure travel business. I had been trained as a bush pilot in northern Canada and briefly considered a flying career before settling into academic life. We even had our own small aerial tour company, California Ecology Tours. Amy arranged the bookings while I flew tourists along the Monterey and Big Sur coastline in my Cessna Cardinal, keeping up a steady patter of geological and historical information on the land, the tidal pools, and the whales, elephant seals and sea lions we could easily spot from the air. It was fun. I had a great time playing the role of professor pilot. Over Waddell Creek, I would bank above the spot where Mr. Waddell was killed in 1875 by a California golden bear, a now-extinct type of grizzly, and then pull out an old, rumpled copy of the *Santa Cruz Sentinel* announcing his death. We didn't charge much, and barely broke even, but we had a good time and the passengers loved it. It was a logical step to our African airline. We would fly tourists and scientists around East Africa, combining the same mix of sightseeing and natural history. And if it didn't pay the bills, I could get a job at the University of Nairobi. Indeed, I had already been to Nairobi one summer to teach under a university arrangement.

But the truth was, I had no intention of substituting one disappointing job for another one in a third world country at a fraction of my American salary. If I was going to Kenya, I was going for adventure.

"In fact, I have decided that we should fly there in the Cardinal," I told her. "It is a good airplane. It would be much more expensive to buy another airplane in Africa. And the red tape would be a nightmare."

"From California?" Amy looked at me dubiously. I could see that she was not excited at the thought of sitting in a cramped little airplane over the ocean. "Do you really think that's possible? Over the ocean?"

"Absolutely!" The idea had taken root in my mind like an addiction. "Over the ocean. I'm sure it's possible. I've calculated the fuel requirements and it is possible by going up to the Canadian arctic, then over to Greenland, Iceland, and down the North Atlantic to Scotland. I'm sure it would work."

She didn't look convinced.

As my fantasy grew more detailed, it began to take on its own reality. The winter gave way to spring and we sat at little outdoor cafes and made sketches on napkins. To the other diners, we probably looked like a typical couple planning to build a house or a business: a tall, slender man with a neatly cropped beard and Harris tweed jacket with leather patches on the elbows, and a vivacious woman in tight jeans and a winsome smile, giving an uncertain giggle with every new idea. But, if they listened closely, they would hear plans that became increasingly outlandish.

"Remember the Automatic Direction Finder I told you about? Well, the kind they use here in the U.S. is different from the kind you need in Africa. It turns out that I need one with a Beat Frequency Oscillator. But when I went to the avionics shop in Oakland, the guy asked me why I needed it. When I told him, he wouldn't sell it to me! He said there was no way I could fly to Africa in the Cardinal. He said it would be suicide to try and he didn't want to have any part of it."

"Well," Amy gave me that skeptical look again, "has it occurred to you that he might be right? Don't you think he knows a little more than you do?"

"... so I bought one by mail order. Two thousand bucks."

"You spent two thousand dollars on another radio? That you can't even use here? Are you *crazy?*"

It became clear during the spring that Amy's enthusiasm was wavering. Maybe she thought we had played out the fantasy. Maybe she was aware that it *was* a fantasy. After all, we had no access to the sort of money it would take to start an airline. There was also a lot that had been left unspoken about our relationship. Although we had been dating off and on for years, I always edged away from talk about marriage, not ready for a commitment when so much in my life seemed unresolved. In my view, our plans were just a chance to find some adventure. It never really occurred to me that Amy might not feel quite the same way.

There was something else that was driving me, some other longing that did not involve Amy, which I could not explain. I had the sense that somewhere else, there was a rougher, more uncertain world in which I belonged. It was as if I had entered a shopping mall and got too disoriented by all the lights and mirrored windows to find my way back out.

A memory haunted me of an experience I had when I was a teenager. I met a man who had a domesticated wolf, which, he said, was unpredictable and did not like strangers. He would never let people near it. One day at his house, I begged to see the wolf and the man relented. The wolf was larger than I expected, about a hundred and forty pounds, and as he came up to me, he jumped up and put his paws on my chest, staring at me closely with yellow eyes. He had the look of a dog and yet not a dog, and for a moment I was totally confused by a sense of something far away. Some other life that was waiting in a different world. Talking with Amy, I often had that same feeling that I wasn't quite in the right place.

Things were unraveling at the other end as well. Amy's sister in Kenya had encouraged us to come and stay with them while we got the business off the ground, but now her letters were less enthusiastic. Corruption and violence in Kenya were hurting tourism. The war in Somalia, Ethiopia, and the Sudan, and political instability everywhere else, made flying in East Africa especially hazardous. The end to our plans came with abrupt finality. Amy's brother-in-law had a bad recurrence of malaria and had to be evacuated to the United States. Then she got a call in the night to say that he had died. Her sister Susan and the children left Africa immediately to come home to relatives in Philadelphia.

By this time, though, I was too caught up in my fantasy. My position at the university had gradually become intolerable. I was fed up with the constant faculty jockeying for funds and academic perks. The backbiting and pettiness among fellow professors were offensive enough, but the teaching and administrative burden had increased as well. As I became more exasperated with the situation, I started getting careless and outspoken in my opinions about the unprincipled behavior and outright dishonesty that I saw. I was up for tenure and figured my impudence would result in a denial of tenure and probably put an end to my job, but by that point I didn't really care.

Some senior university officials took a different view of this young professor who openly said what they themselves thought. Instead of my ticket out, I was promoted to head of the graduate program. I wasn't up to the challenge. The position came with even more administrative duties and I became a front man for the aggressive intellectuals, a lightning rod for all the malcontents, and a hero to the students who mistook me for a role model. I wanted to get out. Not just from a factory-like university that batch-processed students through a set curriculum. I wanted to get away from academia, from epidemiology and its endless struggle for research funds, from commuting to a job, and from a life that was no life at all.

When you are a child, you have a vision of what you will be as an adult. It can be a dream to work toward, or maybe just something to take for granted. Then one day you realize you are there. You are the grown-up. But it is not the *there* you expected to be. Now you have a choice: either you smile at the innocence of childhood and shoulder the responsibilities of your adult life, or you leave. In my case, the choice, always, was flight.

"There is something I have to tell you," Amy said one evening. I listened patiently when she carefully and considerately told me what I had already long suspected. She had begun to share company with another man. A meek but stable fellow, quite my opposite. "I just don't know," she said tearfully, "but maybe this is better for me ... I'm sorry."

So that was it. I felt the cold draft of bitterness and the whisper of loneliness. For a couple of months I went to work in a daze, my life unraveling even as I tried to stitch together my plans for Africa. I dreaded the drive to the university, knowing the day would be filled with complaints and accusations between students and faculty that I was somehow expected to resolve. In the evenings, I sat alone and wondered about the abysmal life I'd slipped into. As I tried to figure this out, I acknowledged that I had never been committed to my job or to Amy. It was just something that I did out of fear, and so I did it half-heartedly. Fear of poverty. Fear of loneliness.

The playful fantasy with Amy had just been a pretext for something much larger. On some level, I had known all along that I had to make a journey alone, a journey that would lead me to a new life or maybe retrieve something of one that I felt I had lost. Amy was probably aware of this in a way that I was not. As long as I was with her, I wouldn't have had the courage to go. By leaving me, she made it easier for me.

My close colleagues were incredulous when I submitted my resignation to the university. I gave up my apartment, cashed in my retirement account and sold my computer. Planning the trip began to consume my life. I shaved off my beard and cut my hair short.

It was earlier last spring when my plan came into focus. The East African airline idea didn't make much sense, but Africa seemed ever more intriguing. This year, South Africa would be going through the greatest change in its five hundred year history. Apartheid has just been abolished and the world's eyes are upon this country as it prepares for the end of white rule—the first elections in which the non-white majority will be allowed to vote. It would be a great experience just to be there. Flying there in my own airplane would be an incredible adventure.

The University of Cape Town responded with enthusiasm to my letters offering to come and give a couple of lectures on my research. And yes, I would be welcome to volunteer at the university hospital, as I had requested. I figured a nominal position at the university would give me the perfect vantage point to watch the political transformation and the social upheaval that will be sure to follow. The University of Cape Town is the Berkeley of South Africa, a left-wing intellectual center. As I had gone to Berkeley myself, I figured I would feel right at home.

Everyone said the flight would be difficult, maybe impossible. I called the Aircraft Owners and Pilots Association. This organization has half a million members and is by far the greatest authority on aviation matters. If anything exists that relates to flying, they will know about it. But the consultants I talked to had never heard of anyone flying to Africa in such a small airplane and were of no help at all. I contacted the embassies of the African countries I hoped to fly over. Nothing. I spent months trying to acquire the overseas charts and permissions, including a special permit to land at the U.S. Air Force base in Greenland. Every obstacle only reinforced my commitment. The hell with the African flight permissions—I could get them in

Europe. There must be a way. This flight would be the adventure of a lifetime. If I was going to do it, I simply had to go. I finished my preparations and set a date to leave.

⎮

Now, finally, I am on my way. It is a relief to have the long preparation behind me. In an odd way, the trip itself is so much simpler than the planning. Cruising alone, in this quiet night over the Sierras, I think some more about what it means to be in an airplane, in this strange enclosure.

Although the cockpit sustains the body, it was designed for the mind. The body steps on to the aircraft and after a while it steps off, but the journey in between is as much mental as physical. You don't do much physically in a cockpit. Instead, you sit in a cramped room, make a bunch of calculations, twist some dials and knobs and when you come out you are back on the earth. Maybe, if it is clear weather, you look outside at views that no human before this century could ever have had a chance to see. Or maybe, as I do, you spend most of the time daydreaming and otherwise preoccupied with thoughts that come miles above in the sky. The airplane may physically transport you, but it is your mind that conducts the journey.

The design of the cockpit reflects this cerebral function. The panel is like a face. Each instrument with its glass disk is like an eye looking back, with its own individual iris of numbers. Every time I show the panel to someone new to airplanes, I see the same look, like that of a newborn baby gazing on the face of its mother, drawn to her eyes. First there is astonishment—"Wow ... it looks so complicated! "—then gradual recognition as one by one the instruments are explained and become familiar.

The airplane was probably the first machine where the operator had to monitor many different instruments at once. The student pilot is taught to look at each individually and then put all the data together. Each has important information that must be collected in a systematic scan. A great deal of research has gone into improving the design of the instrument panel. Much of it happened by trial and error. In the early years of aviation, panels were designed by engineers, who were more concerned about the aircraft structure and where the instrument would fit most conveniently, than about the pilot. Sometimes instruments that were mentally associated by the pilot were placed on opposite sides of the panel, or even blocked from view by the control wheel. A design that looked good on an engineering diagram could lead to disastrous results. For example, one new model had the landing gear lever placed right next to an identical-looking fuel mixture lever. Reach for the wrong one and ... oops. After quite a number of spectacular and entirely avoidable crashes, the design became more pilot-oriented and standardized so that all cockpits had the same basic layout.

I reach into my flight bag and pull out a candy bar. A Swiss *Linde* with a fine sheet of paneled semi-sweet chocolate. The tin foil reflects the ruby glow and I feel like I am indeed in a space capsule.

At the heart of the cockpit panel is the Attitude Indicator, the instrument with the little airplane that delights children and immediately identifies the panel as belonging to an airship rather than, say, the control room of a train locomotive, a power boat, or a nuclear reactor. Surrounding the Attitude Indicator, in clockwise order, is the rest of the central cluster: the Altimeter, the Directional Gyroscope, the Vertical Speed Indicator, the Turn Coordinator, and the Airspeed Indicator. With minor variations, this is the appearance of the modern panel. Outside the central cluster are instruments that are looked at less frequently. The student pilot is taught to scan the central instruments every few seconds, but it is enough to review the other instruments only every minute or so, depending on their importance and relation to the flight.

After maybe a thousand hours of command flying time, a pilot may lose the deliberate conscious awareness of the instruments. The dials and numbers are no longer scanned systematically, but in groups. Their information is taken in all at once, as a pattern that provides more than the sum of its parts. It is a *gestalt*. It happens instantly and subconsciously. It is a recognition of a familiar assembly, like a chess master who can walk up to a game in progress and see immediately where it is going. The pilot no longer scans, but sees the entire panel and, looking away, can tell you exactly where the needle points on each dial.

I gently bank the airplane to look at the cobweb of lights fringing the darkness. On a moonless night, mountains are sometimes shown only by the absence of light. You know those great shadows are mountains, but you can't see the ground. It is as if the world has become upside down and now valley lights poke up in tiny sharp spikes while the dark masses are abyssal holes.

The entire cockpit is more than just the glass eyes of the panel. It is like a skull. The broad windshield faces the wind like a forehead. The power console is rigid, dominant like a nose and where the nose leads, the body follows. The control wheel slides in and out on its column, lolling like a tongue, talking to you—sometimes tartly, sometimes sloppily in spongy, slow-flight maneuvers. Finally, the rudder petals are like teeth, chewing through air or gritting for a tight landing.

Why, I wonder, do we describe machines like living beings? It is not that we impute human characteristics to them, but rather that we inevitably make machines that look like ourselves. God, it is said, created man unto His own image. We do the same thing. Our whole world view is based on models with ourselves at the center. Don't instruments have a face? In fact, it seems to me, each has more than a face. It has a character. My life depends on these instruments. They speak to me. And if I'm smart, I'll listen.

People like to believe that humans dominate the machine. It's a lie. A bad myth. That sort of thinking has led many pilots to their doom. The truth is that flying, and probably any mechanical operation, is a collaboration between man and machine. And in every collaboration, there is respect. The pilot has to work with the instruments and they, in turn, have all the characteristics of a human partner—at times erratic, cantankerous, even untrustworthy, but generally reliable if treated well. And the moment will come when they will save your life.

The candy bar is gone. Fewer pinpricks of light are visible in the sea of ink below. A string of tiny colons of headlights creep along the Interstate in the distance. Soon, it will be day.

Chapter 2

COMPASS

A feathery light is beginning in the east, edging the mountains below into sharper relief. My route is roughly along Interstate 80 and I am over Donner Pass. In 1846, a wagon train from the east on its way to California arrived here late after a few wrong turns, a lot of personal conflicts, and just plain bad luck. The party of eighty-one pioneers was trapped by snowstorms and drifts up to thirty feet deep. As the winter hardened, they succumbed to starvation, violence, and eventually cannibalism as the remaining members struggled to keep alive. Their diaries are a parable of human desperation, love, brutality, and courage. It is a peculiar, touching combination of bravery and stupidity. Reading their accounts, you find yourself vacillating between awe at their strength and disgust at their squabbling, childish foolishness.

I crank the airplane into a smooth left roll to get a better look at the small valley where the Donner party had camped. Now, the freeway runs right through it in a double serpentine band. The only vehicles in sight are long semi-trucks, staggered in series, laboring up the grades. A large, ghostly form looms into view on the right. It takes me a few seconds to realize that it is Lake Tahoe, enshrouded in mist. The eastern sky becomes brighter and suddenly there is sun glinting off the ice on the peaks.

Reno appears over a rise and I gently slide down toward the lights. The landscape looks completely different from that of just a few minutes ago. The pine forests and alpine meadows are gone and in their place are joshua trees, creosote bushes, and the nakedness of desert. The outskirts of the city look like a mining camp on Mars. Barren, rust-tinted ground strewn with high-voltage power lines and huge rectangular aluminum buildings. It is all rock and sand, with great gashes where new roads under construction are leading to the growing city. In the distance, the twinkling colored neon lights of the casino strip are reluctant to let go of the night.

I tune in the Reno VOR. The Victor Omni-Range is a high-frequency radio navigation system used to direct aerial traffic along the officially designated flight routes of the sky. The station identification comes through in a thin squeal: *dit dah dit ... dah dit ... dah dah dah.* Yeah, that's it, R ... N ... O, the Reno identifier. I reset my course on Elko, toward the other end of the state, and fiddle with the Loran, a long-range navigation radio developed for ocean ships. The sun breaks the surface and I feel its warmth on my face. I settle in for the long flight across the desert. Visibility: hundreds of miles. Long, open spaces with great sweeps of extinct volcanoes eroded into endless valleys. Occasionally, my direct route takes me across the Interstate again and I can see the trucks, now cruising along at eighty or ninety miles an hour. I am doing pretty well myself. The westerly breeze drifting over the Sierras has warmed into a powerful tailwind and I am being swept along at 160-165 knots. Now and then, I catch a real mountain wave and the groundspeed numbers on the Loran flicker 170, 180 ... 200 knots. Two hundred and thirty miles an hour. *Hoooo Baby.* This is the way to travel! A few years ago, I spent an entire day driving from Reno to Salt Lake City, arriving cramped, sweaty, and exhausted from the heat and the monotony. Today, I will make the same distance in less than two hours.

I open my thermos and pour a cup of hot tea into the plastic cap. Last night, Keith ordered a couple of pizzas for my going away party. Now I rummage through the cooler and find the leftover slices I had tucked away. Cold pizza: the modern American breakfast. Under the sloping windshield, the black metal top of the instrument panel is already warm from the sun, almost hot. I lay the slices on it, next to the compass, while I glance at my tea and drink in the scenery. The Nevada desert is a vast basin streaked by mountain ranges with long, graceful shoulders. They remind me of an eighteenth-century Japanese woodblock print. The land forms have an exquisite sensuality from my height, almost erotic, like the graceful slant from a woman's neck to her shoulder. The smooth, sloping curves reveal yet more distant curves, attracting and assuaging the gaze as they carry it out to the horizon.

With each slight correction in my course, the compass hesitates a moment and then dutifully swings over to the new heading. Yes, old friend, I don't look at you much, but you are still the master of the cockpit.

So much of history, it seems to me, is about inventions. I've struggled with a few fat books on the story of civilization and I admire the scholars who can weave the forces of culture, politics, climate and everything else into a tapestry that explains why things happened as they did. But more than wars, it was the development of gadgets—the wheel, the compass, gunpowder, the printing press, the radio—that seem to have changed the course of history almost overnight. The history of humans, I think, is the history of tools, starting millions of years ago when our pre-human ancestors grabbed a stone and beat their rivals into oblivion.

The compass was the first technical instrument of navigation. Around the twelfth century, mariners noted that a piece of lodestone, attached to wood and floating on water, would gently slew around until it oriented itself to the north. From time immemorial, the most important directions had been the rise and setting of the sun, east and west. After the development of the compass, the direction of the lodestone needle, north, became the dominant orientation. In *Feng Shui*, the Chinese art of geographic harmony, north is the direction of knowledge.

It wasn't long before the compass became the essential navigational instrument. The compass housing, the binnacle, had a special place on the ship and was often exquisitely decorated, like a small shrine. Eventually the compass grew more sophisticated and its face was demarcated into 360 degrees. When it was discovered that the magnetic north pole was not the same as the geographic north pole, compasses were made adjustable for the variation and became even more accurate.

The airplane compass is an instrument of elegant simplicity. It is entirely self-contained, consisting of a printed card attached to magnets that align with the magnetic flux lines of the earth. The card is mounted on jeweled bearings and floated in a light oil or kerosene to dampen any motion from the airplane. The thin lubber line on the front is a remnant of its sailing ancestry. It represented the longitudinal axis of the ship and now shows the alignment of the airplane.

For modern flight, however, the compass has lost much of its utility. It has decreasing reliability as you get close to the magnetic poles of the earth, in northern Canada or Antarctica. There are also problems that came about with the high speed of aircraft. The earth's magnetic flux lines cause specific acceleration and turning errors so that the compass is almost useless during the high momentum of aircraft maneuvers. Finally, the metal or electrical components of a cockpit have an influence on the magnetic field, throwing off the compass accuracy, with the result that the aircraft compass must have an additional card, typically shown in tiny print, to specify the needed adjustment for its errant readings.

Despite these shortcomings, the compass remains with us, like a doddering grandfather whose wisdom and experience can be relied upon in time of need. It is used to set or confirm the calibration of other instruments. And, since it is completely self-contained, it can be used as a backup in the event of an electrical failure that would knock out the other instruments. As a holdover from the beginning of the great ships, it has its own special place in the cockpit, not among the other instruments on the panel, but suspended above. I once saw the cockpit of the newest, most technologically sophisticated airliner, the Boeing 777. There, right in the center, above the digital instruments, flight computers, and video electronic displays, was the lowly analog compass.

I remember as a young child seeing my father's compass. It was a beautifully made Swiss military instrument, my father's orientation to the world. With its leather case, jeweled movement, and drop-away mirror for back-course calculation, the compass guided him from farm boy to officer in the army and then to Captain of the Swiss Guards of the Vatican, as the Pope's personal bodyguard. Did he use the mirror, too, to reflect on his change? *Stolz* is the word my relatives in Switzerland used to describe him. By which they meant proud. The pride of the family. *Stolz* is also the word the other villagers used when they thought of the young man who refused his inheritance of the farm and left his home. But they may have meant the other sense of the word. Haughty.

As the oldest son, my father stood to inherit the family farm in the lowlands of Switzerland. But his tall figure, deep voice, and natural charisma attracted the attention of the Swiss army and he was made an officer. He excelled in horsemanship and became the head of the cavalry during the second world war. For a man who loved the great military campaigns, he was unaccountably lucky to sit out the war as an equestrian captain of a small, neutral country. In one of my few memories of him, I hear him mimicking Hitler. "*Die Schweiz*," he thundered, "*Der alte Stachel, Wir nehmen sie auf dem Rückweg!"* (Switzerland, that old thorn, we'll take her on the way back!). Hitler knew his Panzer tanks would take heavy losses in the little mountainous country and shrewdly went around.

After the war, my father joined the Swiss Guard of the Vatican. Then he took his growing family to the new world of America to devote his life to the church, giving talks to colleges and community organizations. My father was a charismatic military officer, a devoted family man, and a dreamer who could barely support his wife and nine children.

Lecturing did not pay much and he worked as a farmer. First as a sharecropper in Wisconsin, where I was born, and then we moved to our own farm, in Canada. He worked feverishly, leaving his wife and young children alone and penniless for weeks at a time while he traveled the country. It was God's work. It pained him to see his family suffer, but so it must be. And then, some might say, God called him home. His fevers and exhaustion were not just due to non-stop farm labor and long drives and sleeping in his car to save a little money between speaking engagements. He had leukemia. Just before he died, he told me to be strong, study hard, and take care of my health. I was five years old.

To a young child, the parent is the sun to his little planet. Warming, illuminating, blinding, at times even scorching; but always there against the darkness. Once a child's parents are dead, they become mythology, no longer human. For me, my father was never human to begin with. He was the ultimate authority. I craved the feel of those mighty arms sweeping me to a giddy height and that deep voice that seemed to shake the walls in resonation. When he spoke with me, I also felt powerful. And when he sat me on his shoulders, I was on top of the world.

With the death of my father, I lost all respect for authority. No uncle, older brother, teacher, or priest had his knowledge or charisma. Authority was nothing but the self-serving manipulations of people or institutions that wanted something from you: obedience, work, money, respect. In the end, I was never sure if what they said was either a lie or their own misinformation. At the age of eight, I stood on a grassy hilltop and challenged God, as the only remaining possible authority, to reveal Himself. The vacant wind told me the answer. I was on my own.

Vast white patches of salt pan are below me now and the sear outline of the Ruby Mountains is on the right. Soon I will be over the Great Salt Lake Desert of Utah. The miles tick by on the Loran. I flip open the lid of the cooler and start munching on some crispy vegetables. Celery. A few broccoli heads. The microphone picks up and amplifies the *krrrch, krrrch, krrrch* of the carrots, so that I have the odd sensation of hearing through my headset the sound of someone chewing. I tune in the pre-recorded weather report, sorting it out from the garble on the voice transmission mode of the VOR. It calls for thunderstorms in the afternoon. Already, I can see the early stages of towering cumulus in the distance. The air is starting to get rough, waking up from the cool night. Not choppy, more like being in a boat on a moderate sea. Sort of an elastic pulling and then letting go, just a bit too fast to be comfortable. With the great time I am doing, I am eager to continue as far as I can. I call in an amendment to the flight plan, to Logan, Utah. It has been four hours since I left and Logan is not far up ahead. I feel ready for a well-serviced airport to get some fuel and stretch my legs.

Logan doesn't look quite the way I imagined it would. Instead of a bustling airport, I cross to the far side of some barren mountains and find an alpine valley in the center of which are the unmistakable outlines of a number of broad runways. Looking closely, I spot a tower and some hangars. Well, the airport directory says it has fuel, so down I go. No sign of life anywhere. No response to my radio requests. Then, just as I touch down, a cursory report:

"Cessna seven four five, Logan active runway two eight, altimeter two niner six one."

Gee, thanks! Taxiing to the airport buildings seems to take forever; it is well over a mile. Obviously, this had once been a grand airport. There is the old control tower, like a great lighthouse, now empty with the wood broken in places but the high glass windows still looking out over the field. It is a little eerie. A bald eagle is standing at the edge of the taxiway up ahead and is staring at me with an almost defiant indifference. He lifts off only when I get to within a wingspan, flapping extra slowly as if to say, "Hey, I was just leaving anyway."

I taxi on to the only new building I can see, the one with the fuel pumps. The moment I pull up, a young man bursts out and comes toward me. I shut down and he immediately starts securing the airplane, waving me away. "Go on inside and get some coffee. I'll fill 'er up." That sounds good enough to me and I go in. A girl of about twenty is at the desk. Her wide-boned features and baseball cap give her a tomboyish appearance. She looks up, smiles, and says, "Good morning. Come on in!" The lounge part of the office has spilled over onto the business side, with the leftovers of a pancake and egg breakfast and coffee cups on the tables and counter. She is manning a complete weather station, with several computer screens flashing and an old teletype printing reports off to the side. The young fellow I met outside, a heavy-set teenager in a plaid shirt and jeans, comes in and both ask me about the flight.

It is warm inside and I relax on the well-worn couch, surrounded by pictures of the early days of the airport. They banter about, apparently doing a good job but not taking their work too strenuously. Probably summer jobs in between high school or college. There are a couple of plates of untouched pastries.

"My mom *always* brings them," the girl says, "it's like, *mom*, what are we going to do with all that?"

"Yeah," the guy laughs. "Help yourself. I sure can't eat 'em all."

They pour out weather information and advice and anecdotes about the local flight conditions.

"Now, you see that canyon? No, not that one, the second one. It doesn't look like it from here, but you can make it up if you angle toward the north. Don't take the first one, a lot of guys have crashed trying to make it out of the valley ..."

Density altitude, I figure. It is a constant worry of mountain pilots. With high altitude, the air gets thin and airplanes don't perform as well and have a much poorer rate of climb. Heat also makes the air thinner. With high altitude *and* heat, the air gets very thin—so thin that you cannot even take off, or, more likely, take off but not be able to climb out of ground effect, the cushioning boost an airplane gets near the ground. Many pilots have learned this the hard way and the result is a common sight around high-altitude airports: the rusting hulks of crashed aircraft that have been stripped of their still useful parts.

With that kind of talk, I am ready to go before the full heat of the day sets in.

Chapter 3

DIRECTIONAL GYRO

I left Logan well caffeinated with a belly full of donuts, crullers, croissants, and eclairs, and a promise to send a postcard from Africa. In the pure morning light, the canyon comes into view just as they described it. I turn and climb carefully between the peaks, looking down at a chevron of arroyos on either side and calculating how I will turn back if I get into trouble. The Cardinal climbs slowly but steadily. I let out my breath in relief as the crest of the mountain slips past below. I am in Wyoming.

Again, an open, seemingly endless expanse of desert. Rock, salt pans, creosote bushes, broken stone and sand. In the full heat of the day, the surface glints and glares and the ground looks like a rubble of kiln-fired pottery. The blacktop highway, with its fine, precise white middle line, cuts the land. It is impeccably smooth, sinuous, almost alive. The highway winds along the contours of the buttes and knobs like a gopher snake seeking clusters of cottonwood trees at a waterhole. But for the most part, the ground below is barren. Maybe a truck stop and then nothing for another twenty, thirty, or fifty miles. Away from the highway, there is no sign of habitation at all. Yet, looking closely, I can see a faint dotted outline across the desert. The scattered, weathered breaks in the sandy crust might be undetectable by a person standing on the surface, but from my view the braided ruts form a halting, struggling course from east to west. It is the unmistakable track of the wagon trains from one and a half centuries ago.

I have always been filled with respect for the early pioneers. It is just unfathomable to me how they moved wagons across this bleak landscape. Most were not even ox-drawn, as the rustic paintings show, but hand-carts pulled by walking pioneers. When people have faith, I guess, they can endure almost anything. They were risking their lives to go into an uncertain world beyond the horizon. West to find their dream. And I am headed east, maybe to find mine. As we pass each other, seven thousand feet and one hundred and fifty years apart, I am aware that I have it so much easier, although the uncertainty is the same.

For one thing, I have much better navigational tools.

To overcome the problems of the compass, a new kind of heading indicator had to be invented for aircraft. This instrument, the Directional Gyro, uses a three-axis gyroscope spinning about eight thousand revolutions a minute and is therefore much less sensitive than the compass to the motions of flight. A child's toy top is a good example of a single axis gyroscope. When it is spinning, its angular momentum keeps it remarkably stable and resistant to outside forces. It was not until the second world war that a gyroscopic compass was designed for small aircraft, but it quickly became the primary directional instrument.

The Directional Gyro, or DG, is amazingly accurate. I remember the training for my instrument rating, when I was told to maintain a heading to within a single degree. "But that's impossible," I complained. "Its compass rose doesn't even show individual degrees, only every five degrees!" The typical DG shows numbers for only thirty-degree segments and longer and shorter bars for ten- and five-degree divisions. "Hell, the needle itself is more than a degree wide!"

My instructor was one of those humorless masters who demanded a higher standard from his students. If the book said proficiency was demonstrated by holding altitude to within one hundred feet, he made you hold it to within fifty feet. "Just look very closely at the needle," he said, "and make only very small adjustments." Sure enough, such a precise heading *could* be maintained and I grew to develop a lot of respect for the DG.

Like any instrument, the DG has its quirks. It is a bit like a brilliant, but hyperactive, teenager. Although highly accurate, it remains so for only a few minutes. Then it gradually drifts off due to the phenomenon of precession, a characteristic of gyroscopes. After a while it needs to be reset by some other reference, usually the compass. It reminds me of the young computer programmers I consulted when I was a professor. These pimply teenagers (who looked like teenagers even when they reached their thirties) could figure out the most obscure programming glitches in my mathematical function algorithms. But if you didn't stay on top of them, they got side-tracked on to some other minor or unrelated item, or even just totally forgot about my problem when the pizza arrived. I like to think of the DG and compass combination as a bit like the old Kung Fu series, where the young warrior can be depended on to go out and kick butt, but occasionally calls on his old master for wisdom and advice.

The gyroscope is typically powered by an engine-driven air pump. This pump sucks the air out of a separate chamber, creating a vacuum so that a stream of incoming air spins the DG and other gyroscopic instruments. A suction gauge, often located on the far right of the cockpit, shows the difference between atmospheric pressure and the pressure in the vacuum system. When the master switch in an airplane is flipped on, that high-pitched whine is the gyros running up to speed. And long after the panel is shut down, you can hear the gently decreasing sigh as the wheels gradually spin down.

As I ponder this, the clouds are building up and the air is getting rougher. Now I feel like a speedboat in a heavy chop, slamming down with each pocket of air. Maybe I shouldn't have eaten quite so many of those pastries. The temperature of the desert floor is probably a hundred and twenty degrees, pushing up convective air currents. Where there is moisture, towering cumulus heads are developing and creating wind shear along their boundaries. I tune in the main airport at Caspar, wondering if I should land and sit it out. It sounds just as rough there and they are predicting worse. I am being thrown around in invisible currents. One moment, I am climbing at a thousand feet per minute—*Whoa baby*—then suddenly dropped as if I've gone over a waterfall. Sometimes the slams come from the side and the Cardinal is knocked over with a wing to the ground. It takes a lot of strength and all my concentration just to keep a heading. The pitching has become so violent, I have to back off on the power to avoid stressing the wings. Each plunge now feels like falling through a trapdoor. All the unsecured items in the cockpit—the cooler, charts, clipboard and camera—lift in unison and crash back as I hit the next current. I'm about to call Caspar to land when I hear the controller:

"All aircraft, Caspar experiencing severe turbulence. Airport operations restricted. Recommend alternate."

"Yeah, no kidding," I want to say. I guess I'll have to ride it out.

There are a few blasts of rain. A sudden whipping of spray that is gone again after a minute. Probably virga, rain that evaporates before it hits the ground. The cumulus is all around and I weave in and out of the fluffy masses, trying to avoid the worst turbulence but not go too far out of my way. But still, it sometimes it gets downright rough. At one point I am shoved up so violently, the force rips the sunglasses off my face. This is really too much. I should not have pushed it so far. I should have waited out the hot afternoon on the ground. If the wings get overstressed, they can buckle from the strain. Crashes due to structural failure are not common, but they happen. I slow the airplane down even more. Maybe too much—now the stall warning horn is shrieking every time I get slammed. Easy does it. I concentrate on the smoothest track through the cumulus, dripping with sweat and my forearms stiff with tension. There is no point in landing now. I have probably penetrated the worse of it.

Gradually it begins to ease up. The clouds are behind me. I can see the Black Hills of South Dakota ahead. I cruise up over the dark pine forests that the hills are named for and start looking for the airfield at Custer State Park. Guessing from my charts and airport directory, it seems like a nice spot to relax for a day and camp out. But I can't see any signs of an airfield. The Loran is worthless now because I am out of its range, too far from the coast where the transmitters are located. And Custer doesn't have a VOR. The only way to find the airport is to look for it in the old-fashioned way, studying the features on the ground. I double back and see a river indicated on the chart and then follow it to a road where the airport should be. I am exhausted, dirty from sweat and strain, and in no mood to play a guessing game about the location of the field. There it is, a pale, open patch in a grassy valley. I drop down for a low pass overhead and see nothing of interest. No buildings, no other aircraft, no cars, just a paved strip in the field. Right now, I want something more hospitable than this and look at the chart again. The county airport is not far away and after a bit more following of the roads, I find it a couple of miles south of the town of Custer.

I land and pull right up to the main hangar, the only site of any activity, and cut the power. Before the propeller stops, a rotund, middle-aged man rushes up to the door. He welcomes me to the airport, and tells me please go into the hangar and help myself to a cold drink—he will take care of tying down the airplane. I thank him and walk stiffly over to the building.

In the shade of the open hangar, a young woman is playing with a baby while keeping an eye on a little girl running around. A mechanic is standing by the wing of a twin-engine airplane, working in a leisurely sort of way among the ducts and wires of the turbo gate and chatting with an older, wiry fellow in a floppy canvas hat, who is sitting on a bench and commenting on everything around him. He turns his attention to me as I enter.

"My name is Leon and I welcome you to our airport." He gives me a mock salute. "What brings you to us?"

"I am just passing through. I've always wanted to see Mt. Rushmore—it's not too far away, is it? I was going to camp out at Custer State Park, but it didn't look like much ... and I could really use a shower."

"Well, you've come to the right place!" he cries. He looks over at the Cardinal and narrows his eyes.

"That is really a pretty airplane, but the tail is awfully large—it looks bigger than the Bonanza." I have never really noticed this before, but it is probably true. Because of the innovative design of the Cardinal, a large vertical stabilizer was required. I am about to explain some of this, when the mechanic interrupts and patiently outlines the advantages of a large tail. I get the impression that Leon is one of those characters that you often see around airports: a bit slow-witted, but friendly and harmless, with a childlike fascination with aviation. Some pilots, especially the corporate bizjet jocks, tend to have little patience with the guys they call hangar rats. But most fixed base operators and pilots don't mind them, maybe because they are a reminder of the excitement flying once held for them, too, before it became a job.

I tell Leon some more about the airplane and what I am doing. Virgil, the good-natured airport operator, joins us bringing a dozen iced cans of beer and we all talk for a while. Virgil says I can camp wherever I like and gestures to a woodsy glade just off the runway.

Leon says he is going into Custer and offers me a lift. As we drive in, he asks about me and I explain about my job as a professor and epidemiologist, leaving out the fact that I have left it.

"So you're going to be here for a couple of days? You're going to need some wheels. If you drop me off in Rapid City, you can have the car. Just leave it at the airport," he says, to my amazement.

Rapid City turns out to be an hour's drive and it is my turn to learn something about him. My initial impression of this modest man couldn't have been more wrong. Leon was a dentist and built up a network of satellite clinics in rural South Dakota. Now he has become quite wealthy and spends his time checking on his holdings. The twin in the shop is his—he prefers to have it serviced by his old friend, Virgil, and to have an opportunity to sit around now and then and talk about flying.

On the return from Rapid City, I stop off for a swim and shower at a motel and then take the opportunity to visit Mt. Rushmore. It is near sunset when I pull up, park the car, and hike the short distance to the viewing area. Most of the tourists are gone. The mountain itself seems both smaller and yet more impressive than I expected. Photographs I've seen are always taken close up, making the monument look imposing against the skyline. In fact, it is quite subtle among the other mountains. The faces of the presidents are remarkably smooth, with meticulous stonework. The silence of the faces is palpable in the failing light. I stand there, pleased to be alone to get a sense of the place. An older man walks across the plaza toward me. For a minute, I think he is a caretaker, about to ask me to leave. Instead he says, "Beautiful, isn't it?

"You know," he goes on, "people think they built this place just for tourism—just another monument. That's not true at all. They chose this place because it was so far away from any city. Most of the guys who did the work didn't even get paid. The blasting and cutting was done by miners who came here after working their shift."

"You seem to know a lot about this place," I say, a little lamely.

"It was all Gutzon Borglum's vision. He never saw it finished. You know why he chose those presidents? Washington, Jefferson, Lincoln, and Roosevelt. It is really symbolic: the birth, the growth, the preservation, and the development of America. That's why I come here every year. You don't see too many people thinking about that anymore."

AUGUST 15: CUSTER, SOUTH DAKOTA

I wake up comfortable and refreshed in my tent at the airport. Today, I'm going to drive south to Wind Cave, reputedly the third largest cave system in the United States and seventh largest in the world. But first, I head into Custer for breakfast. The Chief restaurant is a huge dining hall lined with curios, plastic ferns, and velvet paintings of native Indian scenes. I order a proper mid-Western morning meal: eggs, flapjacks, bacon and sausages, wholewheat toast and, just in case lunch is delayed, a large wedge of blueberry pie.

What is it about caves, I wonder, that holds such a fascination for people? Despite the popular notion of the "cave man" as our ancestor, in fact it is unlikely that people ever spent much time in caves. Early humans probably lived in hide tents, or shelters made of branches, moss, and mud. Caves are dark, damp, and cold, with no ventilation, and are a very poor choice for a home. But when our ancient predecessors did visit a cave, they left behind artifacts that were naturally preserved, while their open-air tents and shelters have long since crumbled to dust. And despite the lack of any good reason to do so, it seems that early humans did visit caves, even quite deep ones.

My guess is people have always been attracted to caves because they stand for the opposite of life. They are the place you go to die, or to be reminded of death. They also signify the subconscious. Mythology around the world speaks of traveling to the underground to retrieve the soul. As you pass the twilight zone of the entrance to descend into the cool, dim chambers, the sharp smell of earth tingles your nose and your voice has a slight echo, as if you were inside a drum. In a natural, unmodified cave, you climb, slither, crawl, or wriggle through rooms or cracks that are chaotically irregular. Your headlamp illuminates only a small area in front of you and the shadows glance and change with every slight movement. It is thrilling and frightening. You want to go back to the warm light of the surface, but you can't resist going deeper.

It is evening back at the airport and I crawl into my sleeping bag, reading Nabokov's *Pale Fire*. I had read the first part, the poem, once when I was teenager, but now I'm fascinated by the rest of the book. Its hero lives in a dream world—or does he? Or is there, I wonder, really that much difference? I like to think that I can shape my reality. I think that if I work hard enough I can realize my dreams. But if I can't, does that mean I live in a world of illusion? Or simply that I haven't worked hard enough? So much of growing older, I realize, is not a matter of changing reality but of reconfiguring your dreams. And if you are lucky, somehow the two will come together.

The light is now too weak to read. I plan to leave Custer early tomorrow. The airport elevation is almost six thousand feet. I want to take off into the cool, calm air and hopefully make it to Canada by late afternoon. With that thought in mind, I set my alarm for four in the morning.

Chapter 4

CLOCK

At about three A.M., I hear a soft tapping of footsteps outside
the tent. I peek out and see a few deer in the moonlight, their
mottled coats almost camouflaged in the dappled shadows of
the pines. I settle back for a bit more sleep and then hear a
chunky clatter of car doors and human voices. I listen, half-
dozing. From the sounds, I guess a man is leaving and his wife is
there to see him off. I am awake now and might as well get
started too.

In a few minutes the tent and sleeping bag are rolled and
I carry them to the ramp. I nod to the other pilot as he climbs
into his aircraft. With a penlight in my teeth, I do a brief walk-
around inspection of the Cardinal—fuel tanks, oil, cables, surfaces,
vents—checking everything. Then I climb aboard. Master switch
On. The instruments wake up and each needle jumps to its
proper position, shifting back and forth slightly and then resting, fixed in expectancy, like a tennis player waiting for a serve.
External navigation lights, *On*. Anti-collision lights, *On*. The
red beacon at the top of the tail flashes like a traffic light in a

one-stop prairie town. It bounces a startled reflection from the aluminum hangars and then is joined by the white strobe of the second airplane in a dance of echoing lights. The engine of the other airplane roars to life. With the sudden noise, the deer jump in a reflex relevé, but don't run far. They're used to airplanes.

The other pilot taxis to the far end of the runway and takes off. I follow a few minutes later, climbing slowly in the thin air. The moonlight sheds a soft albedo on Mt. Rushmore and the neighboring hills and meadows where I saw herds of buffalo yesterday. For a moment, I am transfixed by the beauty, the gentleness of the light over the sleeping countryside. I bank slowly to the east and settle in for a long cruise in cool quietude.

Below, the dark forests give way to the lighter desert and canyon land—the famed Badlands. With the gray light of the coming dawn, they have a chalky appearance, winding gullies and chiseled canyons between towering spires and jagged rock. Then fingers of farmland begin to probe among the canyons, thickening and eventually spreading into the palm of the Missouri valley, beyond which is revealed the river itself, vast and calm.

The radio is picking up commuter airline traffic. The usually terse communications of air traffic control seem relaxed, more informal, and it is obvious that the controllers and pilots know each other personally.

"Delta five oh level at two two zero. Say John, are you gonna be over on Saturday?"

"Roger Delta five oh, maintain flight level two two zero and continue Victor one four eight. Yeah, I better check it with Betty, though."

Now the arid country is polka-dotted with large, circular, irrigated fields. Dark disks on a tawny landscape, with a thin, silver-wheeled irrigation pipe extending in a radius from the center to sweep the field like a quarter mile long windshield-wiper. The disks multiply and then come in honeycomb sheets. And then the drylands are gone, replaced by farms and hamlets with the occasional town or small city. A patchwork quilt. I still have hours to go before my refueling stop in Decorah, Iowa, a place I picked for no reason except that the name sounds nice. I put a tape into the deck which I had hooked up to the intercom. Talking Heads, *True Stories*. Full blast. Through my high-quality headset with the liquid-filled ear seals, the music turns the cockpit into a concert hall.

I am rocking to the beat and feel a wave settling over me of pure happiness. Even the occasional radio communication breaking through seems to add to the music. Every cell in my body is radiating in that single moment when existence is perfect. I have the sense of complete peace and understanding. Everything is true, everything is real. All you sleepy people waking up in farmhouses down there, I want to shout, Don't be discouraged. Look around you! Life is *wonderful!* At the last song, I almost weep with the lyrics,

> *We live*
> *in this city of dreams,*
> *We drive*
> *on this highway of fire.*

For the next couple of hours I stay bathed in that glow of happiness, thinking whatever happens, at this moment my life is complete. This journey, this cockpit, myself: it is all that there is. Everything else is either a memory or an expectation. I am alive. Anything else is an illusion. This sense of *being* is all any living thing ever really possesses.

A moment of time. That is all we have. Normally, this thought makes me slip into despondency as I think of how short, how evanescent life is. Here, over the land of the great Indian chief, Crowfoot, I remember his dying words:

> *What is life?*
> *It is the flash of a firefly in the night.*

It is the breath of a buffalo in the winter time.
It is the little shadow which runs across the grass
and loses itself in the sunset.

There is nothing more sad or more true. But my mood is too upbeat now to be pulled into this melancholic reflection. I tackle it head on. Okay, so life is just a moment. But that moment is elastic. How is it that a minute of sky diving free-fall can seem like an eternity, when years of work slip away in the blink of an eye? I see passing years and decades and an aging body, when I should be looking out instead at the incredible fluorescent beauty of the world. When I hear people lament their lost time, and listen to myself bleating the same complaints, it is a loss not of what was, but of what might have been. My guess is that people want to be immortal, or re-incarnated, because they want more time to do something they haven't done yet, which is to really live. To live to the fullest. What we all really want is not life time, but the time of our life.

人

Time in an airplane, on the other hand, is an entirely different matter. The cockpit is run by the clock. At least one analog clock with a sweep second hand is on the panel and often a second, digital countdown clock is mounted on the control wheel. The clock is the metronome of the avionic orchestra. There is almost nothing in an airplane that is not time-regulated with its own adjustment schedule.

The clock is also the mainstay of all navigation. This is true because of simple arithmetic: Speed equals distance divided by time.

Therefore *distance*, which is what navigation is all about, is *speed multiplied by time*. This very simple equation may sound trivial, but it caused the rise and fall of empires, changed the course of human civilization and created the global political organization of today. It is even the reason why I, as an American, am writing this in English—rather than French, say, or Spanish, or Chinese.

To know distance, you need to know speed and time. Speed is quite easy to measure in an arbitrary sort of way: it is just the movement of one thing relative to that of another. The ancient mariners had no problem with that. They attached a float to a rope with knots at measured intervals. Then they threw it overboard and counted the number of knots paid out on the rope during the emptying of an hourglass. Today, on sea and in the air, the unit of speed is still the knot. One knot is one nautical mile per hour. One knot, or nautical mile, is also one minute of latitude. So even now, the earth is measured by those knots on a rope.

Measuring time was another problem entirely. Big chunks the size of a day were easy enough, but shorter intervals proved fiendishly difficult. Galileo measured brief durations by counting his own pulse—not a bad idea so long as you don't get too excited by what you are timing. The invention of the pendulum clock was the first big breakthrough, but clocks were ponderous and needed stability, not very suitable for a rolling ship. Clocks also gradually lost accuracy as the pendulum slowed, or as the metal contracted and expanded with changes in temperature. A more accurate clock was needed for navigation.

An accurate clock was specifically needed to calculate longitude. Latitude and longitude are the imaginary grid lines used to locate any point on the surface of the earth. Ptolemy in 150 AD had already devised such a system, with the zero line at the equator. After the end of the dark ages and the start of the Renaissance in the fifteen century, the sea-going countries of Europe became excited by prospects of trade with, and plunder of, foreign lands. But, first, they had to get there. Each country had its own version of the Ptolemaic grid lines. With a sextant to determine the angle of the sun and stars, latitude was easy to calculate, but to calculate longitude, they needed to know the exact time as well. For ocean voyages, accurate time keeping became the limiting factor in navigation.

An enormous effort took place among the colonial powers of Europe to develop a clock that was precise enough to allow accurate determination of longitude. The victor in this race was England, which is why Greenwich became the longitudinal reference point and a major reason why Britannia went on to rule the waves. Ultimately, it is the reason why the mostly widely spoken language in the world today is English.

In an aircraft, the timepiece serves a number of functions. The clock is the policeman of the cockpit. He is the good cop who stays in the background, but when there is a problem he lays down the law. Other instruments might malfunction and you can rap your knuckles on the glass plate or just slap a placard over it to ignore it, since an inaccurate instrument is worse than no instrument at all. But you don't argue with the clock. For that reason, I have up to half a dozen timepieces in the cockpit: in addition to the panel-mounted clock, there is a stick-on clock set to local time, a digital timer on the control column, a glow-in-the-dark travel alarm and, of course, my wristwatch. The main clock is usually set at Greenwich, or Universal Time, called Zulu in air traffic control. This avoids the problem of time zones, which can pass quickly at the speed of modern aircraft.

Where the clock really comes into its own is during instrument flight, when it is used for reporting points, holding patterns, and non-visual approaches. When you are heading to an invisible runway at two hundred feet per second, believe me, time matters.

Now my stomach rumbling tells me it is almost lunchtime, so we must be getting close to Decorah. This part of Iowa is classically rural America. Incredibly green fields and forests on rolling hills, with pretty, red-brick farm houses and wooden barns. I touch down on the smooth, paved runway and feel like

I have dropped into a Grant Wood painting. Everything looks so carefully tended, from the tidy country roads and hedges to the neatly plowed acres. The runway lies in a manicured field of clover. Horses stand nearby and cows chew obliviously in the distance. For a minute, the unnatural stillness makes me think the airport might be deserted, but I see a tractor-mower trimming the grass near the hangar. I pull up next to it. The driver is a plump woman in checkered gardening clothes with her hair in a kerchief. She waves me on to the hangar, a meticulously clean building with planted petunias along its borders.

The door says Pilots Lounge. I leave the airplane parked by the fuel pump and lug my cooler inside. The lounge is clean and air-conditioned, well-stocked with cold drinks and flying magazines and a direct telephone line to the weather information service. A man in blue coveralls walks in and introduces himself as the owner and mechanic of the airfield. That's his wife on the mower and they run the place together. I tell him how pretty Iowa is, like a painting. He doesn't know who Grant Wood is. When I mention *American Gothic*, he guffaws, "Yeah, that's me alright."

I make a lunch of most of the remaining food in the cooler and use the telephone to get a weather update and file an international flight plan. Then I take a leg-stretching stroll around the airfield outside. The scene is wonderfully bucolic—hay fields with large round bales dotting the freshly cut stubble, old barns and silos, a gabled farmhouse with the big front porch—it is an image of American farmland nostalgia, when the reality, nowadays, is more likely to be agribusiness and migrant labor.

It reminds me of my childhood. Not the truth, maybe, but the image I carry in my mind. I also grew up in a red brick farmhouse, with plowed fields, a little forest, and the wind soughing through the orchard. But it was not quite so pastoral.

My parents were born in Switzerland, the product of a quaintly Swiss heritage. My father grew up on a small farm, herding cows, goats, and sheep to the alpine pastures. My mother was the daughter of a cheese maker. What they had in common was their ambition to move beyond their humble origins and to emigrate to America. In a mountainous country, whether it is in Europe or the Himalayas or the South American Andes, there are not many ways to survive. Only one child can inherit the family plot of land. For men, the other traditional options are the military and the monastery. As it happened, my father chose the first and an uncle chose the second.

After my father had achieved his goal to become the leader of the Pope's private militia, he was inspired by visions of farming in America, the land of growth and opportunity. My parents emigrated in 1952, but, unable to afford even a small holding, they became sharecroppers. This almost feudalistic arrangement allowed the great waves of European immigration to the United States. The newcomers were asked for nothing but their labor and were given little except a place to live, a fraction of the fruits of their work, and a hope for a future for their children. Which was, nevertheless, considerably better than what they had left behind.

I was born in Wisconsin while my father ran a dairy for an absentee owner. A couple of years and many moves later, my parents found inexpensive land in Canada and settled down to their own farm and growing family of nine children. The vision had reached maturity, but nature had other plans. The winters were vicious, with blizzards that seemed to last for weeks and cold more intense than anything they had experienced in Europe. Wild animals killed the sheep. When equipment broke down, it was a long way into town and the neighbors, from a dozen different countries and speaking English no better than my parents, were virtual refugees themselves and not inclined to be generous. This was not Switzerland, with its dependable climate, tight social organization, and short walk to a nearby village. They persevered. Then, just when things started to improve, my father died. It was our good luck to have a mother who was determined and shrewd enough to keep our family together and to marshal every resource to succeed in that heartless country.

Replenished, refueled, and invigorated, I climb back into the Cardinal for a flight back in time, to the land of my youth, Canada.

Chapter 5

ATTITUDE INDICATOR

"Cessna three zero seven four five, this is Green Bay Radio. Do you read?"

Finally. I filed an international flight plan in Decorah, planning to continue on over Wisconsin, Lake Michigan, and across the border into Canada. But, once in the air, I have had trouble contacting the flight service station to activate it and thought I would just let it go for a while. Now they are coming through nice and clear.

"Three zero seven four five reads you five five. Could you activate my flight plan please?"

"Roger seven four five. Report crossing the border."

"Thanks Green Bay. Wilco. Seven four five."

At nine thousand feet, the city of Milwaukee materializes underneath. It isn't quite the brewing capital it once was, but I can easily smell a yeasty aroma drifting up from the factories. A funny thing about flying is how smells loft up above the countryside. Over Texas, I sometimes felt like I was right in a cattle yard and once over Gilroy, California, the odor of garlic was so strong I could smell it in my clothes hours later.

The shoreline of Lake Michigan marks the end of the land. In the thick haze, the light blue of the water merges imperceptibly into an identical light blue of the sky and soon I am suspended in a cerulean world where I can no longer make out direction, up or down, front or back. An envelope of blue that has no depth, nothing to focus on. I have a tiny thrill from the feeling of complete disorientation. But I only need to look at my instruments to know exactly where I am.

The attitude indicator, often called the artificial horizon, is the primary instrument when flying without a natural earth horizon. For that reason, it is smack in the center of the panel. The instrument shows the aircraft's *attitude*, its position relative to the world outside. The little airplane in the window banks or tilts to show the way it approaches the horizon. If the little airplane's wings are banked or the nose is high, that doesn't mean that the real airplane is turning or climbing—only that that is your position relative to an outside world you cannot see and it is up to you to do something about it.

Now the little airplane indicates that we are in stable, level flight and I easily calculate that the eastern shore will be reached in eighteen minutes.

Seventeen and a half minutes later, the blue begins to split and a shoreline is drawn through the haze.

My father died at thirty-nine, the age I have just achieved. After his death, my mother continued to run the farm as far as possible, leasing out some of the land, and as soon as my brothers and sisters were old enough, they were sent out to work to bring in some money. I was the middle of nine children and began picking crops when I was eleven. By fourteen, I was missing a lot of school to help support the family. I worked for other farmers and lived in their barns, since I was not old enough to drive. At fifteen, I went to work full-time.

I didn't mind leaving school. The Catholic school was run in strict fashion by monks, the Brothers of St. Louis. I hated having to sit inside when there were so many other interesting things to do. Outside, the rabbits were running, the birds were soaring, and I was jammed into a plywood desk with a speller. It felt like a prison.

I had a lot of friends, farm-toughened, some of whom had it a lot harder than I did, with an alcoholic father who beat them or jobs that gave them a permanent stench of manure and the slaughterhouse. We tried to ride the young bulls, dodging their horns when we fell. We played games, such as seeing who could hold on to electrical cattle wire the longest, trying to look nonchalant every time the shock hit our arms like a sledge hammer. If anyone showed a hint of pain or fear, we mercilessly taunted and ridiculed him.

With that kind of fun, punishment at school was no ordeal. I had learned to ignore pain. On the farm, if you hurt yourself, the other laborers thought you were stupid. Or worse, that you were looking for an excuse to get out of work. If you cried or whimpered or showed any sign of pain, they laughed at you. Later, as I grew older, I laughed myself when I got hurt, as if getting injured was a slapstick joke. I learned a couple of useful things about pain. First, pain goes away eventually, usually faster than you think. Second, the amount of pain and the actual injury don't always go together. I found, as any boy knows, that getting kicked in the testicles can be a nauseating agony even when there is no real injury. But when I once had a pitchfork stabbed entirely through my foot, it was oddly almost painless. So if you yell and scream over what turns out to be a mild injury, you will only embarrass yourself among your coworkers. And that is one thing that has always amazed me: there are few forces stronger than the threat of embarrassment.

There is no point in fighting pain, or in trying to deny it. You simply acknowledge it and leave it alone. The pain may still exist but it doesn't seem to hurt as much. Time and again, my school friends and I would be called into the principal's office for our unruly behavior. As the red-faced monk slammed the leather strap on our open palms, it was all we could do to restrain our laughter.

When I was in the seventh grade, the teachers organized a chess tournament. I was a poorly attentive and barely average student, but I had learned to play chess and I liked the challenge. The whole town was caught up in the competition. A pretty trophy was bought and put on display with the name plate blank. The wealthier kids had private lessons and the monks surreptitiously tutored their favorite students. I hunted down every book I could find for playing strategy and clever gambits.

To the consternation of the monks, I won. They decided that the contest had not been adequately prepared and that they would hold the "real" contest a month later. When I won it again, they were furious that this kid who was such a bad example was ruining their plan to showcase the clever students. Again, they nullified the results and decided to have the tournament at the end of the school year. By that time, it was clear that I would not be returning in the fall. Like a couple of my classmates, I had to drop out to work, but I had little regret in leaving. There was a mutual contempt between the monks and me and it wasn't helped when I began to wear an old army jacket on which I had stenciled the words KING KONG DIED FOR OUR SINS.

When I won a final time, the principal determined that, since I was no longer a student, I was technically not eligible for the trophy. The following year, interest drifted away and the tournament was forgotten. The trophy, its name plate never imprinted, ended up in the garbage.

⏄

Flying over Michigan, some of the bitterness of childhood seeps through me. It has been a long time since I was in Canada and now that I am crossing the border to my boyhood home, the memories come flooding back.

"London approach, November three zero seven four five is with you over Sarnia at five thousand five hundred."

"Cessna seven four five, London Approach. We have your flight plan. You are cleared for landing on zero nine. Report left downwind to tower, one one nine decimal four."

Such a nice welcome. Quite the opposite of my first twenty years in the country. With only a grade school education, I was limited to whatever unskilled work I could find. When I applied for anything more than a labor job, the answer was always the same: you are not qualified for the job because you didn't finish school and if you want to finish school you have to start where you left off. Canada did not have equivalency pathways. Once you were pegged as an uneducated laborer, you stayed there.

I did try to go back. My mother helped me by talking to the nuns at a nearby Catholic high school, convincing them that her boy deserved a chance to try the ninth grade.

The old school stood next to the railway crossing in the industrial town of St. Thomas, Ontario. On September 15, 1885, the great Barnum and Bailey circus came to the town, with the largest elephant in the world, an African giant named Jumbo, from the Swahili greeting, *Jambo*. It was a foggy night and the elephants were disoriented in the rail yard, trumpeting in fear. As Jumbo ran along the track toward them he was struck by an on-coming train. I could see from my classroom to the site where Jumbo died and I felt a tremendous sympathy for him. Captured from the African savannah, shackled, shuttled around dreary industrial towns, and then killed during a final valiant gesture.

My brief time in high school turned out no better than my earlier experiences. Once again, the combination of missed school and stifling classrooms was unbearable. I left after a year, sorry to have let down my mother and my teachers' expectations.

The economy was bad and unemployment was high. Between work, I read a lot, especially Solzhenitsyn and George Orwell. I became so obsessed with Orwell that I read every one of his books and the four volumes of his published letters and diaries (years later, I went to Spain to visit the scenes he described in *Homage to Catalonia* and even slept in the same seedy hotel rooms). From age fifteen to eighteen, I often hitchhiked to nearby universities and walked among the ivy covered buildings. The freedom of being out of school had worn off and I missed the enjoyment of being allowed to study in clean, comfortable surroundings. To me, the universities were a refuge where people worked for the pursuit of knowledge, not just to get a bigger house or a four-wheel drive truck. I gazed at the pretty girls playing tennis in short white skirts. I was terribly shy and didn't know how to play any sports. Instead, I slunk around the lecture halls, occasionally joining a class on population genetics or film history. Sometimes, a kindly professor would beckon to me, "Come, come in. Sit wherever you like. You don't need to be registered to join my class." Sometimes, I provoked the curiosity of the other students. "You mean you're going to these lectures and you're not even getting *credit?*" a buoyant young woman exclaimed when I sat next to her in an astronomy course. "I wish you could take this course for me!" I did, too.

Until I was eighteen, I worked on farms, living either in a tent or the barn. Barns, in particular, are very pleasant places to read: quiet, large and open with the fragrance of alfalfa and sage. The rats become almost tame after a while. I would look up from a book to see one sauntering across my old mattress on the hay, stopping to sniff at my little toe, and moving on with its postman-like rounds of the neighborhood. Reading, anything and everything, kept me going as I hitchhiked between farms to follow the growing seasons of different crops.

I graduated from hitchhiking around Ontario to traveling thousands of miles across the country, joining the great baby-boom diaspora of the sixties and seventies, when every young adult, it seemed, shouldered a backpack and put out a thumb. There was an oddly self-imposed etiquette in hitchhiking: you couldn't stand too close behind someone else and you certainly couldn't stand in front of someone. I remember walking to the outskirts of Sudbury to thumb a ride west on the trans-Canada highway. As I trudged past the line-up, I counted over seventy individuals, couples, and occasional threesomes, each with their brightly colored frame packs and sleeping bags, standing at their posts a dozen yards apart, patiently waiting for their lucky ride. The end of the line was almost a mile away and I thought I would never get out of there, but no sooner did I reach it than a pickup truck pulled over.

"Jump in, son. I figured the guy at the end waited the longest, so I picked you."

Hitchhiking took a long time and one day when I saw a freight train slowly trundle past the road, I vaulted aboard. That was much better. Freights covered an enormous distance and you could actually plan your trip if you learned their times and destinations from a friendly railyard worker. I discovered one thing right away: the stories of hobos in boxcars may or may not be true, but hopping into a moving boxcar is a very awkward and dangerous way to jump a freight. If you miss, your legs might swing underneath the wheels, with gruesome consequences. If you get in successfully, you rattle around in a wooden crate with only a half-open door to look out of—and heaven help you if someone should slam it shut. The best way to take a freight, I quickly realized, was to grab the low-hanging steel ladder of a tanker car. The recessed ends of these cars provide a comfortable shelter with a superb view on either side. And for a really spectacular view, you can climb the steel rungs to the top. Sitting up there, twenty feet above the ground and rolling across the prairie, you feel as if you are on a great ship on an ocean of grain. Sometimes the train crew let me ride in the secondary locomotives, with their roomy cockpits and gangways on the outside. Standing at the rail of one of those thundering leviathans, I could only feel sympathy for the hitchhikers on the road.

⊥

It feels strange to remember that time now. Bright Canadian flags flutter as I taxi up to the terminal in London, Canada. The customs officer is polite and smiles with approval when he sees the toys I have brought as gifts for my nieces and nephews. He waves me through without checking the airplane or even my identification. My mother and oldest sister, Maria, are waiting by the parking lot. After hugs, exclamations and a little ribbing, we drive into the city. My mother now lives alone in an apartment. I have the feeling that I am really visiting her and not just returning to a family home. It is a chance to see her as an individual, in her own place as she likes it, rather than as a mother concerned more about her children. It is also a chance to have plenty of time to talk without having countless other demands and interruptions. I need a rest and take advantage of her hospitality. For a couple of days, I lie around happily indulged and reminiscing on the changes since my youth.

AUGUST 17: LONDON, CANADA

I am curious to have a look at the old farm from the air, so this morning I take off for a local cruise. In twenty minutes I have covered all the ground of the first couple of decades of my life. As a pilot, I am used to seeing land forms from an aerial perspective. But I am unprepared for the experience of seeing the entire world of my childhood zip by in a few minutes. The town passes in an eye blink and I am already over the farm. Turn and bank to have a look and I am almost ten miles away over Lake Erie. It is necessary to slow the plane down, drop some flaps, slower, lower, more flaps, a bit of power, and slower yet to a nose-high chugging plow through the air. This time I come up about six hundred feet above the town. In the film, *2001: A Space Odyssey*, there is a scene at the end where the astronaut returns as a fetal astral body to gaze upon the planet he left behind. I feel like that astronaut. The tiny town below hardly seems to have changed, but I look down as if I am staring into one of those glass ball Christmas ornaments, picking out the church and school and the streets I walked, to the fields and the farms and ... Hey! Where did all these houses come from? Scattered bits of suburbia dot the land. Our family farm, once remote, is now half engulfed by tract housing of neatly land-scaped ranchettes. The old brick house is still there, but it looks dilapidated and almost hidden behind the newer buildings. The orchard has completely gone, the swamp has been drained and is overgrown, and the only remnants of the once dense forest are just a few thin trees. I jam in the throttle and rocket out of there.

Chapter 6

Turn Coordinator

California has the colors of earth: gold and pecan, ochre, sienna, and cinnabar. When it rains, the amber hillsides turn a bashful green, like the color of potatoes left in the sun. To residents of the American west, the iridescent verdure of the east comes as a shock. The leafy forests of maple, elm, and oak are luxurious and comforting. I remember the carpet of trilliums under the canopy of the trees and the joy and sense of virility that comes with the efflorescence of spring.

As I drive with my mother along the country roads, visiting another brother and sister and their families, she is happy. We reminisce about my childhood and my roaming after I left home at fifteen. It is clear that she feels the relief of survival, of having weathered the storms, vindicated by her optimism. Hadn't my success put those hard years behind us? But I want to turn my face to the memories.

When I was seventeen years old, I worked the summer in the tobacco fields outside the town of Aylmer, just as I had done for the previous six years. Picking tobacco is brutally hard labor and one farm I worked on still used horses. While most farms had changed to picking machines where the pickers rode on a metal seat and slung the leaves into a basket in front, the traditional method required you to walk along, hunched over, collecting the leaves under your arm. When you had as much as you could carry, you ran over to a horse pulling a trough on skids to drop in your load, then back to the row. Since it was much harder, there was a certain pride among tobacco workers for the old way. You could recognize them immediately by their dark tans and bulging back muscles from working stooped over all day. I personally preferred it simply because it was a lot quieter. You felt more alone in the field, without the noise of a diesel engine, and you worked at your own pace as long as you kept up with the horse.

The Belgian work horses had huge, hairy hooves and my own big feet occasionally got in the way of them. I still have deformed, horny toenails that never grew back right. I liked the physical work and the rhythm, the feeling of muscles rippling, moving to music in my head and thinking of things I had read. Sometimes, you had the row next to the horse and had to come within a couple of feet of its tail to deposit your leaves. If the timing was bad, you might look up just after the tail lifted and that big black sphincter opened to a fluttering whoosh of warm, moist fart right in your face.

In the little towns in tobacco-growing areas, it was well known that picking tobacco was hard work. No matter what your age, if you were a picker, the bars would let you drink. I had a '63 Chevy Biscayne at the time. It had a crunched-in side door from a minor accident, but it was a good road machine nonetheless. My fellow laborers and I got into the habit of jumping into my car around sunset and heading into Aylmer for a few beers.

On the farm I worked, there was a chicken, a capon, that was exiled from the flock. Chickens have a very tight dominance structure. An obstinate chicken can run afoul of the rules of the roost. When that happens, the problem chicken is usually pecked to death by the others. First, it is given an irritable poke by the dominant chicken and then, as soon as blood is drawn, all the others jump in like a street gang. This particular chicken was smart enough to know what was in store for it if it went back to the roost. So it wandered around the farm alone.

I felt a great affinity for this chicken and it became my pet. I named him after Hank Williams and he walked alongside me all day as I worked in the fields. At night, Hank would roost on my car, hooking his claws into the crevice between the hinges of the trunk.

One Saturday night we got off work a little later than usual and it was after dark when we roared into town, ready for the weekend. At the traffic lights people pointed and stared and someone yelled at us, "Hey, there's a chicken on your car!" But we figured they were joking and thought nothing of it.

We drove up and down the main street a few times before deciding on the right bar and then joined the noisy crowd. Pretty soon we overheard other drinkers: "That car outside ... it's got a chicken on it," and I had a sudden realization. Sure enough, there in the moonlight was Hank, claws jammed in the trunk edge, a few feathers shy but otherwise looking unperturbed.

Driving down these familiar roads, I regret the suffering I put my mother through during those years. With nine children to worry about, she couldn't do much to help one who drifted around the country with hardly any news for months at a time. Looking across at her now, the gentle, white-haired lady with the deep wrinkles and European accent, she seems like a different person, with the fragile features of old age.

The thought occurs to me that it would be nice to take her on a flight to show her a different view of the land and a glimpse of my world. In the past, she always graciously declined the offer. I plan to fly to Ottawa tomorrow, where more of the family has settled. It is a seven-hour drive from London.

"Mom, why don't you come with me? You haven't been there in years. It'll be a surprise!" She looks at me dubiously, but I know I have caught her.

AUGUST 18: LONDON, CANADA

I am thankful for the clear weather this morning and we depart into a heather-blue sky with wisps of high cirrus. My mother is a little timid in the cockpit and hesitates to speak into the voice-activated microphone, afraid that she might interrupt some critically important communication from air traffic control and make us crash.

"Don't worry, Mom, I'll let you know when it is safe to talk."

She points like a child and exclaims when she spots places she recognizes. I am so happy at the unexpected opportunity to be together with her this way. A distant thought creeps in that with my upcoming journey, this might be the last time I ever see her.

Canada's largest city, Toronto, lies under our route ahead and the controllers give me tight vectors to fly. By luck, we are directed right over the city, low and out of the way of the jet approach paths. My mother looks on in amazement as we angle among the skyscrapers, almost eye level with some of them and actually looking *up* at the CN tower.

She looks over at me, still a little unsure that I'll hear her through the headset, and says, "Now I understand why you like to fly. This is just ... wonderful."

The sprawl of the city gives way to the rugged country of the Canadian shield, a sparsely settled and seemingly endless expanse of spruce forest. Glacial moraines and drumlins corrugate the land. These mile-long ribbons of gravel were left over from the ice age. Along here, it looks as if the ice had retreated just last year, with the ground still sharply gouged and the gravel freshly heaped into clean, gray mounds. We drone on for a couple of hours, fighting a quartering headwind. My mother drifts off to sleep. I attend to some fuel calculations and try to find an altitude with more favorable winds.

Like a sailing ship, the best way to fly an airplane is in partnership with the wind. With enough power, you can just bore a hole through the air directly from point A to point B. But with a little finesse, you can save a lot of fuel and stress to the airplane by feeling what the wind is doing and taking advantage of it. The turn coordinator is especially useful for this. It is really two instruments in one: a turn and bank indicator, and a slip and skid indicator. Together, they give you precise information on the efficiency of your flight path and your motion relative to the wind. The turn coordinator is invaluable in instrument flight and sits right next to (usually below and to the left of) the attitude indicator. Like the AI, the turn coordinator has a little airplane in the window that tilts with a bank. The two instruments are like brothers, each acting like and complementing the other, and if one should break the other can take over much of its function.

I hear a soft crackling sound. Ever attuned to the subtle variations in the sonance of the engine, I immediately perk up. There it is again, crackles coming a few seconds apart. I pay more attention to my scan of the instruments. Everything is normal. I adjust the propeller pitch control to see if that changes it. Sometimes a particular combination of pitch and RPM can cause a harmonic, a rhythmic vibration that can be damaging to the engine. No change. It is getting louder, a crescendo rasping sound like a long plank being ripped from the side of a building, *rrrrAAAP*. I suddenly realize where the sound is coming from. My mother is fast asleep, the active microphone a half inch from her open mouth.

Ottawa's airport is not especially large but quite busy and we are told to remain in a holding pattern for a few turns. Then we land, sandwiched between a couple of jets. I taxi to the visitor parking apron and pull up next to a de Havilland Beaver, the quintessential Canadian bush airplane. My brother, Peter, has been waiting for an hour. We rumble into town in his classic old truck with the slit grill and wooden flat bed.

The Cockpit

AUGUST 19: OTTAWA, CANADA

Peter is a craftsman and is working for a theater company building their stage sets. His house and workshop are tiny but very comfortable, with just enough room for a couple of extra cots for my mother and me.

Today he takes us to the grandly named Museum of Civilization. The architecture is beautiful and the backdrop of the parliament buildings across the river even more so. I am a little puzzled by the museum itself. If anything, it seems to be misnamed. It is a display of Canadian Indian artifacts and of the handiwork of the waves of explorers and settlers from Europe who had to adapt to the Canadian climate. None of this is *civilization*. More puzzling is why this heritage is housed in a modern building. It is just too weird to see a colonial house inside a huge concrete and glass enclosure, like a ship in a bottle.

Peter explains how many of the items in the museum are reproductions, but each was crafted with careful attention to authenticity. One of his own works is on display, a replica of a sixteenth-century Quebecois door. He had spent months painstakingly building it with the same kind of tools the original settlers had used. It looks solid, all right. But I am amazed that such effort has been taken to produce something that I am sure is unappreciated by most of the museum visitors. Do they know how hard it is to plane wood with an adze and augur? With Peter's skilled workmanship, the result looks no different than if he done it in an afternoon on his lathe. Do they realize that the glass windows of the Maritime House, which look like ordinary glass, were made at great cost the same way they made glass in the eighteenth century? Do they care?

Perhaps Peter puts so much emphasis on authenticity because he needs to balance his stage work. He wants his craftsmanship to have integrity. And so the entire Quebecois door is made of oak, when an oak veneer over a cheaper wood would have looked identical. The stage sets he builds are the opposite:

the elaborate constructions are the flimsiest facade. Just some plywood, paperboard, and a splash of paint. Make it cheap and make it quick. The sets will be discarded after a few performances. Peter tells me that he has to fight his natural, perfectionist tendency to build a precise and durable structure when all that is needed is a crude form. It bothers him sometimes to produce such artificial work. Is this life? You throw up a bunch of junk that looks good in the moment and move on, close the curtain, before anyone notices what a gimcrack job it is. No one will remember it, anyway.

On the other hand, I wonder, what is the point of sacrificing your life to a labor that serves some abstract principle but provides benefit to no one? Sooner or later, tourists will be bored with looking at a replica of an old door and the museum will want the space for something else. The workmen will carry it out to be sold or junked, saying, "Man, this sucker is heavy. It must be made of solid wood!"

It is a question that has bothered me my whole life. Where do we find the balance between shoddy work and an impossible ideal? How do we create a life that has meaning and integrity, but not get lost in a hopeless *Don Quixote* pursuit of some unachievable fantasy? After I finished a master's degree, I spent another three years working on my Ph.D. Years working feverishly to write a two-volume dissertation on the environmental basis of disease that was probably read by no one except the dissertation committee. I forced it to completion long after I had lost interest, just to prove that I could do it and because I wanted the title of Doctor to get rid, once and for all, of the ignominy of not having finished high school. Sure, it got me a job as a professor. But I could have done so much more with that time. I could have built something meaningful with my life. Instead, my career has been an ever more elaborate stage set meant to fool everyone, especially myself, with the grand performance taking place. The illusion is no longer good enough. I want to walk out of that performance.

Chapter 7

AIRSPEED INDICATOR

"Ria, say hello to your Uncle Paul. He flew in an airplane by himself all the way across the country to come and see us," my sister Margrit says to the three-year-old girl shyly clinging to her skirt.

"Why?" says Ria simply.

Well now, that is a good question and I pause a bit to think of an answer.

Margrit interrupts, "She says that to everything these days," and laughs, throwing out her arms in a feigned helpless gesture. "Whatever you say, she'll ask you 'Why? Why? Why?' It's driving me nuts!"

And indeed she does. Ria seems to hide behind her page-boy blonde hair, but her blue eyes catch you and won't let go until she gets an answer. I love talking with her, walking with her hand in hand through the garden and answering all her questions as well as I can. But sometimes, as my sister warned, it gets to be a bit much.

"We have to wait about another hour before we have lunch."

"Why?"

"Because Grandmommy will be ready then and everyone will be hungry."

"Why will they be hungry then?"

"Because we ate this morning and it takes a while to get hungry again."

"Why?"

"Because when our blood glucose levels go down, the chemoreceptors in the anterior hypothalamus of the brain are activated and they stimulate the ventrolateral nucleus, the 'hunger center', that makes us want to eat."

"Why?"

"*Grrrrr....*"

As much as I enjoy visiting with the family, I know that I am putting off the real journey that lies ahead. I am totally committed. But I am also scared and well aware that I might not survive. Trying to fly across the Atlantic in a small, single-engine airplane is reckless, everyone has told me, and to South Africa it is probably impossible. I am pitting my personal calculations against the experience of the aviation authorities. But maybe the real wager is between my luck and my destiny. It gives my visit here a peculiar feel, like that of a soldier going off to war. I have tried to hide the details from my mother and the others, but my sisters sense the danger. Margrit gives me an amulet she has made.

"Wear this around your neck," she tells me. "It will protect you."

Another sister, Trudy, is more challenging. "You really don't have to do this, you know. You don't have to prove anything."

She has some understanding of what I am going through, and she points out that there are much safer ways to seek my goal. "Why don't you go on an expedition, instead, or with one of those adventure travel groups?"

But I have to admit, I don't really know my goal. My life has been reasonably successful and yet I don't feel quite right in it. I don't really feel at home in it. I feel that I have lost a sense of purpose—if, in fact, I ever had one—and that somehow this trip will restore it by forcing me to face something. This flight is the only way I know to do it.

My next destination is Bangor, Maine, where the aircraft will be prepared for the ocean flight. In California, I had a lot of trouble convincing aviation experts that it was possible for the Cardinal to make it across the Atlantic. The facility at Bangor specializes in modifying aircraft for ferry flights. They have no objection to doing the work for me, though their track record isn't especially good. A few months ago, one of their ferry pilots was forced to ditch in the ocean off Greenland. He was extraordinarily lucky to have a ship nearby and barely survived. The experience turned that hard-bitten airman into a born-again Christian.

In the evening, I say goodbye to my mother and my sisters Margrit and Trudy. Peter takes me back to the airport. I am glad to be finally underway. These last few days with the family have felt like packing up the photo albums before a move. Pack up my former life. Put it in boxes for storage. There is another life ahead.

It is a cloudy, moonless night and there is not much to see. The darkness gives me some time to consider what I am doing. For now, I am on a pleasant cross-country jaunt, like so many others I have done before. In Bangor, the aircraft will be transformed. After that, flight will become very different and there will be no turning back. I fiddle with the Beat Frequency Oscillator unit on the ADF radio, the unit that the avionics shop had refused to sell me and which I finally got by mail order. I can't really tell if it works, since the North American non-directional beacons (NDB), the radio signals that the unit homes in on, don't use the BFO. The rest of the ADF seems to work satisfactorily. I play with it for a while and manage to tune in some AM radio stations, which use the same frequency range as the NDB, and listen to country and western music.

A few hours pass and then the parallel lines of red lights

of the huge runway at Bangor appear from a long way out against the dark countryside. Bangor is a major cargo and military trans-shipment point, but has very little passenger traffic. The vast airport is quiet as I land and taxi past the miles of hangars and warehouses to the ferry company building. I pull up near the door and shut down. In front of the office, there is a neatly cut lawn. I set up my tent and roll out a sleeping bag. Might as well get started first thing in the morning.

AUGUST 20: BANGOR, MAINE
Daybreak. I walk a couple of miles to the outskirts of town and find a Howard Johnson restaurant. Its large plastic menus show pictures of the usual American breakfasts composed of the basic four food groups: sugar, fat, grease, and caffeine. I order up an ensemble of eggs and sausages, waffles with maple-flavored syrup, buttered toast, orange juice and tea. Maybe later today I can find a grocery store and get some better food.

By the time I walk back to the airport, the mechanics have arrived. They have been expecting me and have already started to take some measurements. We pull the airplane into the hangar and empty it out. Over the next three days, the interior is stripped to the metal. The back seats are removed and replaced by a fifty-gallon auxiliary fuel tank, with a conduit that runs from the back through to the front cabin where it joins the main fuel line, with a valve at the pilot's feet. On top of the fuel tank is mounted a large, black, High Frequency radio unit with more knobs than a Japanese stereo and a two hundred page instruction manual. The antenna for this radio stretches from the right wing tip to the top of the empennage. Together with the lengthy antenna wires of the ADF, dual VHF navigation and communication whip antennas, and additional antennas for the Loran, the marker beacon and the transponder—the airplane is beginning to look like one of those spiny science fiction spaceships.

The interior is almost complete. Today, I reload the airplane, carefully packing equipment in order of emergency usage. For the over-water flight, I rent an additional Emergency Locator Transmitter (ELT), a survival suit, and a life raft, all of which I plan to ship back once I arrive in Europe. The aircraft has a built-in ELT, a unit that is activated in a crash and automatically sends out a signal on an international emergency frequency. But if I were to ditch in the ocean, the soft impact of the crash might not be enough to activate the ELT. Even if it were activated, the salt water would destroy the electronics, and the airplane would undoubtedly sink within a few minutes, anyway. This extra ELT is portable, waterproof and can be activated either manually, or automatically by exposure to salt water.

The survival suit was specially designed for workers on the oil rigs and fishermen in the North Atlantic. It is heavy and bulky, a fully watertight outfit that looks like an orange space suit. It takes quite a bit of wriggling to get into it, but once it is sealed, so they claim, you can survive for hours in freezing water. The life raft was also specially designed for the rough ocean, bright orange with an enclosed shelter topped by radar reflectors. It has its own built-in emergency equipment and is tightly bound in a heavy package, set up to inflate automatically if you pull a handle.

This morning, I meet the ferry pilot who ditched earlier in the year. Bill is a reserved, middle-aged man with the barrel-chested look of someone who had once, I guess, been a laborer. In a relaxed and measured voice, he describes to me how it happened.

"My co-pilot, Steve, had flown the Bonanza here from California—it was a real beauty, almost brand new. It flew real nice to Newfoundland. We were about two and a half hours out from land at eleven thousand feet, when the oil pressure started reading kinda high. Both of us thought that it might be a gauge malfunction. Then it dropped back to normal, then to real *low* pressure. We turned around to go back, but it was too late. The prop went into an overspeed, and you could tell, it ripped the hell out of the valves. Then something blew. *Bam!* Smoke came into the cabin. The engine just totally seized and we went down."

He continues in an oddly calm voice, given the predicament he is describing.

"We had a hard time getting into the survival suits. By the time we dropped to the surface, we almost got 'em on but Steve and I, we couldn't get the things to seal. We cracked open the door so it wouldn't jam when we hit. The plane landed on its belly. Man! I tell you, it is a real wake-up when you feel that ice-cold water."

"That was really lucky," I say, knowing that sea ditchings almost always cause the aircraft to turn upside down when the heavy nose strikes the water. "I'm surprised you didn't flip."

"Yeah, we were lucky alright," he drawls, and goes on in the same relaxed manner. "We panicked. I was stuck on something and couldn't get out of the sinking airplane, and I guess Steve was stuck too. We were going under. One of us, I don't know, maybe it was me, must have pulled the handle on the life raft and it inflated inside the cabin. Then the heavy nose tipped the plane vertically into the water, and we got pulled completely under. I figured I was gone.

"But you know," he now looks at me seriously, "that is when I knew it wasn't my time yet. I just knew that someone was watching over us. Steve and I just came loose and popped up to the surface. I knew then that we had never been alone, all along. And that I'll never be alone again.

"The life raft also budged loose and we could see it come out, but then it got snagged by the tail of the aircraft and pulled under again. I can't tell you how hard it was. The ocean was rough. We were pitching around in about a twelve or fourteen foot swell.

"Somehow, the life raft got free. I guess we got lucky again," he adds with a hint of irony. "It was all we could do to get into it."

They were exhausted, soaked, and almost comatose from hypothermia when they were picked up by a nearby fishing trawler. Had they not been helicoptered to a hospital, they would certainly have died.

There is a high-pitched whine of a drill and both of us look over at my airplane. The mechanics are cutting holes in the fuselage for the fuel conduits and vent ports. With cables snaking along the floor and the swinging booms overhead, the plane looks like a child in a dentist's chair. Exposed and partly dissected, it seems small and fragile in the white open space of the hangar. Bill's aircraft had been larger, almost new, and far better equipped with a radar altimeter and other instruments I can't afford. And they were two highly qualified pilots. He gives me a sympathetic look, and says quietly, "Be careful."

"And," he adds as he turns to leave, "just make sure you don't open the life raft inside the airplane."

Sobered by this encounter, I review every detail of the preparations. The flight is risky enough as it is; I don't intend to leave any more to chance than I have to. I plan to *wear* the bulky survival suit, not just over the ocean, but in every flight from now on, just to get the feel of flying the airplane in it.

Inside the survival suit, I tuck the portable ELT, a separate hand-held navigation and communication radio, an extra set of batteries, some chocolate candy, a quart bag of fresh water, and a packet of emergency equipment that I carry when I go backpacking: Swiss army knife, signaling mirror, and some other small items. I put the life raft beside the HF radio on top of the auxiliary fuel tank, over my left shoulder and next to the door. When everything is done, I climb into the survival suit, get into the airplane, and practice opening the door, grabbing the life raft and rolling out in one smooth movement. The mechanics and office staff look on, amused. They chuckle and toss me a few useful comments: "That was a good one! But watch your left foot—it almost got hung up on the step." It may look silly, but if the moment ever comes, I am going to be ready.

AUGUST 24: BANGOR, MAINE

It is mid-morning when I complete the paperwork and taxi away from the shop, a half-ton heavier and a few thousand dollars poorer. The aircraft is fully loaded and all the tanks are filled to the caps. Although I will not need the extra fuel until I reach the long legs of the ocean, I want to see how well this fat goose is going to fly. The airplane rolls along heavily in a slightly nose-high attitude. I am two hundred and fifty pounds over the maximum legal gross weight, but with the ocean ferry permit that allows a ten percent overgross, we are right on the money. The overgross exemption was meant to accommodate the additional fuel that would be burned off during the ocean flight. But I do not want to wait until I am over the water before testing the system. Until I reach the Canadian Arctic, the flight will be mostly over land. I want to get comfortable managing the auxiliary fuel tank and an aircraft shouldering a lot more weight than its designers had intended. In case of a malfunction, I fully intend to use this opportunity to fly over land—and the law be damned.

Full power. The airplane only grudgingly gains speed. With such a heavily loaded craft, airspeed calculations will be critical. Rotate too soon and we will crash back to earth. How often had exactly that happened to the first pilots trying to fly across the ocean? As early as 1913, just a decade after the invention of the airplane, the London *Daily Mail* offered a prize of £10,000 to the first crew to fly across the Atlantic. It was a magnificent sum for those days, but the first world war intervened. After the war's end, the race to claim the prize excited adventurers everywhere.

The problem they faced was a simple one. It is the same problem we face today with manned space flight to Mars: fuel vs distance. They just didn't have an airplane with enough fuel capacity to cover the distance. Dozens tried and dozens failed, usually by crashing from overloaded takeoffs. And if they didn't crash, it was only because they jettisoned anything available:

spare oil, equipment, *nothing* was unexpendable ... as I read in the account of a crew led by the U.S. Naval Commander Towers, making the attempt in a flying boat from Trepassey Bay, Newfoundland, on Friday, May 16, 1919:

> *Unable to climb away from the bay, Towers had begun ripping equipment out, first a long-range radio, then a bag of mail being carried for the benefit of philatelists. Finally, his eyes lit on one of the two engineers they were carrying, the heavier one, Lt. Braxton Rhodes.*
>
> *"What do you weigh, Rhodes?" he inquired.*
> *"No, Commander, no!" Rhodes replied.*
> *But Rhodes was bounced along with the other cargo.*

To little avail, as it turned out, when the flying boat crashed in the ocean a few hours later, with its remaining crew rescued by a ship.

It is a good thing I have this long, smooth runway to get up to rotational speed. I keep a careful eye on the creeping airspeed indicator. Yes, my friend, without you we would have no way of knowing when to lift this stuffed bird into the air. At the point of rotational speed, I tug back on the control wheel just enough to clear the landing gear, then drop the nose slightly to float in ground effect, building up a little more crucial speed without the friction of the runway. Then, with a comfortable reserve of airspeed, I ease the Cardinal into a shallow climb.

The airspeed indicator soon reveals a normal speed. This instrument, just left of the attitude indicator, is one of the most important and has a complicated design. The busy markings and colors on its face show the critical airspeeds under various operations. Underneath that dial is a clever bit of engineering that compares the force of air passing under the wing, the *dynamic* pressure, to the pressure of quiet air, the *static* air pressure, and the difference is interpreted as the speed of the plane through the air. This means all those pieces must be working perfectly. The dynamic pressure is gained from the pitot tube, that little missile that projects from under the wing on small aircraft, and from the sides of the fuselage on big jets. It can get iced up during flight and has its own special heater. The static pressure is taken from a number of different ports, tiny orifices on the sides of the airplane. If they, in turn, get iced up, the only recourse is to smash the glass of the instrument to allow a static reading of the cabin air.

Once up to seven thousand feet, I level off and begin to experiment with the behavior of the airplane. What happens when I drop a wing? How soon does it stall when I pull back on the control column? After I am reassured that the airplane is well balanced, I practice twisting the stopcocks and managing the fuel pump, in the prescribed order—*one*, boost pump on; *two*, auxiliary fuel valve on; *three*, twist the conduit valve from main to auxiliary—to shift fuel flow from the main tanks to the auxiliary and back again, until I can do it without looking. I have plenty of time, and the skies are clear.

The destination today is Moncton, New Brunswick. Before any single-engine over-ocean flight departing from Canada, the Canadian Ministry of Transport requires that the pilot and aircraft undergo an inspection and test by an office at the Moncton airport. If the flight fails, it is the Canadian Coast Guard that mounts the rescue mission, and the Canadian people that end up footing the bill, which can easily run to a million dollars. So it makes sense to demand a thorough inspection to weed out the unprepared adventurers or outright lunatics who want to fly to Europe. My inspection is scheduled for tomorrow morning, so I have the day to prepare for my interview and hopefully convince the no-doubt skeptical Canadian authority that I am neither inexperienced nor insane.

Chapter 8

ALTIMETER

Flight. According to the dictionary, it means, "an action of moving through the air, as with wings." But it also means, "soaring out of the regular course, or beyond ordinary bounds," or, "an excursion of the imagination," as in a flight of fancy, or flight of ambition.

The word comes from the Old English *flyht*, which came from the Old Saxon *fluht*, which in turn originated from the early Germanic and much earlier Indo-European languages of thousands of years ago. I'm sure that the first humans, maybe being chased by a bear or a lion, looked up at the birds and exclaimed something like *ffuuuhhkk*, meaning, "I sure wish I could fly." It is an exclamation people still use in similar circumstances.

But the word also means "to flee," to run away from. Flee has an origin that is very different from flight, coming from the Old Dutch *vliegen*, but by the time of Old English a thousand years ago, the two meanings were already confused. Thus flight is both a venture and an escape. In the Greek myth, Daedalus was a brilliant artisan who built the labyrinth for King Minos.

When he fell out of favor with the King, he was imprisoned so that he could not offer his skills to some adversary. "Minos may control the land and sea," said Daedalus, "but not the regions of the air." So he fashioned wings from feathers and wax, for himself and his son, Icarus. Daedalus warned Icarus to be careful, to not let the thrill and power of flight lead him into danger. But despite his father's warning, Icarus flew too close to the sun. The wax melted and he plunged to the sea and drowned. For Daedalus, flight was an escape from a prison. But for Icarus, it was a flight of vain ambition and, like all such flights in mythology, his had to end in tragedy.

I also escaped by flight. At the age of eighteen, my future in Canada held no promise.

"Don't you know what the word Canada means?" a friend joked. "The Spanish explorers arrived and said *'aca nada,'* there is nothing here."

There was certainly nothing for me, an uneducated farm laborer. Nor for my friend, who hanged himself that spring. I decided that I had to leave. Go back to my roots.

In October, after the harvests, I collected my savings and bought a ticket for Switzerland. I arrived in Zürich with an ability to speak the Germanic Swiss dialect, a vague sense of birthright, and fifty dollars. Within a day, I found a job in a town next to the airport, scrubbing the racks and ovens in a bakery. The hours were long and after a couple of weeks I quit to work in a bar at night. That left the days free to do a bit of exploring, but I didn't make much money and couldn't compete for tips with the sultry hostess with the slit black dress. After I saved a small sum and got to know more about the country, I left that job as well and took a train to St. Moritz, looking forward to being in the mountains.

In Chur, at the foot of the Alps, I transferred to a smaller, meter-gauge train that chugged its way through picturesque tunnels and gorges until it came to the glacial valley of the Engadin. Then it unexpectedly stopped in the village of

Samedan, just eight kilometers from St. Moritz. It was midnight. The remaining passengers quickly left, and the jovial conductor walked through the carriages, swinging his metal ticket folder. He informed me that this was the last stop that night. The train would continue on in the morning. No, there was no youth hostel in Samedan, and the station building would be locked within an hour.

I stepped out into the cold night air and paced along the platform. A night at a hotel in this ski resort would take my entire savings. On the other hand, I couldn't very well wander around until dawn or sleep in the bushes. Switzerland, so tightly controlled that you have to notify the police whenever you rent a room or apartment, does not allow that sort of thing. There was a silhouette of an old woman at the end of the platform. I discreetly strolled past her to get a better look. Her hunched back, black coat and pointy black hat made her look like a hag. She stood still, resting a gnarled hand on a wooden cane and, when I drew near, I saw that she had a long, beak-like nose with an ugly wart on her chin. I quickly retreated to the other end of the platform. "This is just great!" I shuddered. "I've got to spend the night on a freezing railway platform—with a witch!"

One thing I learned a long time ago is that every situation, no matter how bleak, also presents an opportunity. In this case, the opportunity was obvious. After screwing up my courage, I walked over and introduced myself. "*Grüezi,*" I said, in the usual Swiss greeting. "It is a chilly evening, isn't it?"

"My, it certainly is," she replied with a twinkle in her eye. If she thought it was odd that I should be there, she certainly didn't let on. "Where are you staying tonight, young man?"

"Well, I ... ah ... I thought the train would continue to St. Moritz, and I hadn't ... made any plans." As soon as I spoke, I regretted exposing my situation. I had a quick vision of Hansel and Gretel and thought, Man, this is just the sort of opening a witch looks for.

"Well," she said, a little too cheerily. "Why don't you come with me?" And before I could answer, she pointed a bony finger. "Here is our ride now!"

A white Volvo pulled into the parking lot. "Come," she said firmly, "come, come, come." A bear-like man was at the wheel. "This young gentleman would like to join us," the old crone said. He nodded hospitably and we sped off, away from the town and up along narrow mountain roads. The man had a heavy foot and must have noticed me suck in my breath when we hit some of the curves, a granite wall on one side and the ink of darkness on the other. "Moose tongue," he said when he found out I was from Canada, and continued in Swiss, "that is a good car."

Huh?

Oh, I realized, the *Mustang*. "Yeah, the Mustang is good, but I think what you need here is a Jaguar."

"*Ja, ja!*" He thumped the wheel "*Der Jaguar*," pronouncing it "Yuck-var," and I could see that this might work out. Maybe I could get a warm bed for the night, a meal or two, and save a few francs while I looked for a job.

We arrived at a large stone chalet, four stories tall and set into the mountain side. The house was much too big for a family, I thought, and then learned that it was a communal house for some kind of religious sect. I was shown to a small room and, after once again expressing my gratitude, said goodnight. The room had nothing but a desk with a Bible and a plain wooden bed. The bed was covered with the traditional Swiss down comforter, a big, fluffy, pillow-like object that invariably lets your feet get cold. I tucked up my legs and fell fast asleep.

After a pleasant breakfast the next morning of *müesli*, bread and jam, and coffee, I again expressed my gratitude and murmured that I must be on my way. "Not at all, you just arrived here," a kindly Frau answered, "and besides, Herr Baissier is working on the driveway today. We were hoping you might give him a little help." I could hardly refuse, I thought, and besides, another day here wouldn't hurt.

The house had a large auditorium on the ground floor. That evening, people began to arrive, singly and in small groups, until perhaps fifty or sixty had collected. They were locals, old and young, well dressed professionals from the village and shy mountain herders in their rough garments. The service began without introduction, with several individuals spontaneously coming to the lectern and giving a prayer, or relating an inspirational story. After a half hour, the group was settled and in a peaceful, religious mood. Herr Baissier then came to the front, looking more bear-like than ever. He began in fatherly tones, chastising the group for their sins. His words gradually became more forceful, yielding to visions of God and punishment, forgiveness and the glory of redemption, the coming of the Pentecost. He paced it masterfully, building, ebbing, and building again and the crowd responded with cries and Amens. He continued for over an hour, raising the power in his voice until he thundered, his face purple with strain, and smashed the air with his meaty fist. The crowd was in rapture. People tried to stand and fell, some convulsing. I shrank into my seat at the back, fascinated by the spectacle but hoping I would not be expected to participate. A man next to me fell to his knees, gushing nonsense syllables.

What the hell have I got myself into now? I thought, and vaguely remembered having read something about this. Glossolalia. Speaking in tongues. Nearly everyone was in a delirium, rocking, muttering, witnessing an unseen sight.

"The Holy Spirit will come down and you shall be *possessed!*" Baissier bellowed, and people cried out and wept in remorse and in ecstasy. I slunk even lower in my seat.

Gradually, it quieted and people drifted off into internal meditation. Some curled up asleep on the floor, emotionally spent with their catharsis. By midnight, everyone had gone and another man and I cleaned up the room.

The next day, I again was steered into some work on the stone walkway and it was evening by the time I could broach the subject of my departure.

"Where are you going, then?" asked Herr Baissier. When I admitted I had no job, he said, "Well, stay here until you find one." His reasoning was quite logical, but I was beginning to feel trapped. I had no way to get to town and every day seemed immediately filled with work duties. Every scheme I came up with was quickly refuted and he could see through my weak descriptions of jobs I said I had heard about and wanted to investigate. The life there wasn't so bad, really, and other than the gnawing feeling of having stepped into a cage, I enjoyed the communal atmosphere. Sometimes the old woman at the train station, Anna, came to breakfast. Without her witch outfit, Anna looked like the kindly dowager she was and I enjoyed chatting with her. But I often felt like saying, "You know, you ought to do something about that wart."

Three weeks passed, with a now-familiar revival session each Sunday evening. One afternoon, I met a man who worked at the regional hospital. He said they needed assistants in the surgical suite. I jumped at the chance and asked to go with him to meet the nuns directing the hospital. Not tomorrow, *now*.

The convent was next to the hospital. After evening prayers, I found the chief administrative nun and told her I would do any work available. She brightened up and said, "Yes, we do have need for a young man. You can start immediately." The resident doctors and other staff lived right in the hospital, an arrangement that was extremely convenient for the lengthy and irregular work hours. The nun gave me a small room on an upper floor with a wood-shuttered window looking out over the valley. I wasted no time going back to Herr Baissier to collect my things and thank him once more for his hospitality.

Six o'clock the next morning, I was in the surgical suite. Some pretty nurses helped me with the sterile gown and gloves, tittering among themselves about my lack of familiarity with the procedures. They patiently instructed me for the coming operations. As an assistant, it was my job to disinfect and shave the patient and assist the anesthesiologist in the preparation for surgery. Then, during the operation, I was to suction off blood from the incision, pass sponges, hold retractors and generally assist as called upon.

It was not a complex job. The patient was brought in and I did as I was told. Then I watched, transfixed, as the surgeon took a scalpel to the woman's pale, naked belly and drew a ribbon of blood from her chest to her navel, parting the flesh and exposing tapioca mounds of white fat and smooth red muscle. Blood pooled and I leaned in to suction it off. The surgeon noted the small bleeding vessels and zapped them with a cautery instrument that looked like a soldering iron. There was a crackling sound with a smell of barbecued meat. My mouth watered involuntarily. I hadn't had time for breakfast.

Jesus! I thought. What am I doing here? The Pentecostal thing was bad enough, but what the hell have I gotten into now?

The next operation involved stripping varicose veins from an obese lady, and I had to do a lot of disinfecting. It is amazing how heavy the limbs are of an unconscious person, especially a fat one. In those days, the hospital used ether, and I poured it on generously. The air shimmered as the stuff quickly evaporated and I poured on more to be sure that I had covered the area. After a little while, I began to feel woozy. The color of the room turned to a dense golden hue and a high-pitched buzzing filled my ears. I caught myself on the table. At the edge of consciousness, I said loudly that I was going to pass out. Someone grabbed my shoulders and quickly helped me away. The fresh air of the hallway brought back my senses and the nurses clustered around. They sat me at a table laden with coffee and cheeses, yogurt, chocolate, and pastries. I felt no hurry to get back to work as they fawned over me, loosening my clothes and wiping the sweat off my face.

"Oh, don't worry, it was the same for all of us when we first saw blood," they giggled. "*Eeyuu*. But then you get used to it."

After a month, I took the train to Zürich for a weekend.

I returned to the hospital with a pack full of books from an English language bookshop I found there, mostly philosophy and psychology. The books caught the eye of an eighteen-year-old girl, a physiotherapy intern, who had a room down the hallway from mine. Her name was Beatrix, Trix to her friends. She had straight blonde hair to her shoulders and an athletic, shapely figure that radiated a cheery confidence. Her gray-blue eyes seemed to take in everything and delight in any novelty. Trix was fluent in German, English, French, and Italian, and had studied Latin and ancient Greek as well.

We began to spend time together. I learned that her father was the head of the International Red Cross and her mother a prominent socialite in Zürich. Trix was the product of the European upper class: a personal nanny, ballet school, classical music, a private tutor in the arts and sciences. As a little girl growing up in the Zürich suburb of Küsnacht, she was friendly with the old men who were her neighbors, Herman Hesse on one side and Carl Jung on the other. I was completely in awe of her fluidity in a world I had only glimpsed, and by her angelic beauty.

The snows of winter deepened and turned Samedan into a Christmas fantasyland. Horse-drawn sleighs pulled shoppers and tourists along cobble-stoned streets lined by gabled shops with frosted windows. Trix and I went for long walks in the moonlight and snuggled close as we talked about things we read, told each other stories and made up jokes about people we saw.

We were so opposite in background. I thought I could never compete with the innumerable other young men of the hospital who vied for her attention; the suave doctors, elegant musicians and handsome skiers. All I could offer her were my thoughts, my whimsical humor and a singular desire to make her happy. For some reason, it was enough to make her fall in love with me. And I, I was swept away; completely, hopelessly infatuated with her.

Her family had a tiny cabin in a high mountain valley

and we often spent the weekend there. I met her father, a man I was a bit intimidated by. Because I had grown up speaking Swiss almost exclusively at home, I mistakenly used the familial form in addressing him. Trix hurriedly apologized for my gaff and explained that my language skills were a bit rough.

"Oh, not at all!" he laughed. "I wish everyone would address me this way."

He seemed very considerate. Whatever he actually thought of me, it was clear that he respected his daughter's judgment.

Her mother, on the other hand, detested me and everything I represented. I was uncultured, uncouth and, worst of all, uneducated.

One evening at the cabin, her mother was delayed on her return to Zürich by a blizzard and the three of us were alone.

"Why don't you two play chess?" Trix asked brightly.

Her mother considered herself quite a capable chess player. She lifted her eyebrows and seemed to wonder if it was beneath her dignity.

"Oh, I guess there is nothing else to do." And then she perked up with the thought that this was a chance for a little humiliation. "If you know how," she said cuttingly and looked over at me.

I was irritated enough by this crap to take the game seriously and trapped her into losing her queen.

"No," she said, stunned and angry, "you can't do that."

"Why not?"

"Because you didn't say *'Gardez'* first."

So. Evidently, it was the custom in Europe to say *"Gardez"* before attacking the queen. Very well. I let her have the piece. It only served to delay her loss of the game. She was furious. We played two more games and I might have been a bit more tactful. But I was in no mood for our more profound little power game, and beat her decisively.

She no longer spoke to me and the following week forbid her daughter from seeing me again, threatening to get the police if I came by. Trix and I surreptitiously continued to spend time together and she begged me not to leave her. I was torn between my love for her and my feelings that I had nothing to offer her. How long could we continue? She had everything, within her and ahead of her. I toyed with the idea of going to school in Switzerland so that we could stay together, but where would I begin? Grade school?

Work at the operating room was becoming more intense. My own inner turmoil was reflected in the brutality of the surgeries I assisted. It was the height of the ski season and some days the halls were lined with gurneys overflowing from the emergency room. The injured were mostly tourists, not quite prepared for the steep powder of the Alps, moaning in shock and disbelief at their blood-soaked jacket or glistening bone jutting out of a thigh. And there were highway accidents with whole families crying from fear and pain, then shrieking in hysteria when they learned that one had died. As the only native English speaker in the hospital, I was called to assist and translate for the doctors, the families and the police. Every day I was faced with so much suffering that the patients became just more meat on the table. I was crumbling from the horror of work and from the emptiness of my self-worth.

Flight. Flee. Fly away.

I returned to Canada in the spring, leaving Trix weeping in anger and confusion. We knew the goodbye was permanent. We knew that our lives would go in entirely different directions. My trip to the land of my ancestry had been to find some sort of identity, my self-worth. What I had found instead was my worthlessness.

"November three zero seven four five, Moncton Approach."

I snap out of my reverie. Holy Cow, I am almost in the Positive Control Zone! I've been so completely lost in my thoughts, I've flown right across the border and almost blundered into the protected airspace.

The altimeter reads seven thousand feet. Seven, the number of the virgin, the number of love. Yeah, good buddy, you know where my mind had drifted off to. I can't believe that, after all these years, I still think of her.

Now it is time to get back on the ground.

Chapter 9

VERTICAL SPEED INDICATOR

AUGUST 25: MONCTON, CANADA

Yesterday, the inspector at the Canadian Ministry of Transportation suggested that we meet at the airport coffee shop. "I don't get out of the office much," he added, "and after we're done we can just walk over to your airplane to have a look."

I am a little nervous about this inspection. I imagine him flipping through my logbook with an unimpressed look, saying, "What makes you think you can fly across the ocean?" To be ready, I arrive at the coffee shop early and arrange my notebooks, binders and charts on the table, along with neatly printed lists of radio frequencies and fuel calculations. A middle-aged man with a strawberry-blond crew cut and checkered sport jacket strides in and spots me immediately.

"Jack McCallister," he says and holds out a hand. He signals the waitress for coffee and takes a seat.

"I'll bet you're a little nervous, Paul, but don't worry, this isn't an interrogation."

I laugh. This guy has got my number, all right, and I clearly am not the first to come through here.

"I understand the difficulty of flying across the Atlantic and I have a great respect for the problems that can come up. But my airplane and I are ready. I've studied every detail of the flight," I emphasize, patting the stack of binders, "and I'll be happy to go over them with you."

He settles back and looks pleased. "OK, Captain. Let's get started."

We spend an hour and a half reviewing the trip. Beginning with my pilot qualifications, we go on to the legal documents and then discuss each approach plate and low altitude enroute chart for the flight itself. He raises his eyebrows a few times over my unimpressive instrumentation, but I assure him that I have what I need.

"You've done a good job," he says finally. "Let's have a look at the airplane." As we walk out to the flight line, I notice that the clouds are building in the north. It is midday already and I wonder if I should spend another night or start the flight to the Canadian Arctic this afternoon, as I had hoped. After a cursory outside inspection and a few minutes poking around the interior, he is satisfied with the airplane. We return to the coffee shop, where we finish some paperwork and have a late lunch. He shares a bit of advice:

"Don't depend too much on the radios. We've had reports of a lot of problems with the HF lately because of high sunspot activity. If the radios don't work, use your head and do what you know—dead reckoning."

Dead reckoning, I think, over the North Atlantic? Before radio beacons, before instruments and before navigation by the stars, there was the age-old system of calculating your position simply by estimating winds and bearing and drift. "Deduced reckoning," which the sailors shortened to dead reckoning. That is what the Polynesians used a thousand years ago to cross the Pacific to Hawaii. And that is what Charles Lindbergh used on the first solo crossing of the Atlantic on May 20, 1927. Even Lindbergh had access to a radio, but chose not to take it to save weight—a testimony to his skill and his courage. It is one thing to practice dead reckoning over corn fields when you are a student pilot, but it is quite another to do so over a featureless ocean, in darkness and cloud. This is the modern age. I intend to put my trust in my instruments.

I leave Moncton under threatening skies, eager to be on my way, regardless, with an elated sense that my real journey is just beginning. Again, a long takeoff and climb-out in the overloaded aircraft. I am beginning to get the feel of it. The carpet of spruce forest underneath resumes, now occasionally hidden as I pass into and out of light rain squalls. A glimpse of Miramichi Bay between clouds, then Chaleur Bay and Bonaventure. The ADF localizer needle flips as I pass overhead the Bonaventure NDB, once more in cloud, and I know that somewhere down there is the rugged country of the Gaspé Peninsula.

ZONE II DE VOL TACTIQUE, the chart says. Ah yes, the Canadian Air Force operations restricted area. Well, never mind. I'm on a flight plan and if they want to know who I am, they know how to call me.

The skies clear and reveal the wide mouth of the St. Laurence River, maybe sixty miles across. I maintain a heading to Sept-Îles on the north shore and cross in a deepening twilight. After the lights of Sept-Îles fade behind me, all traces of civilization disappear.

This is the Canadian north, the land that forms the vast majority of the country but in which very few Canadians have ever set foot. It is the nation's back yard. The history and legends of the north permeate the psyche of the Canadian people, even though their day-to-day lives are virtually identical to those of their American neighbors. Canadians seem to be forever in search of the real meaning of Canada, especially English Canadians who are hard-pressed to distinguish themselves from Americans. Ironically, it is the French Canadians, the Québecois, who provide the most heartfelt Canadian culture. You can hear it in the folk song by Gilles Vignault, *Mon pays, ce n'est pas de pays. C'est l'hiver.* My country is not a country. It is the winter.

Darkness descends and in the shadows I can see that the forests are thinning, with rocky outcrops and countless unnamed lakes scratched into the land. A few snowflakes dance past the cowling of the airplane. A few more and suddenly they are thick and streaming to all sides, like a shower of glinting cornflakes blowing through a black tunnel. I turn on the pitot heat and note the distinct pull on the ammeter needle with the heavy electrical draw. Labrador City is still hours ahead. If I have to, I can turn back to Sept-Îles. I look out at the wing and see an unexpected, pale roughness. Grabbing my larger flashlight, I peer at the wing and can clearly see a white crust building up on the leading edge. *Ice!* For a moment I have an impulse to do an immediate one-eighty. I've read too much about icing in aircraft. It is the terror of northern pilots. Ice doesn't just weigh down the airplane, it changes the shape of the wing and propeller, destroying lift and power. In the many books I've read about flying, ice is considered just about the worst thing to come across. Countless aircraft have crashed from a loss of control due to icing. Larger aircraft have anti-icing equipment, but even airliners have crashed because of ice. I survey both wings closely and see a coarse, ugly crust along the entire leading edge. I have never encountered this before and I half expect to be sinking into a slow dive. Instead, nothing happens. The vertical speed indicator is pegged at zero. Level flight. I warily keep an eye on my left wing. The layer is almost an inch thick now, but it doesn't look like it is getting any bigger. There is ice on the wheel fairing as well. That doesn't matter as much, but it is a good indicator of ice on other surfaces I can't see, like the rudder and stabilator. Meanwhile, the performance of the airplane seems only marginally affected. The vertical speed indicator will let me know if I am getting into trouble. Unlike its cousin, the altimeter, it relies only on static pressure, not dynamic pressure, so it does not depend on the vagaries of the pitot tube. When it dips, you know you are going down.

Well, I think, flying into known icing conditions is considered about the stupidest thing a pilot can do. On the other hand, this might be good experience. At least I'm over land. If the ice gets worse, or the vertical speed indicator dips, I am turning around. But until then, I'd better learn as much as I can about this. If the same thing happens over the ocean, I may not have the option of going back.

The snow stops and returns and stops again as the hours slowly pass under a dark, woolly overcast. With each snow flurry, the coarse layer of ice cakes up and then very gradually erodes when we return to clear air. Finally, the lights of Labrador City appear in the distance, a tiny pearl necklace on black satin terrain. Coming up to the airfield, I see the whole community is just a tight cluster of aluminum pre-fab houses near a hydro-electric plant. The sodium street lamps throw a weak yellow light onto the flat, mostly windowless walls of the metal buildings. I land and pull up to the airport terminal. As I tie down the airplane in a light drizzle, chunks of ice fall from the wings, *splush, splush,* onto the tarmac.

There is no one around, but the terminal building is unlocked. I walk around cautiously inside, slightly worried that I might set off an alarm. Everything is quiet, serene. The baggage carousel, the counters for Air Canada and a couple of local airlines, the odd, freestanding door-frame of a simple metal detector at the departure gate—it all seems ghostly in the shadows of the outside lights. In the passenger lounge, I roll out my sleeping bag on the carpet and try to calm down enough to sleep. But my mind is still on the move. Maybe it was all that caffeine in Moncton, as we drank cup after cup going over the charts, envisioning scenarios, and debating whether I'm really able to do this flight. Maybe it is worry about the airplane— didn't the engine cough a bit before it started? What if I have engine trouble in the Arctic? Or over the ocean? Then again, maybe it is just being back in the Canadian north. The desolation and rocky terrain take me back to memories of my first venture into this region.

$\perp$

When I was eighteen, after my return to Canada from Switzerland, I drove to Niagara Falls. Niagara College was a newly built community college, still littered with construction debris and rutted unlandscaped grounds. To build up its enrollment, it advertised for "nontraditional" students. The administrative clerk asked for my highschool transcript, but I explained that I had just immigrated and hadn't attended Canadian high school, though I would be glad to write an entrance examination. She then instructed me to take a test in English competency, to insure that I would be able to understand the lectures. Perhaps it didn't surprise her that I spoke regular English without an accent, but I was delighted to get into college and didn't mind playing along.

I signed up for a full course load as a day student and another full load as an evening student, ten courses in all. Going to classes was a pleasure. It was my only chance to make something of my life. I couldn't bring myself to write to Trix, but someday ... someday when I could face love without shame, maybe I would see her again. And so I came to school with the fervor of a poisoned man for the antidote. At the lectures, I sat in the middle of the empty front row, prepared with notes of not only the required reading, but all of the elective reading as well. Many evenings I hid in the library at closing time so that I could spend the entire night reading without interruption. At the end of the semester, a professor came up to me.

"You don't belong here," he said. For a moment I thought they had finally discovered my lack of entrance qualification and I would now be expelled. "You should be at a university. I'll see that you get in."

Even though Brock University was hardly a major academic center, it was enheartening just to be an authentic student. I worked in the evenings as a movie projectionist at the theater in Niagara Falls, studying with a tiny reading lamp while I kept an ear tuned to the reels. Then, after a year, I moved to Vancouver, British Columbia, and enrolled as a philosophy major at Simon Fraser University. Two years later, I had almost finished my Bachelor of Arts degree, but I was getting jaded with the subject. It wasn't really philosophy that was being taught, I complained, but the history of philosophy. I appreciated learning about the development of western thought. But that was not why I had come to study at a university. I was full of questions. There were problems about reality, about God, about the mind-body difference, and countless other issues I was trying to get a grip on. I expected an aggressive intellectual atmosphere, where smart people made you think. Instead, I found a bunch of meek professors, clinging to hopes of tenure and writing papers on some trivial aspect of philosophical classics that they dared not question too closely. It reminded me of medieval monks, tediously copying the venerated manuscripts and maybe adding a few of their own illuminations on the side.

The students were better. In my Philosophy of Religion course, I particularly liked a reserved young man with a pale complexion. He had a constant, rumbling cough that kept him from talking much, but one day he stood up in class and declared that God is an asshole. "You might find this offensive," he said, "but how can God be offended? Respect? Hah! Respect is for the weak. You show respect to the old, the frail, *ahh-huck*, or maybe something you put on a pedestal. Why do you put it on a pedestal? Because otherwise it might be damaged. If God is all-powerful, He doesn't need respect. In fact, it's patronizing. *Ahrrk*. It's an insult! How can God need our respect? We are the ones who should be respected!"

He dropped out of class just before the end of the year. A few months later, I heard he died from tuberculosis.

I was beginning to think that my courses were a waste of time. On the other hand, there were a lot of non-academic benefits of being a university student. At Simon Fraser, I spent as much time learning rock climbing, ice climbing and white-water kayaking as I did in the classroom. My roommate was a graduate geology student. Chris was a small, energetic, muscular man with a ragged beard that made him look like a leprechaun on steroids. His father was a professional NHL hockey player and Chris had learned to skate before he could walk, but he was most comfortable in hiking boots. I had a lot of opportunities to go on field trips with him. We jounced around the country-side in my old Volkswagen Beetle with the rusted-out floor boards, while I listened to his explanations of everything from plate tectonics to gold mining. The highlight was a week exploring and mapping caves in West Virginia, a thrilling experience that combined rock climbing with a childhood delight of being underground.

Although I hadn't finished my degree, I left the university. It was time to get back into the real world. In keeping with the classic Canadian tradition, I decided to look for money and adventure in the north. Chris had told me so much about mining, I figured I knew enough to bluff my way into a job without too much difficulty. But my applications were all returned with a brusque apology, "Sorry, we're only looking for experienced miners." I took a gamble and flew to Edmonton, a city that billed itself as The Gateway to the North and the location of the mining company head offices. I had no more luck there, and got the same responses. Then I decided to put all the chips on one last number: I spent the remains of my savings on a one-way ticket to Yellowknife, Northwest Territories, over a thousand miles due north from Edmonton. Yellowknife was a wind-swept frontier outpost, a cluster of shacks along Great Slave Lake inhabited by in-between-work miners, prospectors and the occasional native Dené or Inuit who strayed into town. There were also a couple of horrendously expensive hotels for government officials or mining company executives on expense accounts. Yellowknife had only about twelve hundred residents, but boasted seven very loud and boisterous bars.

Over a few beers, I talked to some miners, but they were not very encouraging. It was true that it was easy to get hired there if you were an experienced miner. These men never filled out an application or visited a company personnel office; they just went directly to the mine office on site. Miners were free-spirited characters who roamed around the country, taking and leaving jobs at a whim. After all, no matter where you are on the earth, it is the same when you are underground. "It's warm in winter, cool in summer, and there's no bugs." They formed a loosely connected social group, like sailors who had worked on the same ships and visited the same ports.

One miner told me, "The first question they're going to ask you is, 'Have you worked underground before?' If you say no, you can forget it."

The question was reasonable, in my opinion. There were stories of powerful, strapping men hired without experience, who panicked with claustrophobia on their first descent into the hole, or quit after a single shift, unable to tolerate the danger, depth, and darkness. Why should a mining company take a chance on someone new when they could hire a fully trained miner?

I caught a ride north on a rough gravel road to the Giant Yellowknife Gold Mines encampment. It was already late afternoon by the time I got there, almost five o'clock, and I cursed myself for getting a lazy start. Now I would probably have to do it all over again another day. Luckily, the office was still open. I told the elderly receptionist—probably the only woman in the camp—that I was looking for work and, like a reflex, she asked in a no-nonsense manner, "Have you worked underground?"

"Of course."

"Well okay then, Mr. Trencher will see you." She hesitated, looking at the old clock on the plywood wall. "You better go right in."

Mr. Trencher was a pleasant, elderly man whose leathery, creased face and swollen knuckles disclosed a life of hard work.

"Well, son, tell me what other mines you've worked."

There was no point in trying to bullshit this man. He probably had a personal familiarity with every mine in Canada and in any case, the North is so replete with liars, con-artists, hustlers and nut cases that no story goes unchallenged.

"Well, I haven't worked in a *mine* before but," I hastened to explain in my rehearsed speech, "I worked for a geological survey exploring caves and have a lot of experience underground. You know, the equipment we used, carbide lamps, is the same that miners used before electric headlamps, and a lot of cave layout is similar to the stope and drift system of the mines. And of course, in caves we were not allowed to use power drills, so we'd break into a room with a jack-leg and sledgehammer, just like they used to do in the mines before the high-pressure air lines came in ..."

"Carbide lamps!" he exclaimed. "I remember using those when I was a boy."

This good man, who had worked in the mines since he was a teenager, had never in his life been in a cave. He was fascinated by my descriptions of stalactite formations that looked like a hanging pipe organ and underground rivers that connected cave systems hundreds of miles apart. After a half hour, he said, "I'll show you the bunkhouse. The commissary is by the headframe; you'll have to go there first thing in the morning to pick up your gear—they'll give you credit and take it out of your paycheck." As we stepped into the thin twilight, I was so delighted I could have done cartwheels.

I walked on alone to my bunkhouse, one of the long aluminum trailers a few hundred yards away. The very moment I opened the door, there was an ear-splitting crash of rent metal and glass. Light flooded into the dim hallway from the only open door, evidently the source of the noise—and, I guessed, directly across from my assigned room. As I walked gingerly toward my door, I could hear the sound of a drunken party across the hall, with an occasional smashing bottle.

Oh shit, I thought. The North, in addition to its share of liars and con-men, also was replete with tough guys and brawlers—in fact these categories had a considerable overlap. There was not much law in the Territories. The Royal Canadian Mounted Police took care of the serious stuff, but everything else was left to a kind of frontier mentality and you were on your own. Mining camps had their own police, the bulls, typically sadistic law enforcement rejects who were a little short on intelligence but good at restoring order without a lot of talk. A camp bull wasn't allowed to carry a gun. Instead, he wielded a three-foot-long leaded hardwood nightstick that could do as much damage as any firearm—and he was far more likely to use it.

My attempt to sneak by was of no use. "You! Get in here!" a voice from the room yelled. All right, the one thing I was worried about in coming north was keeping my teeth. Among these guys, introductions were often made by throwing a right hook to the other guy's jaw. Just about every man in northern Canada had dentures by the time he was twenty. I turned as if I had just noticed them and did my best to look like a guy whom you would rather talk to than throw a few punches around, just for laughs. There were two men in the room, both of them pretty drunk, and the room itself was in a shambles. Broken glass littered the floor and there was a gaping hole where the window had been, now lined with twisted metal, making a large porthole into the twilight. I guessed that the missing chest of drawers, somewhat larger than the window, had gone through that hole.

"Have a beer!" One of them took a fresh bottle and swung it abruptly against the table edge, leaving a small gouge in the wood as the bottle cap neatly popped off. He jammed the brown bottle into my hand. He drained the one he was holding and, without looking, hurled it through the open window space. I heard it bounce off a truck and break on the rocky ground.

I introduced myself and explained that I was moving in across the hall.

"That's good," the other guy said, "because today is my last day. Ya got gear? No? I'll sell ya mine." He pointed at a burlap sack. "That's right, the whole works. You can have 'er for ten bucks."

I couldn't believe my good luck. The muck boots alone would have cost sixty dollars and they fit me perfectly. He had everything in that bag: slickers, gloves, eye shields, hard-hat, safety belt, the requisite miner's pocket watch, even the heavy thermal underwear.

"Take it all, I'm done wit minin', never goin' in the hole again."

The other guy laughed. Miners were always saying they were done. But it paid well and it was the only work they knew how to do. Everyone understood that within a month or two, this guy without a doubt would be back working in some mine. I felt bad about taking his gear, especially at the ridiculously low price, and made a half-hearted attempt to talk him out of it, but he waved me off.

I sat by the door and, happy with the good fortune of the day, allowed myself to get drunk. But what I saw next caused the color to drain from my face. A huge mine security officer loomed over me, his face contorted in fury. The other guys were yelling foul epithets and throwing bottles through the hole and hadn't noticed. Before I could say something, or draw their attention to the problem, the bull smashed his nightstick on the back of my chair, showering the room in splinters and landing me on the floor near the door frame.

"What the hell is going on here?" he bellowed.

"Are you a fuckin' idiot?" one of them replied, completely nonplused by the crumpled chair. "What d'ya tink is goin' on here?"

"Have a beer!" the other one said and held out a bottle. And to my astonishment, the bull took it and relaxed. It turned out that he was a friend of the man who was leaving. I made a mental note to keep on his good side, as well, and soon after excused myself to get settled in my own room.

Next morning, I joined the others at the headframe, was issued my headlamp and metal dog tags for the shift, and entered the cage. My assigned level was twenty-one hundred feet below ground. Because the shift started when the worker left the surface, the mining company wasted no time in a gentle elevator ride to the site. I had been warned about this. I hung on when the cross-bar to the cage was latched and felt the floor drop out from under me. Minutes later, there was a spongy, oscillating stop as we reached our level. A dim amber bulb illuminated the shaft entrance. Drifts, tunnels up to two or three miles long, radiated out from there, lit only by the search-light beam of our headlamps. I quickly learned to look to the side when talking to someone. If you look the other person in the eye, your light will blind him. (Eventually I could pick out miners in Yellowknife just by looking at their head movements in conversation.) Few of my fellow workers had finished grade school, but they knew everything about mining and were generally good humored. I felt right at home with them. Many were immigrants from eastern Europe and I felt a natural affinity on that level as well. One of them, Mustafa, was a short, tightly muscled man of about fifty who had been on the wrong side of some military conflicts in one of the Russian republics. The other miners had a lot of respect for his intelligence. His darting black eyes could take in a situation very quickly. Mustafa was a trammer, driving the ore train, and jokingly boasted that his locomotive was the fastest in the mine. He called it Sputnik.

I liked the physical work. It felt good to be swinging a sledge hammer. When you do it right, it feels oddly effortless even as you sense a tremendous power to the movement, smooth and flowing like a firehose. I loved the rhythm of the swing. The ebb and flow of pulling back, raising and releasing, then the smashing follow-through as iron connects with rock. It's a physical meditation, like walking, or breathing.

I learned that the greenstone type of granite that formed most of the rock had a grain to it, almost like wood. You could whack a piece all day and just crumble the edges, or you could hit a chunk the size of a refrigerator just right and it would crack in two. The miners referred to the unbroken rock walls as the living rock, having a sort of life energy until it was blasted into rubble. Mining was a satisfying combination of very basic labor and simply walking along the drifts, enjoying the quiet, dead-still air and the surrounding darkness. As the short, arctic summer gave way to winter, it became incredibly cold on the surface, as low as seventy below zero; a painful cold like sandpaper on your face and you could actually hear the rasping sound of your breath instantly freezing into a fog of ice crystals. But at my level underground, the warmth of the earth's core kept the temperature pegged at precisely fifty-nine degrees, and this gradually increased with depth to a sweltering seventy degrees at the five thousand foot level. Sometimes, working off alone somewhere, I would lie on a plank and turn off the headlamp. The resulting absolute darkness was almost hallucinatory and I would meditate on the fact that there was a half-mile thickness of granite above me.

But what I liked the best was blasting. As soon as I could, I applied for a blasting license. "Now, you have to write a test for that," the older miners warned. The test was ten questions, with true or false answers, and to help me study for it, they gave me the test sheet with the correct answers. There was a short practical test as well, where I demonstrated using both fuse and electrical explosives by blowing up some furniture-sized pieces of rock. The next day, I had a nice official certificate stating that I could use any manner of explosives at my discretion.

There is a wonderful satisfaction in blowing something up. It is really gratifying to destroy a huge obstacle, all in the guise of work. Kids nowadays play videogames where they blast apart their opponents. The games are no comparison to the hair-prickling, gut-slamming force of a real explosion. There was a tiny erotic thrill as you packed the explosives in the cracks just so, leading the fuses or blasting wire to your detonation box, or connecting them for multiple charges. Then a little ritual. Walk a hundred feet in each direction to clear the area. Yell, "Blasting one ... Blasting two," crouching behind a barrier with your hands cupped over your ears. And then, "Fire!" With the explosion, the air became brittle as if you were inside a clap of thunder and you could feel the pulse of the shock waves in every cell of your body, your skeleton resonating and your tissues buzzing with a tingly orgasmic intensity.

Despite safety precautions, accidents happened. Improperly placed explosives could cause the resulting rubble to hang up, unstable, only to come loose with the vibration of a footstep and crush the unwary miner. Fuses got snuffed and you weren't sure if they were still burning. Or the electrical detonation box shorted. Blasting caps were especially dangerous. A young guy I worked with blew off his right forearm packing them too forcefully. I saw him months later unloading boxes at a Yellowknife store, using a hook that was fashioned to his stump.

One day I was sloshing along a drift—the mines were always trickling water and puddles lay among the tracks—lost in my daydreams, when I heard, or thought I heard, a vague *Fire*. I was puzzled, because I wasn't looking down the drift but at a rock face straight in front of me. Then I felt wet. Soaked. It took me a while to realize that the rock face was the ceiling and I was lying on my back in the muck. My ears were ringing and there was a *whoosha, whoosha, whoosha* sound dying away. A man came around the corner and gave me a horrified look.

"Christ almighty! Are you all right? I thought I was alone." He helped me up. I felt a little unstable, but nothing broken. My chest felt tight. I coughed deeply and spat out some frothy, bloody phlegm.

"Yeah, I'm fine. Hey, isn't it about lunchtime?"

I always enjoyed having lunch with the other miners. We usually worked alone, or in pairs, and it was fun to get together.

Mustafa told hilarious stories of Russia, but generally had nothing good to say about his homeland. The lunchroom was warmed with an open flame heater that also provided illumination, so we could turn off our headlamps. Most of the time, we all fell asleep after lunch, sometimes for an hour before going back to work. It was only later that I realized that the burner was probably using up the oxygen in the room.

My blasting skills improved and I developed a small reputation among the stope miners, those who worked at the large ore face. One day, Mustafa and I were called to a remote site. It was a room the size of a concert hall, with a steep floor of jagged boulders like a heap of junked cars. At the back upper end was the face, a wall forty feet high and wide, with a loose crust. Our job was to take off that crust so that the stope miners could go to work drilling into the fresh surface. We spent the entire morning packing the face, making frequent trips to the locomotive we had with us. Climbing each way through the rubble took about twenty minutes and it was exhausting. With all the charges, this would be a tremendous explosion so we elected to use a long fuse. That way we could be a mile or two off when the face blew. Finally, we surveyed the completed work. The face was draped with a great gossamer web of fuses that were linked to several slow-burning master fuses. We were using nitroglycerin, so the shock of the first explosion would quickly detonate the other charges, but the network of individual fuses would provide a neatly controlled blast.

When we were done, Mustafa waited at the locomotive while I set to work lighting the master fuses. There was no room for error and I calculated that we had thirty-five minutes: twenty for me to get down, and fifteen to give ourselves plenty of distance. I carefully lit each master fuse. I was almost finished when I saw that one of them had twisted and curled back up on itself as it burned. To my stunned gaze, it touched another fuse about four feet over my head. The fast fuse crackled to life, reached a split and suddenly there were three fast fuses burning toward the charges. It was too late to try to stop them. I had maybe five minutes to get out.

I bolted down the slope, vaulting and clawing my way over the rocks. Somehow I covered the distance in a couple of minutes, expecting any second to feel the impact that would be my last sensation. Mustafa saw my panicked scramble, figured out immediately what was happening and when I got to the locomotive, he slammed the power on. We rocketed out of there, bent over with our hard hats against the firewall, bracing against the coming impact. With a sudden crack of thunder, a wall of dust and pressure swept past us. For a second I felt as if I had been plunged under water and then tossed up into a hurricane. The storm dissipated as quickly as it had come, and I released my tension when I felt Mustafa had cut the power. We coasted to a walking speed in the dusty tunnel. Mustafa looked at me grim-faced, but his eyes were twinkling and I found myself grinning back. "Son of bitch," he said. "Next time you give me warning." And we both burst into laughter.

A few weeks later, I was invited to meet with the foreman. "We're going to a new system in the mines," he said. "These trains are the old way. They don't even use them in the States any more. We are going to get diesel bucket loaders. I figured you'd be a good man to handle one."

The bucket loaders, huge earth-moving vehicles with tires higher than a man, were impressive machines and I looked forward to the opportunity of driving one. But there was something about the change that bothered me. I would be working completely alone, without the camaraderie of the other guys. Diesel underground also didn't seem like such a good idea. Where is all that exhaust going to go? Besides, any idea that came from the United States was generally inspired by the American owner's attempt to extract ever more gold for less cost, and any possible detriment to the miners was not a big consideration. There were no liability lawyers in Yellowknife. With American mining companies in Canada, the saying went, "The

U.S. gets the gold and Canada gets the shaft." But when the boss invited you to do a job, you thanked him, because the alternative was finding yourself with no job at all.

Driving the Euclid was just as I had suspected. It was a big power trip, climbing up into the seat and maneuvering that huge machine, the thousand horsepower engine roaring as you picked up tons of ore in a single scoop. It was also lonely. Every shift, at some arbitrary time, I would set the Yuke to idle and eat a solitary lunch. There was a taste of diesel smoke at the back of my throat.

One day—or was it night? There was no sense of time underground and as the winter gave way to summer, it was light twenty-four hours a day on the surface—I worked the Yuke in a narrow sloping passageway. Creep down the twisting tunnel to the rock face, load, and then back up a quarter mile to dump the load at the chute. No need for level drifts here, as there were with the train system. Just a wormhole that twisted its way to the face, barely big enough to accommodate the Euclid. Not even room enough to turn around. When I backed up the length of the tunnel, I had to turn my head to face behind me, keeping my eyes on the rock walls to avoid jamming into them. Spending eight hours driving back and forth alone in a distant, dark tunnel left plenty of time for spooky imagination. A few hours into the shift, backing up, I had a thought. What if the devil were sitting on the front of the loader? It was one of those silly thoughts I used to have as a child, when I imagined there was a bogeyman in the barn or in the cellar. It would take all my courage to go down there in the dark. As I got older, I liked to think that I was afraid of nothing and forced myself to look at the cellar as just a dry storage room. That took away the thrill of going into a creepy space, too, and it wasn't as much fun anymore. The long, boring hours in mines had to be filled with something and when I ran out of the usual day-dreams, I tried to think of scary stuff like the roof caving in, being buried alive, or discovering some grotesque carnivorous creature and being torn apart and eaten. Now, backing up, the thought came that the most terrifying creature, the devil himself, was sitting right behind me. The notion gave me goose bumps. Don't look! If I turned my head, I'd run into the wall. The thought came back. The hideous devil was sitting, grinning at me on the hood. I could feel his hot breath on my neck. The temptation to look was unbearable. I was breathing heavily, my heart raced and my head swooned. No, no, this is ridiculous, I told myself, I'm just making this up. But the image was overwhelming. I couldn't see clearly. The goddamned devil was right behind me! I spun around to look and the Yuke immediately crunched into the wall. There was no devil on the front. Instead, there was a long thin pipe, twisted and broken, dangling from the bucket. The loader had snagged the fresh air conduit near the face and torn it out the length of the tunnel. I was being asphyxiated from carbon monoxide. I staggered off the machine, my head pounding and feeling that familiar orange glow as I knew I was about to pass out. "I've got to make it to the landing," I told myself, "or I'll die." I crawled, breathless, disoriented and almost blind, up the rocky slope, fighting the sleepy weight that felt so peaceful. When I finally reached the fresh air near the shaft, my head cleared to a throbbing ache. I took the cage to the surface and quit.

August 26: Labrador City, Canada

Morning creeps over the collection of pre-fab aluminum buildings and quonset huts that calls itself Labrador City. For a large airport, it is remarkably quiet. I lie in my sleeping bag, drowsy, enjoying the cosy feeling of goose down. Not much sleep last night. From now on, I have got to go easy on the caffeine, I tell myself. I need the rest. It is foolish to fly exhausted. Around eight o'clock some people show up and open the cafeteria. I arrange fuel for the airplane and review the weather charts over hash browns and eggs. No further icing conditions forecast. It looks good to the north.

The engine coughs a few times, then turns over slowly. I stop and wait for a minute. It catches the second time. This is starting to worry me. Before I left California, I had a new impulse coupler installed to ensure easy starting in cold weather. Now the same damn problem is happening again. I can't afford to have engine trouble in the Arctic. Maybe if I just go easy on it. Maybe it is just some carburetor ice that developed after I shut down. Yeah, that must be it, I figure. But I don't feel reassured.

As I lift off the runway and climb out, the land below looks more desolate than ever.

Chapter 10

TACHOMETER

For hours north of Labrador City, the terrain below has looked the same. Striated rocky outcrops and nameless, amoeba-shaped lakes. But the trees are gradually thinning. Even at ten thousand feet, I can see that the black spruce, firs, birch, and aspen have given way to arctic dwarf spruce, twisted and withered by the cold wind. And soon there are no trees at all. The airwaves are quiet as well. In the United States, there is always something to listen to if you want, with a range of frequencies competing for your attention. Now I am on a long haul to Iqaluit, the administrative and commercial center of the eastern Canadian Arctic. It is a five-hour flight and for much of that time I might be the only small plane in the air on that route. So the radio is quiet. I call in position reports to Montreal Center. There isn't much to do otherwise but watch the terrain, laced to the horizon with rock and water, become ever more inhospitable. There are streaks of snow near the rocks now. The landscape is a Jackson Pollock painting, a limitless spatter of gray and white.

The continent of North America ends at the top of the Ungava Peninsula. Near the coast, I look down onto the native settlement of Kuujjuaq. Just a few aluminum huts next to a runway; a makeshift, desolate outpost. I could stop here for fuel but decide not to. I want to test my ability to do a long flight with the auxiliary fuel tank. My strategy is simple: take off with the fuel flowing from the main tanks, because they are the natural, reliable, fuel system for the airplane. Then, once I am established at cruise altitude, switch to the auxiliary fuel tank. In severe turbulence or in critical conditions, I could switch back to the main tanks. Otherwise, I should continue on the auxiliary tank until that supply is close to exhausted, and then go back to the main tanks for the remainder of the flight. There is only one problem: it is difficult to tell when the auxiliary tank is exhausted. If I switch back to the main tanks too soon, I will leave unused fuel in the auxiliary tank. This will shorten my range unnecessarily and I'll have to carry the dead weight of the unusable fuel.

It is time to check the auxiliary fuel level. I unbuckle my seat harness, disconnect my headset and climb over the HF radio, the life raft and other gear, into the back of the airplane. I spin the large cap off the tank and peer inside with a flashlight. I just manage to get a glimpse of fuel sloshing at the bottom, but the cockpit immediately fills with fumes, so I quickly spin the cap back on. This definitely is not going to work. Not only is it impractical to be crouching in the back trying to guess the depth of the remaining fuel while no one is flying the airplane, but any electrical spark will turn the whole ship into a fireball.

I clamber back into my seat and re-hook the harness. For a while, I ponder about what to do, then start munching on some granola bars from my cooler, washing them down with a root beer. It would be cheaper just to chew on some cardboard and the taste would be about the same. Suddenly the engine dies. No sputtering, just an abrupt stillness, with the propeller windmilling as the aircraft slowly loses speed and noses into a shallow dive. *Engine failure!* My mind snaps into gear. *Stabilize the airplane.* Done. *Look for a landing site.* Nothing below but rock and ice. *Leave it for now. You got ten thousand feet. Check*

the problem. Master switch. Ignition. Mixture. Fuel flow ... Snap
the fuel boost pump on. One, two, three, I twist the valves to
the main fuel tanks and the engine purrs right back to life as if
nothing had happened.

Whew. I take a few minutes to let my heart slow down. So
that's it. Fly the auxiliary tank until empty, then switch. It had
never occurred to me to actually fly the tank until empty and
the engine fails. It reminds me of when I had a motorcycle.
That was how you did it: you just rode along until the engine
stopped, then reached under the tank and flipped a switch to
reserve and the engine picked right up again. The process is a
little more unnerving in an airplane. What if there is a vapor
lock and the engine doesn't start again? You can't just pull over
and let it sit for a while. Even so, this system should work okay
with calm air, plenty of altitude and a reliable engine. This
morning's worry about the engine returns. I better take some
time to look into this in Iqaluit.

The stony northern shore of the continent comes into
view, crisp and clear in the sunlight. Hudson Strait lies beyond,
the scene of so much history in the early exploration of North
America. How many ships had come through here, in a fruitless
search for the northwest passage to the Indies? I try to picture
the tall-masted vessels sailing below, but the strait is littered with
icebergs and I can hardly believe the ships came so far.

An hour later, the bergs cluster up in a solid pack against
the shore of Baffin Island and I am over land once again. At the
tip of Frobisher Bay, named after one of the great explorers, lies
the town that also used to be called Frobisher Bay. The name was
changed to Iqaluit a few years ago, when the Canadian government agreed to recognize the traditional names. Eskimo is also
no longer used. It was an old, derogatory Indian name for the
people of the Arctic. Instead, these people call themselves the Inuit,
which in their language, Inuktitut, simply means The People.

The compass swings around lazily, not much use so close
to the north magnetic pole. Iqaluit has a VOR radio naviga-

tional transmitter as well as an NDB. I tune in both and follow
them over the low mountains, festooned with snow fields and
crumbling glaciers, until the town slides into view. If it were
located a couple of thousand miles further south, it might be a
pleasant resort. The community is nestled along the side of a
hill abutting the bay and the gaily colored buildings are strung
together along a single street, within walking distance of the
airport at one end and the hospital at the other.

I taxi up to the terminal. People are bustling about.
Mechanics in orange coveralls, businessmen with navy blue
overcoats and briefcases, and Inuit women in *kamiks*, sealskin
boots, carrying their babies in the elongated hoods of their fur-
lined anoraks. In 1576, the English artist John White made a
drawing of an Inuit woman with her child at Frobisher Bay. He
could have sketched it yesterday. Many of the women I see now
look no different than the one in that drawing. After relaxing in
the coffee shop for a bit, I stroll on over to the hangar. Ray is a
tall, blond, handsome man in his mid-thirties, wearing a bright
red Montreal Alouettes sports jacket. He owns the only small
aircraft maintenance facility. A few years ago, Ray tells me, he
had come up to Iqaluit on a visit, then decided to stay when he
saw the opportunity to open his own shop here. Business certainly seems good, but I get the feeling that he is a bit mercenary
about the operation, and his heart is still in Montreal. I explain
my concern about the hard starting and the impulse coupler.

"No problem. Pull the airplane into the hangar. I'll
have one of the mechanics get started on it first thing in the
morning. By the way," he looks at me pointedly, "I don't accept
credit cards. Cash only. U.S. dollars."

I hesitate. So that's what happens when you are the only
game in town. Canadian dollars are worth thirty percent less
than U.S. dollars, but there is no point in arguing.

"Do you take traveler's checks?"

"Sure." He gives me a slightly predatory smile. "No problem at all."

Iqaluit is a lot like Yellowknife. The town is more modern, though, and the only bar I see is a subdued room in the main hotel, with a few businessmen sipping whisky and a couple of guys in jeans and lumberjackets playing shuffleboard. Otherwise, it has the same feel of being a crossroads in the tundra. A meeting place of different cultures: federal government employees, businessmen, grizzled prospectors, native Inuit, and an occasional tourist or adventurer. I hike up to the top of the hill overlooking the town and the bitterly cold wind whips my breath away. My hands are freezing and my feet are numb. And this is *summer!*

I have no interest in spending down my financial reserve to stay at one of the hotels. The air terminal building is open all night, so I roll out my sleeping bag off to one end, away from the arrival and departure gates, and settle down to write in my journal.

A few minutes later, I can sense some cute dark eyes looking at me and it is easy to guess who they belong to. Three young Inuit girls are shyly scampering around the terminal, daring each other to come close to me. I pretend not to notice and wait until one of them is about ten feet away, then look directly up at her and say, "*Unnusa'akut.* Hi! Come on over."

She lets out a little squeal at being caught, and then timidly comes over with the other two cowering behind her. They exchange a few phrases in Inuktitut and one asks me, "What are you waiting for?" She is maybe eight or ten. Lithe copper body and straight, raven-black hair to her waist. Her cheap, discount-store nylon clothing can't be of much use against the polar climate. But these people have a phenomenal tolerance to cold. This girl might well have been born in an igloo and an icy wind probably feels like a fresh summer breeze. In her smooth, plump face, the oriental eyes are little slits of friendliness.

"I have an airplane that's broken. So I'm going to stay here until it is fixed."

"You don't sleep?"

"Yes. I'll sleep right here."

One of them is fascinated by my fluorescent yellow highliter. "Can I see, can I see?" she peeps.

"You can have it—" whereupon the other two clamor to say they want one too. I hold up my hand, "—but first I want you to tell me your name and you have to write it here," showing them my journal.

The first one again is the boldest. "I'm Mary Petooloosie." And she writes it out in a neat, schoolgirl script. "I'm Nulu Siutiapik," says another, but has trouble writing it. Mary helps her, pronouncing her name Noodloo, then prints it out again for her. Linda Kanuweepi writes her name in the Inuktitut script, a series of triangles and squiggles. It strikes me how different they are from the greater population of the south. These people have lived here thousands of years, yet so few Canadians or Americans know much about them. I give each girl a highliter and a colored felt-tip pen. Outside, the wind is soughing over the rocky landscape. I feel like I am on a moon base, but this is their home.

Back to the journal. As I record the events of today, the words take me once more to memories of Yellowknife.

After I left the mines, I thought I would stay and pick up some other work in the north. I went to the Territorial Administration office to ask for a local driver's license. "What kind do you want?" the secretary answered. There were only four gravel roads in the Northwest Territories, a region over half the size of the continental United States. Along with the airport and a few streets, that was it for driving. There was not much point in a road test for a driver's license; anyone who wanted one could get one just by paying the nominal fee.

"I'll take a Class I license," I said, indicating the one for tractor-trailer operations. It couldn't be that hard to run one of those, I figured.

The next day, I got a job driving a White Freightliner with a forty-foot trailer, hauling frozen foods and beef carcasses from the airport. I bought a few beers for a driver from another company to show me how to operate it. The air brakes were like the Euclid. The thirty-six gears were simple enough to master. "Just remember," he said, "when you're drivin' the Fruitliner, take your turns *wide*."

There was a bush-pilot training school at the airport and one day I went over to inquire about it. As a child, I had been fascinated by the pretty crop-dusting aircraft parked in a nearby farmer's field. The opportunity to actually learn how to fly, however, seemed about as likely as becoming an astronaut. I walked up the hangar that said Spur Aviation. Mr. Jensen, a soft-spoken man in his mid-fifties, came out to greet me. He wore a maroon down jacket, even though it was the end of the summer and quite warm that day. The bush-pilot school was operated by him and his wife, with a half dozen training aircraft.

"It's his lucky jacket," Mrs. Jensen explained. "He *always* wears it. He just don't feel comfortable without it."

They invited me in to their little office and classroom in a mobile home next to a hangar. To my mounting delight, they laid out the flight training plan. I felt like a bridegroom at the wedding altar, knowing that, whatever comes, life would never be the same again.

I took back to the bunkhouse an armload of manuals and charts. The next day, Mr. Jensen directed me to a Cessna 150, a small, two-seat airplane. It had a very modern appearance, all aluminum and with tricycle nose-wheel landing gear, not like the old, fabric-covered, tail-dragger cropdusters. Mr. Jensen had a wide reputation as a pilot in the Arctic and had trained most of the local airmen. He edged himself into the tiny cockpit beside me.

"Now do *exactly* what I tell you, and when I tell you."

He patiently led me through every step. We taxied out, took off, flew around a little bit and landed. When I shut down the engine, I realized that I had done the entire flight. Mr. Jensen had not even touched the controls.

I became obsessed with flying. When the weather was bad, I hung out with the air traffic controllers in the tower or dogged the mechanics in the hangar. When it was time to fly, I absorbed every word and gesture from Mr. Jensen. He had an almost Zen-like approach to the airplane.

"Feel the airplane! Don't just fly it. Close your eyes. Now listen to the motor. Listen to the wind over the wings and the struts and the cowling—can you hear the difference? Each one has a different sound. Listen to the creaking of the metal in the fuselage. Feel the vibrations from all those things—each one by itself—coming through your seat and the floor and the control yoke. Put your hand on the metal. Use your guts. Feel what the airplane is telling you!"

His ability to be relaxed in the air was truly amazing. One afternoon, he was teaching me how to do a crab approach for a landing.

"In the old days, we didn't have flaps, so this is how you came in. Now, a lot of the schools don't even teach it. But I think you should know how to do a strong sideslip. You can make a very steep approach this way, if you have to, almost vertical."

The sideslip involved using the control wheel and rudders in an opposite, contradictory way so that the airplane moved in a sideways hermit crab-like fashion toward the runway, losing altitude rapidly but stable otherwise. The crossed controls were psychologically counter-intuitive and I had a lot of trouble getting it right. On one approach, I thought I would exaggerate the maneuver and ended up tipping the airplane over on its wing, the nose perpendicular to the runway just a few feet away. I stared in horror at the pavement and braced myself for the impact. Out of the corner of my eye, I saw Mr. Jensen gazing calmly out of the passenger window. With his baby finger, he lightly poked the control wheel, just enough for us to clear the runway. "Why don't you take it around again," he said casually.

My flying skills improved. The airport staff assumed that I was headed for a job with the airlines. But the routine, highly regimented work of an airline pilot didn't sit well with my wandering attention and innate rebelliousness. I wanted to fly for beauty. I wanted to fly for the feel of the earth dropping away and with it the cares of terrestrial life. And I wanted to fly to go somewhere, not in a straight line, but to caress the rugged hills and silent forests and the white-caps of windy lakes, to drift among the cloud mountains of the sky and to float in the ocean of night.

Commercial flying is like driving a bus. You went by the book. Entirely by the book. An airline pilot is really a flight manager. Three-axis autopilots and slaved instruments take care of much of the aircraft's operation. Nowadays, computers could even fly an airplane from terminal to terminal without a pilot on board and might do so if it weren't for the anxiety of the passengers. There is not much room for creativity in an airline flight.

⅃

In 1975, I left the Territories and took a job as a logger on the mountains of Vancouver Island. Eventually, I got discouraged with my part in leaving a forested mountainside looking like a battlefield of stumps, shredded limbs and gouged earth, so I switched to planting trees for the same company, on the same slopes. At the suggestion of a friend, I took a course to become a paramedic. It was a two-year program, but I managed to convince the course directors that my experience at the hospital in Switzerland qualified me to take just the month-long re-certification course rather than the full program. The training was pretty simple, anyway, mostly common sense, and I had seen far more trauma as a surgery assistant than most of my re-certifying classmates. The program was designed for the remote logging and mining camps. We were trained in air evacuations, splinting, suturing and basic medical skills, such as how to treat a human bite in contrast to an animal bite. I hadn't expected to deal with the consequences of people biting other people but, as I later learned, it was not all that rare.

I got a job running the ambulance and first-aid station at the Leo Creek logging camp, seventy miles from the end of the road in northern British Columbia, a few hundred miles inland of Alaska. The camp had about eighty men, most of whom were Carrier Indians native to the region. The non-Indians were flown in for two-week rotations from Fort St. James, then out for five days. The pay was good and I had plenty of time to read—a great combination.

The camp, like all such camps, had a very strict no-alcohol policy. Mac, the camp director, and Johnny, the burly logging foreman, were jovial Scotsmen who had a bit of trouble with this, even as they understood, and enforced, the regulation. The solution lay eight miles away through a rough cut in the forest.

Erich Hauptmann was a German immigrant who had built a hunting lodge. He came to Canada shortly after the second world war. It was generally said that he had been a Nazi officer, but no one was stupid enough to ask him about that. I accompanied Mac and Johnny on a trip over there. The lodge was a log structure next to a small lake with a dock for a float plane. Erich served up the beer as we came through the door, with a controlled friendliness that made you want to return the laughs but watch what you say. His English hadn't improved much for all his years in Canada, but it was enough to guide the American tourist hunters to kill whatever trophy they came for, and relieve them of about five thousand dollars for the experience.

"*Ja*, vee get close to da bear, maybe fifty feet, and I tell him to shoot, shoot, but he shake. Den he shoot, but he hit da bear in da het and da bullet bounce off skull, *k'nick*, and now bear angry and come tovart us. I hat to brink him down. Hunter angry. 'I vant to kill him! I vant to kill him!' But I say, 'You already kilt him. You see, you shoot him in het!'" He laughed uproariously and we laughed along at the pathetic stupidity of the tourist hunters. But when Erich turned away, he moved with an unsmiling efficiency.

The run to Erich's lodge became a weekly event. Because logging vehicles were not supposed to be used at night and I had a four-wheel drive ambulance for use at my discretion, it seemed logical that I should drive. It took an hour to make the trip over the stumps and gullies, occasionally winching the ambulance up a muddy ravine, but on the way back we would take twice as long, drunk, yelling and crashing through the underbrush as we tried to stay on track, with the lights flashing and the siren wailing.

After a half year in the camp, I had saved up enough money for a big trip. Freeze-up was coming, the onset of winter. The camp would be shut down for a couple of months anyway and it seemed like a good time to leave. I had become interested in anthropology and decided to travel for a year in Southeast Asia. After reading so much philosophy, I was fascinated by the possibility of seeing humans in a primeval type of existence. The French anthropologist, Levi-Strauss, wrote of these tribal people as if they were child-like beings, living in a world of magical realism. What were they really like, I wondered? My suspicion was that the great philosophical dilemmas of the world were not those of all humans, but simply of a bunch of cranky old white men. I wanted to meet people who were not part of this modern world. Maybe I could learn something from them.

I made elaborate plans for the trip, assembling maps and writing away for visas. On my last day at the camp, Mac and Johnny came up to me after dinner.

"We got something for you."

I followed them to the bunkhouse and they brought out a fifth of Scotch.

"Hey, you shouldn't have that here."

"Come on, it's your last day. We figured we couldn't talk you into going to Erich's, so," Mac took a pull on the bottle "—we had to bring the party here."

I took a couple of hits, feeling the burn followed by a warm glow.

"Why don't you go to Erich's yourself? You don't need me. Hell, you could walk about as fast as the ambulance." I took another long swallow. The whiskey was smoother now and the glow reached to my toes.

"That's ridiculous. You can't walk to Erich's. Not even an Indian can make it to Erich's faster than the ambulance."

I thought for a moment. Eight miles. I used to be able to jog that in less than an hour. "I'll bet I could run to Erich's faster than the ambulance."

Both men immediately perked up. "That sounds like a fair wager to me," Johnny said. "I'll put down fifty bucks, if you will."

"Count me in," seconded Mac.

Maybe this wasn't such a good idea. I was partly drunk and had only some light camp sneakers rather than proper running shoes. It was already night. But there was a full moon and I knew the way pretty well. I should be able to beat these clowns and I could sure use an extra hundred dollars.

We settled it. I would go first and they would follow in the ambulance a half hour later. I jogged off into the darkness. The cool evening air lent just the right crispness and the broad moonlight illuminated the forest track like a stage lamp. A few miles passed easily. I had settled in my stride and was starting to feel confident that I would win the bet. There was a soft rustle in the brush. Probably just disturbed some night creature, I thought. Then more rustles, the movement of a large animal, following me. Christ almighty! Maybe it was a bear. I stopped and listened nervously. A black bear wouldn't chase me, unless I crossed a sow with cubs, and I hadn't seen any sign of bears. A grizzly would and there were plenty of grizzlies in that part of the country. If a grizzly was coming after me, I was dead meat. Climbing a tree was the best thing to do. Climb and wait for the ambulance. But the sound had stopped and I couldn't see anything in the forest. A grizzly would have charged by now, I figured, or at least growled.

I started running again, slowly, my heart pounding. The rustling came back, now not only behind me, but alongside in the brush, on *both* sides. There was no doubt about what it was. Wolves. Take it easy, I told myself, you've got at least three or four miles left to go. Don't sound too winded. It is often repeated that wolves will not attack a man unprovoked. I went to a wildlife meeting once, where a wolf biologist complained about the unfair portrayal of wolves as voracious sharks. Then I saw a Jacques Cousteau special where he denounced the view of the misunderstood shark as a "wolf of the sea."

Running in the forest, those lectures on the peaceable wolves suddenly didn't seem so convincing. I had seen caribou wolves, which I guessed were my invisible companions. They are a huge strain of gray wolf, much bigger than a timber wolf, and can bring down an elk or moose without difficulty. I thought about going up a tree again, but there was something strangely unthreatening about the wolves running alongside. They didn't seem to be chasing me. I focused on making my breathing as deep, relaxed and smooth as possible, trying to project a rhythm in my gait that was powerful and positive. The rustling came closer and I could easily hear their panting breath. The moon was going down, but my eyes had adapted to the darkness. Then, grayish silhouettes materialized alongside. Feel strong, feel strong, whatever you do, *don't stumble*. I tried desperately to radiate confidence, but the wolves didn't seem to care. They loped on both sides and behind me, letting out little huffs and occasionally switching places. I would have liked to look at them closely, but I was too terrified to stop. For a few miles, they casually accompanied me like big German shepherds running beside a jogger in the park.

The light of the lodge poked through the trees and the wolves vanished. When I got in, Erich served up a pint and waited for my story. In an effort to calm my nerves, I took a few big shaky swallows. Then I threw up on the floor.

Just over a half hour later, the ambulance pulled up. By that time I was lubricated enough to tell what happened. Johnny and Mac each took out a fifty dollar bill and slapped it on the counter.

"Lad. It sounds like you earned it."

The next morning I got on the Twin Otter float plane, sitting in as co-pilot for the flight to Fort St. James and then on to Prince George. An hour later, I caught the commuter airline to Vancouver and that night flew to Japan. The Canadian north was in the past.

AUGUST 27: IQALUIT, CANADA

And now I am back in the north. I walk around Iqaluit, looking at the Inuit handicrafts and chatting with some government men at the coffee shop about the problems and plans for arctic Canada. At the airport, the mechanics confirm my suspicion that the impulse coupler needs to be replaced again. They say it is a common problem with cold starts and they usually have a few spares on hand. But they are out now and won't get any until the Montreal flight comes in this afternoon. Replacing it is a small job, maybe an hour, and I still should be able to leave tonight.

My plan is to depart around three o'clock in the morning. If possible, I want to make it across to Greenland, over the ice cap and all the way to Iceland in one day. It is not practical to stay overnight anywhere en route and if something were to go wrong with the airplane, I would not have any mechanical support. So I have the day to wander around Iqaluit.

I stop in at a little museum. A dark, wiry Inuit man with a black ponytail and indigo tattoos on his face is sitting in the corner office. Simeone Kurangansalik, he introduces himself. He is from Nunatak, in the Pangnirtung region of Baffin Island, and had spent his childhood in winter igloos and summer skin huts. As a young man, he came to Iqaluit to be trained to work in the Defense Early Warning stations set up by the United States during the cold war to detect a Soviet nuclear strike. When the DEW line shut down, he stayed on, proud to run the museum.

"Don't you ever think that it might be nicer to live in the south? I mean, if you could live anywhere at all, where would you live?" I feel a little silly for asking, but honestly can't imagine why anyone would choose to spend his life in this bleak environment.

He chuckles. "I've been to the south a few times. To Montreal, New York, and once I went to Miami. The city is very beautiful. I like the parks. I like to go to Montreal. But," he stops, searching for the words, "I have to come back. I love it here. Sometimes, I have to get away even from Iqaluit. Too many people here."

He remembers my question. "If I could live anywhere in the world, I would live in Nunatak. But Iqaluit is nice, too, don't you think?"

In the late afternoon, I walk back to the airport and talk to the mechanics. The engine starts up easily. An hour's work. A fifty dollar part. I go in to settle the bill with Ray. He writes out a long invoice.

"Let's see ... labor, supplies, GST tax ... it comes to thirteen hundred eighty-one dollars," he says cheerily.

I gasp as I study the invoice. "But it only took an hour. I talked to the mechanics. Why is the bill so high for the shop time?"

"The impulse coupler," he says matter-of-factly. "Ten hours at one hundred dollars an hour."

"But for nine of those hours, he wasn't working on my airplane. He was waiting for the part!" I protest.

"He wasn't doing anything else. It doesn't matter what he was doing. He was here for your airplane. Who else should I bill for his time?"

It is futile to argue. He can charge a thousand dollars for one hour if he wants to. He knows, and I know, that I have no choice other than to fix it myself, which without knowledge or tools is impossible. I write out the traveler's checks, seething.

"What's the problem?" he asks cattily. "Everyone knows that airplane owners are rich."

AUGUST 28: IQALUIT, CANADA

Two o'clock in the morning. I wake up, wriggle out of my sleeping bag, and walk over to the weather office. The warm room is enveloped in a soft, reddish glow and a pleasant duty officer hands me the weather teletype report.

"A few alto-stratus layers. You probably won't be able to get on top, but it should be calm and icing doesn't look like a factor."

Typical weatherman, I think. Every word is qualified with an indeterminate modifier: might, should, possible, probable, potential, a chance of this and a likelihood of that. Well, weather is an indefinite science and why should he be blamed if things turn out differently?

An hour later, I fire up on the unlit, dark apron and lift off into the night sky. My route is north, to stay over land as much as possible, then near Angijak Island take a dogleg over the Davis Strait to Kangerlussuaq of Greenland. I am in clouds right away, but the air is calm. Occasionally, there is a break in the layers and I catch a faint glimpse of glacial ice and rock in the dimness below. I notice that the ammeter is showing a discharge. Maybe there was some sort of overvoltage in the shop. Sometimes you can see a brief discharge on start-up, especially after work has been done on the avionics. I keep an eye on it, a steady but weak discharge for an hour or so. Not a good sign. I debate returning. But it could turn out to be something trivial and I can imagine Ray's glee as he presents me with another thousand-dollar invoice.

"All the mechanics were thinking about it over lunchtime," he would probably say.

The ammeter needle stays pegged on discharge. I flip on some electrics: carburetor heat, pitot heat. I have been in clear air between cloud layers and turned off the pitot heat. Now with it back on, the ammeter shows a substantial discharge. An alarming thought: I am draining power from the battery! I should turn back immediately. The ammeter suddenly goes to normal and I breathe an unconvinced sigh of relief. Maybe the problem has fixed itself.

The cockpit lights start dimming. Now I know there's a real problem. I have been draining battery power all along. The reason the ammeter is now normal is because there is not even enough juice left to run it! Cursing my idiocy, I immediately initiate a turn back to Iqaluit. The cockpit lights continue to fade until they are gone and then, one by one, the radio lights blip out. The transponder goes dead. The turn coordinator, powered by electrical suction, starts to spin down and then tumbles to the side like a spent toy top. I quickly shut off all unneeded electrics. The cockpit is now completely dark. I get on the HF radio and call Montreal Center.

"Mayday. Mayday. Mayday. November three zero seven four five estimated six five three zero north, six two zero zero west. Electrical failure. Mayday. Mayday. Mayday."

There is a faint response in heavy static. "Aircraft in distress, say again."

I repeat the message, but the radio is failing.

"Seven four five," a distant voice announces. "We have you on pan frequency. Squawk seven seven zero zero and ident." The emergency code for the transponder.

"Unable. Electrical failure. Radios inoperable. Will attempt return to Iqaluit."

I listen for a response, but there is only burbling static, then nothing.

A quick inventory. The aircraft is stable at eleven thousand feet, between solid cloud layers. I estimate that I am over the ocean, not far off the coast of Baffin Island, a couple of hundred miles north of Iqaluit. It is dark and virtually all instruments are dead. I look at the panel with a flashlight. The fuel gauges, unpowered, now read empty. The engine instruments are off. It looks like an airplane shut down on the ground. I am flying a dark shell in a black sky that has never felt more desolate.

If I can get over land, I might survive a crash. The compass swings lazily. It is too erratic to set the gyro compass, so I have only the vaguest sense of direction. But the gyro is still powered by engine suction. I can at least use it to fly straight. I am in and out of cloud now. The pitot tube has iced up and the airspeed indicator needle is pegged. *Don't even look at it*, I warn myself. The altimeter is still functional. I've got to have that. The mountains below—if I am over land—are almost seven thousand feet. I have to know my altitude to stay above them. Most of the time, I am in cloud now. There is no way of knowing how far those rocky peaks are below me. I could smash into one any second. I've got to know my altitude. It's all I have. The altimeter depends on the static port, a tiny hole on the side of the fuselage. If the static port ices up, I'll have to smash the glass on the instrument and use the cockpit cabin pressure for an altitude reading. It won't be as accurate, but it will work. It will be enough. I reach for my heavy flashlight, the Maglite with the long black handle, and tuck it under my thigh.

I've got to fly level and straight. The attitude indicator is the only other instrument still powered and, as long as I am in clouds, my life depends on it.

I lean forward and study the tachometer. The engine is running well, seemingly oblivious to the problems behind the firewall. Like the galloping horses of a stagecoach whose driver has been shot. The sound of the engine is the heartbeat of the airplane. It gives me courage. If the engine is good, I should be able to survive. Maybe even get out of this mess.

I zip my survival suit a little closer. The careful preparations that were made fun of in Bangor might now save my life. I pull out the portable nav-com radio, the expensive unit I thought I would never use, and tune it to Iqaluit. There is no response. The short antenna probably restricts me to fifty miles at best. I broadcast over the communication frequency of the nav-com. The power it takes to broadcast on a radio is much higher than for reception. After a few tries, it sounds like the portable radio batteries are weakening, so I back off.

A nauseating urge to panic sets in. I don't want to believe the position I'm in. Total electrical failure in instrument conditions. In the Arctic, no less. It's an unthinkable situation that can only end in a crash. *Easy, easy*, I tell myself. *Focus.* I search for a break in the cloud layers to give me a chance to think. A narrow plain of clear air opens to the left, almost impossible to make out between the shades of darkness. I'm in a sandwich of black, layered masses. It may lead me away from Iqaluit, but will give me time to assess my predicament. I have lost all of my navigation instruments, my radios and most of the flight instrumentation. The only way to get back is by dead reckoning.

I grimly recall the warning in Moncton. Jesus, I never thought it would come to this. With the small flashlight in my teeth and the chart spread out on my lap, I pencil in wind and estimated airspeed vectors, with widening circles of inaccuracy as I fly south. If I miss Iqaluit, I will become completely lost and eventually crash, either in southern Baffin Island, the frozen ocean, or somewhere on the Ungava Peninsula. I push back another wave of panic. Looking for the tiny settlement in the featureless Arctic is like searching for a golf ball on a glacier.

Iqaluit is at the end of Frobisher Bay. Even in the stratus layers, I might be able to pick out the huge body of water. Then I might be able to follow it to the airport. It will be a longer flight, but it will avoid the risk of overshooting the town. The thought of overshooting the town, lost in clouds, gives me a sickening feeling of despair. It is a death sentence. I've already angled slightly to what I guess to be the east, to follow the clear layer, and now I angle even more, to correct my estimated course to be sure to intercept the bay.

The cloud layers are very gradually becoming a gun-metal gray. Dawn is not far off. With the airspeed indicator out, I can't tell how fast I'm going and my attempt to stay out of solid cloud is disorienting. I see that I have dropped three thousand feet. If I'm over land, I could slam into a mountain peak. I pull back on the wheel and there is a sickening sluggishness. A stall now will be fatal. I've got to have a sense of how the airplane is doing. It is hard to fight off the panic of not having my instruments. I rip off my headset and a rasping roar of engine and shrieking wind fills my ears. *Listen.* Listen to the wind. Listen to the crackling fuselage. Now I know that I am not in a climb but in a dive. I pull back some more and the shrieking tones resolve to a smoother, hissing sibilance. I can handle this, I've got to handle this, I can do this, I tell myself.

Please, please let there be some opening. Let me find a way down. Let me get out of this. Let there be some way, however hard. Let me find the way back.

Each passing minute is a minute I've survived. Each minute is another minute farther south, to where I hope the weather will be clearer. Another minute toward Iqaluit, or another minute of less fuel, closer to the inevitable crash. Another minute of borrowed life.

Gradually, very subtly, a thin, grayish light probes through the stratus. There are some breaks. I catch a rip through the layer, showing a grayer layer below it. I've flying between gray woolen blankets, overlapping, woven, becoming lighter. More light ahead. Broad, beaming light enfolding waves of cloud. Then larger breaks, and then I catch a fleeting glimpse of blue. Again, a rent in the blanket below me, exposing a huge bay. It has got to be Frobisher. I gently turn towards it, careful to avoid getting lost in another wall of gray, and the nav needle on the portable radio jumps to life. Contact! For an hour, I follow the bearing directly to the airport. The walls thin and separate. I am out of cloud. Frobisher Bay is clear below me. A wide, utterly desolate body of water shored by ice-encrusted cliffs. The bay gradually narrows as I follow it up towards Iqaluit. The radio is quiet. There is no traffic at all. No sign of life. When I make out the town, it seems like an image, a prayer, a still-life vision. But it is real, and I going directly for it without bothering with the normal approach procedure.

I make a cursory call for a straight-in landing and then drop the airplane heavily on the runway. I taxi right up to the maintenance hangar and shut down. It is quiet. I remain sitting in the cockpit, sweating lightly in the survival suit, listening to the whirring gyros slowly spinning down and feeling the stone deadness of the ground. After a long time, I climb out, trembling in relief and anger.

"I didn't expect you back so soon," Ray quips cheerily when he arrives, an hour later. I feel like ripping his face off.

"Well, I'll be damned," he says when he has heard my story. It has taken all of my restraint to give him a logical account. "I'm sorry about what happened, but it is the mechanics, you know. I hire the guys, but they do the work, and they are usually pretty good, too."

"Yeah, and they are going to fix it right this time," I insist. "And I'm not paying a dollar more." I get up and turn at the door. "And if you have a problem with that, I'll be the biggest asshole you ever met."

I talk to each of the mechanics. No one knows what could have caused the problem. One thinks the alternator has burned out. A few days to ship the part and a couple of hours' labor will fix that, he says. Another wants to tear down the engine, disregarding the fact that the engine was one of the few things that continued to work. I am not convinced by any of it and storm around the entire morning, demanding answers. It adds up to nothing. I ponder the problem over lunch and arrive at a solution. I look for the young mechanic who installed the impulse coupler. When I find him, I pull him away from a Turbo Centurion he is working on and suggest that we reinstall the impulse coupler, exactly as he did yesterday. Everything the same, I emphasize. The look in my face tells him the Centurion can wait. He goes to get permission from Ray and comes back with his evident approval.

We go through the procedure and I question every step. At the end, he replaces the voltage regulator, which we have tested and found satisfactory. He twists it on casually.

"Don't the points have to line up?" I ask.

"Oh ... yeah ..." He looks puzzled. He walks off to find the shop manual and studies it for a while before coming back. "I guess it goes on this way," he says sheepishly.

After an hour of ground run-ups, trying every electrical combination, I am satisfied that the problem is solved. The battery is being recharged and I re-pack my supplies. My anger has dissipated. The incident is over and I am just thankful to be alive with my airplane intact. After all, it wasn't really Ray's fault. I give him three hundred dollars for the additional shop time. He winks and says he will pay the GST himself. Sure, buddy. And I give the young mechanic twenty dollars for a gift for his kids.

AUGUST 29: IQALUIT, CANADA

Three A.M., I walk out into a light drizzle on the dark apron once more. This time, the flight is effortless. With a nervous eye on the gauges, a gradual reassurance settles in when everything goes smoothly in a velvet sky. I watch in awe as a vermilion crescent of daybreak slowly illuminates the coast of Greenland.

Chapter 11

MANIFOLD PRESSURE

In the year 986, an outlaw fugitive from Iceland named Eiríkur Rauthe Thorvaldsson landed on the southwest coast of a great island. Better known as Eric the Red, he was a murderer exiled from Norway and again from Iceland for avenging the killing of his two slaves. He called the settlement Vesterbygd, the Western Settlement, and the island Greenland, in the hope of attracting others to join him in his new home. At the same time, native people from the Canadian Arctic were migrating eastward and began to populate the northern parts of Greenland. Today, the island's scant population reflects the heritage of Inuit and northern European peoples. Greenland is an autonomous province of Denmark, supported by Copenhagen and the rent from the United States Air Force bases at Thule in the north and at Søndrestrøm, at Kangerlussuaq near the head of Søndre Strømfjord.

As I see it now, Greenland is anything but green. I have a sweeping view of the west coast, brilliantly clear in the early morning light, and as I come close I can appreciate that this is one of the oldest and most rugged landscapes on earth. Multi-hued gray mountains arise from the ocean in sharp relief, the colors of flint, shale, pewter, and agate. They are cut by deep gorges, choked with icebergs, with ribbons of the prettiest diva-blue open water leads where the ice has broken. Beyond the rocky coastline, I can see the great ice cap of the interior. Virtually all of Greenland is covered by a two mile thick sheet of ice, tying up a tenth of the earth's fresh water. From a distance, the ice looms over the coast like the cloud bank of a gathering storm.

The flight from Iqaluit has taken almost five hours. I am ready to land and prepare for the next leg across the ice cap, about four hundred and fifty miles to Kulusuk, a tiny Inuit encampment on the eastern coast. My plan is to refuel at the air base, built in 1941 to service the bombers flying to Europe. It took months to get the landing permission from the U.S. Air Force. When I finally got the documents, it became clear that the stop-over would not be cheap, either: five hundred dollars for the landing permit itself, and fuel at about six times the price in the United States.

The airfield lies far up the Kangerlussuaq fjord. It is close to the base of the icecap, very strategically protected. I had ex-pected to find the entrance to the fjord and follow it to the airport. But the visibility is superb and I can easily make out the entire coast of the region. I tune in the Holsteinsborg NDB on a coastal promontory. The needle jumps to the eleven o'clock position. I now see that I am north of the fjord, near Kangerdluarssuk. With the excellent visibility, there is no need to sidetrack south and I continue straight over the jagged peaks and plunging ravines. I spot the airfield first by a number of large oil tanks, and then the broad runway on a small plain at the head of the fjord. On three sides, the mountains rise to seven thousand feet.

My thumb keys the broadcast switch and the sound of my voice is reflected in my headset, "Søndrestrøm, seven four five is ten miles out and has the field in sight."

"Seven four five is cleared for one zero," the approval comes back in an Oklahoma drawl, so strangely out of place here.

I glide down the lengthy, straight-in approach toward the big block numbers, 10, at the base of the runway. As I gently land on the broad pavement, I can see a long, two-story white building, the air terminal evidently, and a few military aircraft: a couple of C-130 Hercules, a C-141 Starlifter, and a twin-rotor helicopter in mottled green camouflage paint. A pickup truck with a FOLLOW ME sign on the back is waiting near the end of the runway. As my rollout slows to a taxi speed, the truck swings out ahead and I follow it, like a cow led from a pasture, to a faded red square painted on the tarmac a couple of hundred yards from the terminal. I shut down and awkwardly climb out, my survival suit open to the waist. An orange falls out and rolls under the airplane. It is good to stand. The sun feels warm and there is a fresh breeze, slightly chilly, coming out of the east, the direction of the ice cap.

A tall, blond man steps from the pickup truck and comes over. He has the broad chest and smooth, pale good looks of the Danish. At six feet, I am used to the perspective of being the taller person, slightly nodding my head to talk to most people, and I always feel a little odd, almost like a child, when I am next to a person much taller than I am. This man is probably six foot eight.

"I'm Lars, with Scandinavian Airlines. We run the operations here." He speaks in heavily accented but well-articulated English, as if he were pronouncing each letter. "Did you have a nice flight?" He peers inside the packed airplane and chuckles. "The food here is really not so bad. You do not need to bring your own."

I shrug myself out the survival suit and do some stretching. The sun feels good on bare skin. There is a fresh, nose-tickling scent of spring, reminding me of an Easter morning when melted snow has left the roads dry and dusty.

"I'd like to get going again in an hour. Do you think I can get refueled in that time?"

"I think so. I will order it for you. You are allowed to go inside the terminal, but nowhere else. May I see your papers?"

Before I left California, I prepared a packet with all the appropriate documents. I have it ready now and describe to him each Department of Defense form, knowing that he is certainly very familiar with them and has no need for the introduction. But I believe it is useful to go through this little performance. It seems to add a measure of reassurance. In my attempt to learn of others who had tried to fly small aircraft across Greenland, I read that the Danish authority has occasionally refused permission. The aircraft were forced to return to Canada and in some cases had to be freighted out by ship.

Crashing on the icecap is usually not fatal, but the rescue expeditions are horrendously expensive. The surface of the ice is not well known. It generally runs from eleven to thirteen thousand feet above sea level, but even my military chart acknowledges the inaccuracy. The Greenland interior is one of the very few places on earth that has not been completely explored. On most of it, humans have never set foot. The service ceiling of my airplane is only fifteen thousand feet, leaving a rather small margin of flying just one or two thousand feet above the ice. The cap is also often overlain by a thin layer of ice-fog, so that the featureless terrain is impossible to see. I read of a small twin-engine aircraft in which the pilot became unsure of his distance above the surface. With a jarring noise, he saw that his propeller tips were curling and he realized that he had flown right on to the ice.

I don't want to take any chances with Lars or his supervisor. As I list each document, I emphasize the capability of the airplane. Lars listens to my explanations with a look of bemusement.

"Good," he says. "Why don't you have some breakfast while I get the fuel."

The restaurant on the second level of the terminal is surprisingly large and well provisioned and has generous triple-paned windows looking out onto the fjord. I order a plate of eggs and sausages and write a few postcards, which can be sent from here.

Relaxed and refreshed, I walk back to the airplane, inspect the outside, the engine, and the fuel. Tidy up the interior and then climb once more into the survival suit. I radio for a weather update, but the information is no better than what I got earlier this morning in Iqaluit: a variable northeast tailwind with indeterminate conditions over the ice cap and the Iceland Strait. If I can make good time, I hope to pass Kulusuk and fly all the way to Iceland. But now, the challenge is to depart from sea level and climb to fifteen thousand feet before approaching the ice.

The long runway and cold headwind help ease the airplane into a steady climb. I follow the westerly wind, flying directly into it to ascend the maximum amount. After eight thousand feet, I begin a slow rotation to face the ice. I am ready to begin a shallow turn back to the fjord if I need the extra room to gain altitude, but staying on the eastern side of the valley gives me a bit of orographic lift, making the turn unnecessary. The strategy works well and by the time I reach the first fingers of ice, I am already at thirteen thousand feet. Twisting the knob to the frequency of the Kulusuk NDB, I am relieved to hear the tinny squeak of the signal. Navigation over the ice is difficult at best, and I will have to keep a close eye on the instruments.

The ice sheet itself looks like an enormous blanket, ruffled as it reaches the coast in great corduroy folds but smoothing out towards the interior. After an hour, I can see only a sweep of white. Utterly featureless. Here and there, wisps of ice-fog drift in a diaphanous veil over the smooth marble surface. The entire world is reduced to two colors: blue above, white below. The sun provides an angle of reference, but throws no shadows, just a sharp piercing of the delicate blue.

"Iceland Radio, November three zero seven four five, position report."

The radios are quiet. I had some concern about this. Leaving Søndrestrøm, I was using the VHF radio to make the position reports, but now, an hour later, I am beyond VHF range. The HF radio is not working either, giving only intermittent static modulated with the rhythmic tones of a human voice, as if someone was shouting through a pipe, too far away to hear. I try a half dozen other frequencies and get only a glissando howl. Position reports are mandatory for legal flight and, if I crash, these reports will be the only indication of where to begin a search. Now it has been forty-five minutes since I have had radio contact. Suspended in this ethereal world, I can do nothing but watch and wait. Scan the instruments. Over and over. I am a black dot, a speck of pepper on a white porcelain dinner plate.

I reach into the cooler and pull out a loaf of carraway seed bread, a half wheel of Camembert cheese, and a couple of slices of Arctic char. Some crumbs from the crusty bread fall into the open suit. Like eating in bed. It is cosy and comfortable, but you can't help but make a mess. Each bite of the char fills my mouth with a luxuriant, salmon-like flavor. I ease the top off a bottle of Pepsi, slowly so the carbonation won't foam over. The taste is no match for my fruit juices—I have cans of pear, mango, and a delicious guava that isn't too sweet—but I need the caffeine. I have to keep alert.

In this elemental space, I feel that I am at the dawn of existence. There is only ice and sky. And in this featureless world, a tiny metal nut with a fleshy seed. What is life, I wonder? What makes something alive? I remember a big discussion about this in biology class and, as I recall, there was no simple or agreed-upon definition. Now I think I know the answer: power. The "unmoved mover," Aristotle had called it. Take some metal or tissue, add power and, like Dr. Frankenstein throwing a switch, you have life. Food into my body. Fuel into the airplane. My tissues breathe, fizzing with chemical reactions, while a tide of blood courses in and out bringing nutrients and carrying away wastes. The engine breathes as well, each cylinder exploding a mist of fuel and air, while a tide of oil brings lubrication and carries away heat and debris.

I look at the manifold pressure gauge. While the tachometer shows the power the engine is putting out, the manifold pressure shows the power going *into* the engine. This instrument specifically shows the intake air pressure of the engine, the lunging inhalation of an athlete. It is the breath itself. After all, the word throttle originates from that for the throat. Closing the throttle is literally choking, strangling, the engine. Now I have the throttle wide open but in the thin air, the manifold pressure reads fifteen inches of mercury, barely half of what it would read on the ground. A turbo charger would solve that problem, but few airplanes of this size have one. Instead, the engine and I are tramping together on a high-altitude plain, breathing deep in the thin air, reassuring and keeping an eye on each other, "Oh, I am fine. *Fine.* How are you doing?"

So, I think, if life is power, then death is simply the end of that power. The flow is interrupted. The rhythmic tide collapses into stagnant pools and the chemical fizz goes awry. One by one, by the billions, each complex chemical disintegrates like a drop of oil in a detergent bath. The tension, the focus, is lost. The body and the environment become equal and uniform, and eventually indistinguishable.

I don't believe in life after death. I don't believe in any other kind of continued existence after death, either. It is not that I am opposed to this belief, which is probably the core of every religion. It is just that I don't see any good evidence for it. Even more, there seems to be plenty of evidence against it. People are desperate to cling to some hope of continuity beyond death. After all, any living being must be terrified of an end to its existence. Otherwise that type of organism wouldn't be around very long, would it? You don't see a lot of people whose ancestors were kamikaze pilots. The people you see are those whose ancestors worshiped life. It is natural that this worship should extend to everlasting life.

My guess is that life is like a work of music. It exists only as an event, a performance. The notes on paper or the hard phonograph record—these are not the music, only its tracks.

Life is that thrilling moment when the players and pieces come together just right, and a gasp arises, an awareness is awakened, an astonishment of beauty, and then, *bip*, it is over, lost in the oblivion from which it came.

Where does the mind, consciousness, the soul, go when life is over? It goes everywhere and nowhere. It is a Navajo sand painting. The artist carefully dribbles different hues of sand on the ground to form a beautiful image, and then leaves it for the wind to whisk away. What happened to the image? The dispersed sand, after all, is still sand. But that particular image is lost forever.

I don't know why death should be so important. Why should people care what kind of death they will have? A peaceful death, a painless death, an honorable or valiant death—what difference does it make? Any event only seems to derive meaning in retrospect. After all, you can't really think about the whole thing until it's over. But in death, there is no retrospect. Not for the dead person, anyway. No one comes forward and says, "Gee, my death was not as bad as I expected it to be!" And for the others who live on, who will remember the dead person, why should they be concerned? Death doesn't give meaning to life, no more than the final chord gives meaning to a symphony.

Only life can give meaning to life. And yet, sitting here in the thin air between white and blue, I have no idea what gives meaning to my life, or if there is any meaning at all. My friends have a ready answer for this. I can't help smiling at the irony of this: my closest friends tend to be devoutly religious. Christian, Jewish, Buddhist, Muslim. For some reason, they all indulge me when I voice my skepticism about religious matters and usually say something like, "Well, it isn't anything you can rationalize."

I have studied a variety of religions and, frankly, I think they are a mixture of primitive myths and wishful thinking. But I have to admit that the totally rational approach has a few holes. When I look at my own experiences, there is evidence of forces in the universe that bear more than a little resemblance to religious beliefs. If life is so straightforward, how come there is an uncanny coincidence to events? How come experiences chalked up to good luck or bad luck don't happen quite randomly? There are times, as well, when I feel a sensation of something else going on, some other force. I could argue that this is the consequence of stressful emotions, or confusion, or deception. But there is no denying that the universe is not quite as simple or straightforward as it seems. I see no reason to believe in God and yet I have to admit that there have been far too many experiences in my life that suggest some sort of overriding presence. It is not the sense of a spiritual being guiding my fate, but more of a sense that events in life have a flow, or a type of resonance, so that there are unexpected connections. Synchronicity, Jung called it. I've had my share of bad luck. Then something would happen, so completely improbable that it just did not make sense. It was as if something was giving me a message that I did not understand. It happened on that railway platform in Switzerland—how come Anna just happened to be standing there?—and it happened countless other times when my foolishness should have led to some sort of injury or punishment.

This leads me to think about Bill, the pilot in Bangor. What kind of luck was it that he survived? Maybe the luck was that he crashed. That glow in his eyes, that self-realization, right or wrong, is worth infinitely more than a few thousand dollars for a successful ferry flight. He faced his death, and won his life. Am I doing the same thing? Is it necessary to crash to get that awareness? What if it is all nonsense and the near-fatal experience simply causes people to retreat further into a blissful delusion that they have God's protection? If you have to crash to ask that question, the answer will most likely be your death.

A couple of other memories speak up.

When I was a college student, I once packed all my belongings into a battered old Toyota pickup truck with the intention of driving to Mexico. I thought I would spend the summer studying Spanish with a family in Cuernavaca. I had no job that summer and I had always wanted to learn Spanish, the mellifluous sounds of which are a lot nicer than the guttural tones of German. The only problem was that I had just two hundred dollars, barely enough for gas to the border let alone an entire summer of expenses. I picked up passengers along the drive south, some of whom pitched in a few dollars for fuel. When I got to Corpus Christi, the truck starting mechanism broke down and it could only be started by pushing or towing. Neither I nor the local mechanic could figure out the problem. I was destitute. I couldn't afford to store the truck there; even the cheapest storage would have cost much more than I had, and simply parking the vehicle on a country road would have led to vandalism and the loss of everything. I drove to the Toyota dealer, but it was closed. I arranged to leave the truck there for them to fix, and decided just to go on to Mexico and deal with the problem on my return.

Now I had less than a hundred dollars. It was nowhere near enough. In Cuernavaca, the families listed as sponsoring language students wanted fifty dollars a week. I had planned to stay for three months. Moreover, I was told by other, very disappointed, foreign students that the families were merely interested in the money and spent as little time as possible with them, leaving them to congregate with their American friends and learning almost nothing.

I left Cuernavaca and went to Mexico City, even more dejected. A friend had given me the number of a reporter, Dolores, who worked for a leftist radio station. With nothing better to do, I called and was invited to stop by for a cup of coffee. I patiently listened to her diatribes against the American imperialist policies, and then a young woman walked in. She was dark skinned, a Zapotec Indian girl from the Oaxaca region. Dolores introduced her as Mira, who was brought to Mexico City by the radio station to help out and to learn secretarial skills. Mira asked me why I was in Mexico.

"*Yo quiero hablar espanol, pero no puedo, ah, encontrar familia, ah ... Es demasiado caro,*" I stumbled, not making a whole lot of sense.

Dolores came to my rescue and explained to Mira what my difficulty was. Mira brightened up and chirped excitedly to me for a few minutes, the only word of which I understood was *familia.*

"She says her family lives near Xoxocotlán, not far from Oaxaca. You can go and stay with them. They would be very honored."

That night, I got on the bus and by daybreak I was in Oaxaca. It took the rest of the day to get to Xoxocotlán and then hike among the outlying areas to find Mira's family, in the constant company of a pack of snarling pariah dogs. To everyone I saw, I waved the piece of paper with directions to the house, but almost no one knew how to read and it was evening before I found the place, a low adobe shelter in the shadow of the ancient ruins of Monte Albán. A short, well-muscled Mestizo man came out in response to the barking dogs and yipping children that surrounded me. Suddenly feeling silly, I explained in my rehearsed phrases that I had met his daughter in Mexico City and that she suggested I stay with them. Would it be okay if I could spend the night and give them some money for food? He came forward and clasped both my hands. He slowly said that I must come to stay with them and refused offers of payment in a way that made it clear that the subject was not to come up again.

For three months, I lived with them, sleeping on a mat on the floor like the rest of the family. Señor Pacheco was a cobbler, with a workshop behind the house. His wife was a full-blooded Zapoteca who still had her youthful beauty after giving birth to Mira when she was thirteen and four other children later. The younger daughter and three sons were at home. The youngest son, a five year old, took a special affinity to me and I liked him too. He reminded me of myself at that age; I was also the youngest of three boys. At night, he clung on to my back when I tried to sleep. A hot, sweaty little kid competing with the mosquitoes for my discomfort.

Each day, Señora Pacheco collected herbs from the garden and nearby hills and at night she would grind them on a stone *matate* for the next day's meals. The sight of her working and singing softly in the moonlight, below the silhouette of the ancient Zapotec ruins, was absolutely enchanting.

It was the best possible way to learn Spanish. The children had endless patience in coaching me, not only correcting me if I said something wrong but mimicking my accent and phrasing to the giddy laughter of the family and friends. When I got bored, I took the bus into Oaxaca, and watched American movies. The next day, I always had to relate the entire plot in great detail, with long digressions to explain points of confusion. For example, I saw *Dog Day Afternoon,* a supposedly true story about a couple of gay men in New York who rob a bank so that one of them can get a sex change operation. I had to explain about bank robberies, hostage taking, the gay culture in the United States and the actual surgery involved in sex change operations. They listened to all this with wide-eyed attentiveness. Nothing in *el Norte* was too bizarre to be believed.

My vocabulary grew exponentially. By the end of the summer, I had a respectable grasp of the language. When I returned to Corpus Christi, I found that the problem with the truck had been a simple loose wire. Since there was nothing to repair, there was no charge. The truck had been kept in a locked compound the entire time, and I was free to drive it off.

All right. So that was a remarkably lucky summer, I'm thinking. Maybe it is a stretch to ascribe some supernatural force or divine intervention to those events. But was it just luck? Why did I set off with two hundred dollars expecting to spend three months studying Spanish when I must have known how impossible that would be? Was I depending on some sort of magical intervention? Isn't this the sort of foolishness that allowed my father to run around the country and think that God would provide for his family, leading to our destitution?

The Mexico summer was a bit of good fortune, granted. But a second memory makes its way to the surface. It more directly suggests to me that some other force is active.

One spring day in California, five of us from the university decided to climb Mt. Shasta. Just before we left, one had a change of heart and said he was going to a party that night instead. We four men continued and camped out on the flank of the mountain for the next day's ascent. Mark and I were the only ones who had done much climbing and quickly pulled ahead. The snow was deeper than we expected and the going became slow. I could see that the other two had decided to stop at a little hut. Mark started to fall behind as well, but I was determined to get to the summit. I made my way along the western ridge, unroped and moving carefully, and noted that Mark, far below, had also turned back. There was an angry gray line of clouds forming over the Trinity Mountains. I recalled the warnings about Mt. Shasta. It is so high it makes its own weather and climbers have to be very vigilant to avoid getting caught in a storm. Still, I was in clear air and could reach the summit in another hour. As I was climbing my way along a knife-edge, the billowing squall moved over the valley toward me and within twenty minutes I was enshrouded in a bitterly cold fog. The wind intensified to a storm, whipping an icy rain that froze instantly on the rock and snow. I cowered just beneath the ridge on a tiny half-foot square perch of rock, afraid to move. If I lost my footing it would be impossible to avoid tumbling down the frozen wall, thousands of feet to the cirque below. I hadn't been prepared for the cold and wore only a light jacket and canvas boots. My feet and hands were becoming numb and the wind almost pushed me off balance with every blast. I whimpered in anger and fear, clinging desperately and waiting for that little slip that would bring the end, my body plummeting helplessly down the slope. I couldn't believe the force of the storm; even in my terror, a part of me gazed in awe at the billowing, ash-colored masses, like an erupting volcano.

Suddenly, in the midst of this, a warm light seemed to shine from directly above. It was a very odd feeling. There was no break in the dark cloud and the wind slammed into me without letting up, but I felt an abrupt peacefulness and confidence descending on me, an invisible spotlight beam seemed to be projected exactly where I sat. I had an astonished awareness of being in a completely protective cocoon that extended to about a foot outwards of me. The high-pitched whine of the wind continued, but my clothes were unruffled. I took off my jacket and sweat-soaked shirt. I sat down, legs dangling over the abyss, in stunned disbelief, and even took my shoes off. I felt entirely comfortable and content. There was some sort of radiation warming my chest, hands and feet. I stayed in that happy complacency for about a half hour as the storm gradually diminished. Then I climbed down.

When I rejoined the others, all of us were awkwardly silent. For some reason, I couldn't talk about what happened and I wondered if the others had had a strange experience as well. Or maybe we were all just tired. When we returned that night, we found out that our friend, driving home from the party, had been killed in a head-on collision.

⅄

"November seven four five, this is Alitalia flight six four one. Do you read?"

The deep male voice, smooth and relaxed, is very startling. It is so clear, I have a fleeting sense that there is someone right beside me. It has been three hours since I left Søndrestrøm and I haven't heard anything for the last two. I have dutifully made my position reports anyway, in a futile gesture, and now the sudden response takes me by surprise.

"Alitalia, seven four five is at fifteen thousand over the ice cap approximately six six one zero north, four two west. Where are you?"

"Well, you're really down there! You got some guts, there, fella. We're at thirty-seven thousand feet. Read you loud and clear, but I'll bet you're having trouble with Iceland Radio. Want us to make the position report for you?"

"I'd appreciate that. I'm having problems with the HF and can't get through."

"Roger, our HF is unreliable as well. Probably the surge in sunspot activity. Stay on with us and we'll be happy to make the reports."

I feel a wave of thankfulness for this kindly pilot. We chat about the weather, about Greenland and history and flying, and my sense of isolation lifts away in pleasant relief. I imagine sitting up there in the spacious flight deck of the 747 with the rest of the crew, nibbling on snacks brought by the flight attendant. How strange to think of the three or four hundred passengers with you, each a person you have never met and yet whose life is in your hands. While they read a novel, snooze, or watch the inflight movie, the pilot monitors the ship and guides them safely back to earth. And asking me about my location and equipment, he must think it equally strange to be alone in a tiny shell near the top of the ice.

The smooth surface below begins to buckle in great folds and I know that I am coming close to the coast. A few tiny, black, rod-like specks are visible on the ice. I bank over to take a look. Aircraft wreckage. The remains, I guess, of a fleet of B-17s that crashed during the second world war. The wreckage is indicated on my chart and provides a good fix. I've drifted slightly south of my planned track to Kulusuk, but I have made good time. The steady northwesterly has given me a tailwind and I should easily make it to Iceland. I reset the VOR on Reykjavík.

The ice below cracks and buckles in a bergshrund. At the edge of the island, it abruptly drops off to the ocean, calving gigantic bergs into a tumult of frazil and pancake ice blanketing the eastern coast. I am over the ocean once more.

Okay. I don't believe in God. But maybe I do believe in angels.

Chapter 12

ENGINE INSTRUMENTS

A granite slab. Hard bluish gray with white quartz streaks. This is what the ocean looks like from eleven thousand feet. It is too far away to see any motion, swells breaking or spindrift blowing. Instead, the surface looks as fixed as a sheet of rock.

There are icebergs everywhere. Some angle up in a hook, probably hundreds of feet high, casting a translucent crystal blue onto their slopes. Others are vast, mile-long tabular blocks drifting like a mausoleum in a cemetery scattered with thousands of white crosses.

I study the shapes closely. The air is absolutely crystalline and it is possible to see incredible distances. The tiny features of icebergs a hundred miles away are etched into crisp relief. Or are they really a hundred miles away? I have an instability in perspective and suddenly the granite slab is only a few feet outside the cockpit. I can see everything so perfectly. There is no distance. The plane is sitting on the ground. We are going nowhere at all at full power.

I snap out of the illusion. Fata morgana. That is what the explorers called it, after the famous witch. These mirages are common in the Arctic, where the air is so pure that perspective of distance can be lost. From my altitude, the scene outside could be anywhere from an arm's length to infinity. The eyes play tricks. Sometimes, the surface of the ocean looks like the top of a swimming pool, a transparent rippling sheen through which you can see to the bottom. I find myself peering into the depths, trying to make out what it is and realize with a fleeting glimpse of horror that I am staring into an imagined abyss.

The ocean extends forever. There is something remarkably peaceful about heading off into this infinite space. It is a deliverance of sorts, giving yourself up, like stepping off a ledge. Maybe exotic continents lie ahead, as they did for Eric the Red and Christopher Columbus. Or maybe nothing at all but more ocean, as it was for Amelia Earhart, lost in the Pacific trying to find the tiny coral patch of Howland Island. When you venture out onto the ocean, you leave the known world behind. So the ancient Greeks believed; ocean was their word for the great waters circling the earth, beyond which there was nothing.

When I was twenty-three, working as a paramedic in British Columbia, Canada, I left my familiar world to cross that ocean. At the end of the logging season, I bought an airline ticket across the Pacific to Japan. I had never been in such a foreign place, with an unintelligible script, unrecognizable food and millions of seemingly indistinguishable people who swept through the Tokyo subway stations like a flood-tide river. Almost a foot taller than the crowd, dressed in work boots, jeans and a lumberjacket with suspenders, I must have made a comical sight. Everyone I met was remarkably polite and hospitable. Bewildered by Tokyo, I took a train into the countryside and then spent a week in effortless hitchhiking around the main island of Honshu.

Almost invariably the first car that came along would give me a lift, the driver studying me with uninhibited curiosity.

I continued on to Korea, Taiwan, Hong Kong, Thailand, Burma, and Malaysia, replacing my clothes with local garments, shedding my weight and my ignorance, until I was a wiry, sun-tanned traveler, moving efficiently and innocuously. My purpose was to visit the last remaining pockets of people who still lived in the jungle with very little contact with modern society. But they were vanishing rapidly. I had read about the Temiar, a people of the Senoi group of tribes in the roadless interior of Malaysia. They were famous in anthropological circles because, it was said, they believed that the dream world was more real than that of waking consciousness. It was impossible to go there, I learned to my dismay, because of guerrilla activity. The whole region was off limits. The government was in the process of relocating all of these tribes from their jungle homes to tea plantations, where they could be put to work and assimilated into modern society. Most of the larger Senoi tribes had already been reset-tled in towns, the adults trained to pick tea leaves and their children put in schools. Now the last of the Temiar were being rounded up.

I made my way to the office of the Ministry of the Interior, on the twentieth floor of a large tower in Kuala Lumpur.

"I am an anthropologist from Canada, studying the Temiar," I explained to the receptionist. "I'd like to report on the progress in their development, but have not been able to go to the Cameron Highlands. Would it be possible to have a word with the Minister?"

"Yes," she said pleasantly. "You have come at a good time. He is free just now for a few minutes."

Shortly after, I was motioned into the spacious office with a grand view of the city below. To my surprise, the Minister was not a Malay but a jocular-looking Scotsman. As a teenager, he explained, he had joined the navy and fought in Malaysia during the second world war. He stayed on and married a Melakkan girl. His garrulous manner, I guessed, must have been mutually beneficial to him and the Malayan postwar government struggling to get out of the yoke of colonialism.

"It's a pity about the Senoi," he shrugged. "Those chaps have been in the bloody jungle for thousands of years and there is quite a bit of interest from UNESCO in keeping it that way. But it can't go on. We've got some trouble there—terrorists who are still fighting the last war—and the Senoi are caught in between. The plantations will be safe and it will work out well for them.

"Tell you what." He scribbled a note. "The resettlement office has a man going out next week. If you can get to Kampar, I'll have him take you along."

The town of Kampar was swarming with soldiers and jeeps and the hills echoed with the percussive racket of helicopters. I imagined that this is what Vietnam must have been like: an unseen enemy, disinterested locals, and unmotivated soldiers fighting a war for some principle they barely understood. The resettlement officer was a small Malay man of few words. We would be taken by jeep to the edge of the forest, he said, then hike in.

We had a Senoi guide, but it was not easy to find the Temiar. The following day, we finally located the compound by midday, an abrupt clearing deep in the rain forest, no bigger than a basketball court, with several rickety bamboo structures rigged a dozen feet above the ground. It reminded me happily of playing in a tree house when I was a boy and I scrambled up the notched pole without difficulty. At the top, a compact, older man in a loin cloth welcomed me. I sat carefully next to a little fire he was tending, turning a large taro root. Bits of bark and the occasional glowing ember fell through the wide gaps in the floor. While the resettlement officer stayed below and made his notes in a ledger, I tried to communicate with my host, making charade-like gestures and trying the few words I had learned.

"*Ipoh*," he said, pointing to a gourd with a molasses-like substance he was preparing.

Now that was a word I knew. Poison. We spent the next hours munching on the taro root, which was remarkably tasty, and carefully whittling bamboo slivers to razor-sharp darts, then dipping them into the poison and drying them on a little rack. The next day, with two young Temiar men whom I guessed to be his sons, I went hunting with blowpipes and the darts. I looked on in amazement as one of them would nail a monkey thirty or forty feet up in the canopy. I tried the blowpipe, but was unable to do more than a feeble shot, with the dart falling harmlessly a few yards away. What they really wanted was a pig but, after hours of hunting, we found only some spoor and a kind of large rat that we added to our monkey kills.

I had hoped to find people who lived in some pure, primeval way, like our early human ancestors, from whom I naïvely thought I could get some sort of wisdom. I didn't really know what to expect. Maybe I thought they would be so foreign in their way of life that I would not be able to communicate with them. Instead, these people were just like anyone I had ever met—living a little differently perhaps, but underneath it all there was not much that separated us. Even without knowing their language, I felt a kinship. Without saying a word, we understood each other completely. There really is no such thing as a "foreign" person. The few things that distinguish us—language, clothing, food, skin color—these are utterly trivial. I had traveled halfway across the world, but these people were no stranger to me than my cousins.

The experience in Malaysia led me to adopt the persona of an anthropologist. In Singapore, I went to the Raffles Hotel, a classic, grand old hotel that had been the home of Somerset Maugham and other writers. I got a few sheets of the house stationery with a pretty line drawing of the stately manor gracing the top. On this stationery I wrote a number of letters stating that I was an anthropologist and requesting right of entry to restricted areas. In the following months, I used these letters from "my university" or "my government" to get permission to travel to the interior of Indonesia. I took a freighter to Borneo and spent six weeks crossing the island, slogging up muddy rivers and cadging rides on dugout canoes through mangrove swamps. I slept in the jungle in my hammock or at Dayak longhouses where racks of skulls reminded me that these people, not much earlier, had been cannibals. I traded cigarette lighters and other trinkets to hop rides on prahu sailing ships to get to other islands.

It was a good year and I decided on a career. What I had done was for fun and interest, but there were people getting *paid* to do it. I returned to Canada, finished the last year of my philosophy degree and entered a graduate program in anthropology at the University of Manitoba.

Humming to myself, I think during that year in Asia the world became small for me. Manageable. For all of human history, there was a frontier—a place beyond which only the most intrepid explorers and adventurers would go. Now the earth is no longer limitless and the "beyond" no longer exists. For most people in the industrialized countries, a couple of weeks' wages can pay for a ticket to go almost anywhere on the planet. In every part of the globe, you don't have to look long to find not only someone who speaks English, but who will happily accept American money. I learned that it is useful to carry a roll of U.S. one dollar bills whenever I travel overseas. It has become a sort of universal currency. The world today no longer has a frontier. It is like a large garden and every inch of it is under someone's care and control.

It has been almost seven hours since I left Kangerlussuaq. I am making good time and the engine is running well. An hour ago, I burned off the fuel in the auxiliary tank and switched back to the main tanks, getting that little adrenaline shiver as the engine faltered and then charged back to life. The fuel gauges show half tanks—plenty of reserve. I scan the engine instruments. Oil pressure, fine. Oil temperature, fine. Exhaust Gas Temperature, a little high. I had leaned out the fuel mixture to get the maximal range. I don't mind running the EGT on the high side, but keep an eye on the next gauge, the Cylinder Head Temperature. It would be nice to have a full engine monitoring system, with a CHT gauge for every cylinder. But I have only one, sensing the cylinder that typically runs the hottest. If that cylinder is good, it is a fair bet that the other three are fine as well. Now the CHT is running a little hot, so I slightly enrich the fuel mixture. A few minutes later, the needle creeps back into the comfortable zone.

Clouds are building up ahead. Convective activity. And long before I can see it, I know I am near Iceland.

The radio crackles. "November three zero seven four five, contact Reykjavík Control one one niner decimal seven."

A haze obscures the shore, so that I see the piedmont glacier of the interior before I can make out the coast. Reykjavík, "smoky bay," was settled by the Vikings in the year 874, and named for the steam rising from thermal springs percolating through the ground. I follow vectors to the airport on a sprawling lava field near the city. As I turn downwind, I can see the pretty pastel houses and a large white church. There are no trees and the nearby naked hills are an almost fluorescent emerald green.

The airport is modern and efficient. A friendly man with tousled blond hair and a bright blue down jacket comes to greet me.

"Sveinn Björnsson." He reaches out a hand. "Please come this way." He leads me to a comfortably stocked lounge with coffee and assorted breads and pastries. I do my best to sample each one while he taps away on a computer and the dot-matrix printer makes a *scrit, scrit, scrit* noise spooling out the invoice.

Let's see: landing fee, communications fee, customs fee, parking fee. The additional ground handling fee is 5000 Iceland Krónur. Altogether, that's, ah ... what the hell difference does it make? I don't have a choice. I pull out my Mastercard. It is all just numbers on paper, anyway.

"There is a weather warning tonight. We are expecting winds gusting to sixty knots. We can put your airplane in the hangar if you want."

"How much is that going to cost?"

"One hundred dollars U.S."

"Thanks. I think I'll pass. Do you have any extra ropes?"

I pull the airplane behind a hangar and position it in a direction to best accommodate the expected wind, then lash some wooden slats to the ailerons, rudder, and stabilator. Finally I anchor the fuselage and wings separately to some concrete posts. It should withstand a hurricane, I figure.

On Mr. Björnsson's recommendation, I call the Egilsborg bed and breakfast. The owner sends his wife to pick me up. It is a pleasant house with a chic Danish interior, not far from the city center. When I go to take a shower, I see that the hot water has been left on, full blast. Later, the owner explains: the water is from a thermal spring and is limitless, so they usually don't bother to shut it off. He laughs, "Foreigners are always surprised by this."

In a gentle twilight, I walk down into town, trying to remember the streets to find my way back. Let's see, I'm on Skólavörthustígur street—Jesus, how am I ever going to remember that?! But the large white church is nearby and should make a good landmark. I make my way along the Tryggvagata to the very pretty, old section of town. There are a lot of people bar-hopping. I join in and order a beer. Instantly men and women come up and introduce themselves, curious. Everyone seems to speak English very well, with a pleasant nordic accent. It is one of the friendliest places I have ever been and this beer is the last one I will have a chance to pay for tonight. I get dragged to a few other pubs, reminding myself of a difficult flight tomorrow. Maybe I should just stay in Iceland for a few days? But the weather is worsening. If the fall storms arrive, I could be here for weeks—or risk my life in the treachery of the north Atlantic. No, I've got to leave while the weather is relatively stable.

At one in the morning, the sky has settled into a deep violet, but everywhere people are partying. "We love the summer! Tomorrow we will be sleepy but what does it matter? Come! Have another beer!"

I beg off and shamble along, quite drunk, in the direction of the Egilsborg. All the crayon-colored houses look the same. Didn't I come from the direction of the church? There is more than one large white church, I discover. I don't even bother trying to mouth the street names. I stop an elderly lady to ask directions. She points me the opposite way. I'm tired and feel like just sleeping on the pavement. A few blocks further, a man directs me up the hill, at a right angle to where I've been going. This is ridiculous. I find a little pizza shop, still open at two A.M., and do what I always do in times of indecision. I eat.

A couple of slices later, I feel better and my head has cleared a bit. The girl behind the counter looks at me sympathetically when I tell her I am lost. Her straight blond hair, her face and curious smiling eyes, and her slightly athletic body remind me of someone. Well, when you're drunk, everyone looks familiar. She tells me she has a street map and we study it together. And suddenly a memory is jarred loose of someone else I knew with that same mellifluously accented English, soft, not quite German or French, but in somewhere between. For a moment I see Trix, patiently explaining to me how to get home.

The Egilsborg really isn't so far away. Fifteen minutes later, I am snug in bed, with the sound of the still-running water merging with the sloshing in my head.

AUGUST 30: REYKJAVÍK, ICELAND
I wake up with my head feeling like a sack of garbage in a trash compactor. The fluttering blinds suggest that the wind has picked

up, but it is not the gale force of yesterday's warning. When I look outside, the bright sunlight awakens a slumbering pain in my temples. The sky is clear. This weather may not last. If I stay, it might be a few days, a week, two weeks, before the weather is clear enough again. I can't chance it. I will have to leave today. You idiot, you should take better care of yourself, I mutter internally. This is not a flight around the California countryside.

The owner and his wife have a homey breakfast display and I guess that it has been ready for a couple of hours. He winks at me. "I see you came back alone last night." There is already a little knot of anxiety in my stomach. He has no idea what I am facing, I think.

I call the weather office. Things look good, although the briefing attendant emphasizes the unpredictable nature of the North Sea. There is an inversion near the Færoe Islands. "Watch out for icing," he says. This raises my anxiety even more and I am eager to get going. The wife once again offers to take me to the airport. We stop off along the way at a grocery store and I pick up some provisions: pickled herring, some tough-looking rye bread and a smelly cheese that I am assured is very good.

It is ten o'clock as I lift off to the northwest. Even though the weather is clear, I am given a SID, Standard Instrument Departure, and follow the vectors to the west, south and then east. In the morning light, the island is spectacularly beautiful. Braided estuaries of the most delicate shades of green and brown are spread along the coast and rise inland in almost mythically shaped gorges and eminences, reaching up to the glacial ice in the distance. I have never seen such colors. The greens especially, in hues of mint, jade, and lichen, are simply breathtaking.

The fully fueled airplane is heavy and I motor along the coast, climbing slowly. Ahead is the NDB on the small off-shore island of Vestmannæ Jar. Just beyond it is the large glacier of the Myrdalsjökull, its heavy dome streaked with wind-carved sastrugi like a pile of goose down. I pass the NDB and turn southeast, away from the land. I have a reserve flight plan to Vagar, on the

Færoe Islands, but with a favorable tail wind I should be able to make it all the way to Scotland.

There are cumulus clumps below at perhaps five thousand feet. Above, the sky is overcast in a sour gray. Other layers drift by: scattered cumulus at nine thousand, ten thousand, and twelve thousand feet. They don't appear threatening. To the east, a darker line of cloud is developing. Probably cumulonimbus, clouds with rain and, in this weather, certainly ice. Weather far too dangerous to fly into. The Færoe Islands lie in that direction. They are no longer an option.

Four hours pass. I am a little tense. Normally, I have a good measure of confidence and throughout this trip, even setting out from Iqaluit, I have had the feeling that I will survive. But confidence, as the old joke goes, is the feeling that you have before you understand the situation. And logic is the art of going wrong with confidence. My logic tells me now that the airplane is stable at eleven thousand feet, in variable visual flight conditions, almost half the distance to Scotland. With luck I should be there in another four hours. It makes sense to continue.

I open the jar of pickled herring and put a few slimy pieces on a slice of rye. The herring has a delicate, briny taste, not overpowering. It is packed with sweet onions and together they make quite a nice combination. As soon as I open the cheese, the cockpit fills with the aroma of an old YMCA locker room. This stuff smells a lot worse than my socks. I wedge a slice in a poppy-seed bun and take a bite. *Hmmm.* Not bad. That funky taste is not entirely unpleasant, although I'm glad that I got only a half pound.

The scattered cumulus has built up and I am in turbulence. It is the worst just underneath a cloud and I try to dodge them. I drop down to seven thousand to get out of the layer. The air is clearer, but the turbulence is just as bad. I manage to get the SIGMETs, the significant meteorological conditions, on the radio in between periods of squealing static. The radio reports that the North Sea has forty knot winds, freezing level at eight thousand. The engine is fine, but I see that the manifold pressure has very surreptitiously slid back a little. I'm not getting the power I should. Probably carburetor ice. I put on the carb heat and soon after the engine starts to cough, an annoying bronchitic hack like a smoker with phlegm in his lungs. It is carb ice, all right, shooting sprays of water into the cylinders as it melts. After a few minutes, the coughing clears up. Most of the power is back, but I'll have to sacrifice some to keep the carb heat on.

It is exhausting flying in this turbulence. There is no time to think of anything or do anything but work flying the airplane. I concentrate on the conditions and monitor everything closely. A light rain starts and immediately crystallizes on the windshield. After twenty minutes, I can no longer see out through it, but the side windows are clear. I can make out a transparent sheen to the leading edge of the wings, like a plastic food wrap. It slowly builds into a distinct, quarter-inch smooth layer. Clear ice. This is much worse than the rime ice I had experienced in Canada. Rime ice is a crusty mix of snow and air. It is light and falls off easily. Clear ice is solid and heavy. I have got to climb. If I stay here, I'll crash.

Full power. The CHT starts to climb into the red zone. The air intake baffles have probably iced up and the engine is not getting enough cooling air. I open the cowl flaps. Either I climb into sub-freezing temperatures, or turn back. But now, over halfway to Scotland, it is a difficult choice—the conditions are probably no better behind me. The rain falls harder and the airplane climbs very slowly into solid cloud. The ice is heavy. I'm going to have to be very careful. The shape of the wing has been altered and it no longer provides as much lift. The stall speed will increase, maybe up to my climbing speed. A stall in this condition will be fatal.

I'm in trouble, but not quite desperate. At times I can't see out past the pitot tube and then the cloud gets a little lighter and I can see the dull, baleful layer that is caked on the wing. Each gust slams the airplane. I hunt for the abrupt elevator boosts when I enter an updraft and I run from the downdrafts. I've got to use everything to gain altitude, but the airplane is straining against the heavy load. There is no possibility to economize and I leave the engine on full power. Fuel burn has increased to an alarming rate.

I pull out the Jeppesen instrument approach plates, which I prepared by laminating the flimsy rice-paper sheets in plastic for just such an emergency. Flipping through the plates, I find Stornoway, on the Isle of Lewis in the Hebrides. I'm sure that, even at full power, I'll have enough fuel to make it there. I don't have much other choice.

Now I've made it to eleven thousand feet, probably with the help of the loss of the fuel weight. The outside air temperature gauge reads fifteen degrees Fahrenheit. The wing ice is no worse, but it is still there. My hope that it would sublimate off has been futile. I continue on in this way, heavy ice-covered wings, the engine straining with full power, for another hour. On the way up to altitude, the windshield ice thickened to an opaque mass and crept to the side windows as well. I open the tiny camera window in the plexiglass, to scrape off enough ice to see the wing but, as soon as I do, the airspeed falters and we nose into a shallow dive. I need every bit of performance I can get to stay at this altitude.

The radios burble with static interrupted by scratchy bursts. Those bursts can only mean one thing. There is electrical activity. *Thunderstorms!* The thought that I am in a critical situation leaves a cold knot in my gut. This is far worse than the predicament in Canada. I don't have the benefit of special instruments—a strike finder or weather radar—to tell me where in the mass of cloud the storm or lightning might be. If I fly into an imbedded storm cell, I am finished. The aircraft will be ripped apart and the pieces will fall into the empty, frigid ocean.

I punch some numbers into the calculator: triangulation of the NDBs with the wind factor puts me less than a hundred miles from Stornoway. I try the communications radio again and suddenly I hear something: "November three ..." but the connection is lost. I keep trying. I should be close enough. Why aren't they coming through? Maybe the antennas are too caked with ice as well. I don't even want to imagine my airplane looking like the frozen rigging of an arctic sailing ship.

I keep trying, then, finally get a sustained connection.

A pleasant brogue: "November three zero seven four five, severe convective conditions at Stornoway all quadrants. Recommend heading one eight zero to Tango India Romeo."

So Stornoway is out. That is the direction of the storm. I'm desperate to fly to land, but I fight my instinct and angle the airplane away, back out over the ocean. Due south. Tango India Romeo, TIR, is a radio beacon in the Inner Hebrides. The clouds start to become lighter. The air is a little smoother— or maybe I'm just getting used to it. After six hours of a jarring, bucking ride, fighting every minute to stay level and at altitude, I'm exhausted and slow to respond to the concussive turbulence and skewed controls. Gradually, the constant buffeting becomes softer and less frequent. The storm is behind me.

The ADF needle swings over and I have passed the TIR beacon. Still in cloud, I gently turn toward the coast of Scotland. The next phase is a little worrisome. I'm barely clinging to eleven thousand, but I've got to get down to land at Glasgow. When I pass through the freezing level, I'll likely pick up another load of ice. The airplane performance envelope is very narrow as it is; any extra ice will probably make it unflyable. The freezing level is at eight thousand. At that level, any moisture will quickly pile ice on the airplane. When I drop through that level, the extra ice could be fatal. But I can't stay here. At some point, I'm going to have to go down. My reluctance is not helped when I receive the Glasgow Approach instructions.

"November three zero seven four five, descend and maintain five thousand."

"Glasgow approach. Seven four five is concerned about icing. Request delayed descent."

"Roger seven four five. Report two zero miles. Descend at discretion."

Well, thank you. Now I just have to gather my courage. There is only one way to do this: pick a spot for a possible crash and then go down through the icing layer as fast as possible into the warm air below, where the ice will break off. I can't see the airfield near Greenock, but I know it's there. I line up the VORs and call Glasgow Approach. Then I take a deep breath, shove in the control column and drop out of the sky like a frozen eagle.

There is a sudden shattering sound of a smashing sheet of glass. A blast of freezing rain, and another shattering sheet of glass. Again and again, like dishes hurled against a wall. The ice is breaking off the cowling and dashing on the root of the wing. The wing now has honey-combed gaps of white metal and I glance at it just long enough to see a spidery crack rip along the rivets and a doormat-sized chunk of ice tear off. Suddenly parts of the windshield burst clear and I can see out on the craggy highlands shrouded in tendrils of mist.

Whoa, baby, whoa-oh. I haul back on the control column, bringing the aircraft firmly out of its dive, and the extra gravity tugs trickles of sweat from my neck. *Whoa.* Steady. Smooth. The airplane is flying clean, light. I breathe a long sigh of relief.

"Glasgow Approach. Seven four five is over Greenock, inbound for landing."

"Seven four five, Glasgow Approach. We have a lot of airliners coming in. You can expedite direct final for three zero, or hold."

Holding is the wise choice here. It is much more sensible than making a fast entry on a wet runway, sandwiched between jets. But I am in no mood for a leisurely delay. I am exhausted, trembling from the adrenaline and my arms are aching, stiff and cold. I just want to get down.

The glistening black surface of the Glasgow runway is easily visible in the distance. But I don't need to see it to bring in this airplane. I just have to follow the huge Airbus that is touching down right ahead of me. *Power on.* He said expedite, right? I come in fast, high over the touchdown zone, and then slide it in on the last third of the runway, neatly avoiding the wake turbulence of the heavy airliner while causing hardly an interruption in the stacked traffic behind me. Within a minute, I have cleared the active runway and turned on to the taxiway.

"Nice job," says the controller. There is nothing more irritating to air traffic control than having to divert an airliner because a small airplane is tying up the runway.

This is a big airport. Ground control directs me to a dozen taxiways and I pass arrays of airliners, sometimes within just a few yards. I look up at the cockpit of a nearby jumbo jet, eighteen feet off the ground, and wave to the flight crew. They look down, smile, and give me a thumbs up. I continue taxiing past passenger gates, catering hoists, freight lifts, and finally reach a light aircraft transit zone near the terminal. A minivan is there, waiting, along with a small tractor tug, to take me and the Cardinal to our respective shelters.

The survival suit feels heavy. My face is creased with dried sweat. I am still shaking slightly with fatigue and exhilaration, but the coming realization makes me grin in disbelief.

I have flown to Europe.

Chapter 13

TRANSPONDER

AUGUST 31: GLASGOW, SCOTLAND

Morning comes with a golden seepage of sunlight through the curtains of my room at the Stakis Normandy Hotel. I get out of bed, stretch, walk over to the window to look out on the country-side six stories below, and marvel again that I am in Scotland. There is a lot of uncertainty and hard work ahead, with the congested airspace and complex regulations of flying in Europe, but I am relieved that the most difficult part of the journey is over. I'll tackle the work when I get back to the airport. For now, I just want to enjoy the moment of being here.

I shower and dress and take the elevator down to the din-ing hall. An elaborate breakfast buffet is laid out, with steaming copper trays to suit every taste. There is porridge, kippers, black pudding, and "tatties and neeps," mashed potatoes and turnips. After a bit of hunting, I even find a haggis, the quintessentially Scottish dish of a stuffed sheep's stomach. I doubt whether even a Highlander could eat that in the morning and pass on to some-thing a little more tame, loading a couple of plates with oat-cakes, sausages, scrambled eggs, scones and tea. I am quite happy and, when I look at the waitresses and busboys scurrying around, I almost burst into laughter. It still feels too improbable that I can be in Scotland, and the people are almost a caricature of what I expected. They all just look so ... *Scottish*. The men wear kilts and everyone, it seems, has reddish hair and pale, freckled skin and speaks in a thick brogue. It just cracks me up.

A shuttle bus takes me back to the Execair terminal at the airport. My giddy mood is damped down by the business I need to attend to. A Federal Express agent arrives and I work with him to package the survival suit, life raft and the portable Emergency Locator Transmitter radio for shipment back to the supplier in Bangor, Maine. I sort through the documents and bundle all of the Atlantic materials and mail them back the United States as well. The European documents and charts replace them in my flight case.

It takes almost an hour to settle all the expenses. There are separate communications and navigation fees for the flight from Iceland, and these are retrieved by computer from Air Traffic Control. There is fuel, ground handling, and yesterday's arrival and today's departure fees to be paid. Even that little courtesy, yesterday, of the minivan to spare me the walk of a couple of hundred yards, costs £61.50. With the VAT, the Value Added Tax, the total comes to well over a thousand dollars. I'm staggered by the costs of flying in Europe. In the United States, the only cost would have been a much cheaper fuel. Everything else would be free, paid for by the fuel taxes. And in return for the patronage, the Fixed Base Operator would probably give you a "courtesy car" for nothing, usually some old beater, to drive around during your visit.

After chatting with some other pilots, I take their advice and file a flight plan for Ostende, Belgium. It is a large industrial airport with no service charges other than the landing fee. My watch reads almost two o'clock in the afternoon when I depart.

It feels wonderful not to have the survival suit on. The

Cardinal also feels remarkably light. There is no need for auxiliary fuel, so I left the tank dry and the valves closed. With the removal of the survival gear, the cabin is much more open and I can once again see out the back windows. The airplane leaps into the cool air like a colt in the spring.

The radio presents a nonstop patter of communications and I keep a close ear. It begins to rain near Newcastle-upon-Tyne and the land below now looks dreary and gray. I had hoped to see Hadrian's Wall, built by the Romans almost two thousand years ago as a defense against the marauding Celts. At seven thousand feet, I study the ground closely, perhaps paying more attention than I should, because there is a terse announcement:

"November three zero seven four five, state altitude."

I glance at the altimeter. Sixty-eight hundred feet. Okay guys, I know I am assigned seven thousand, but just cut me a little slack, eh?

"Roger London Center, November three zero seven four five will climb and maintain seven thousand. Sorry about that."

"Seven four five, remind you are restricted to within one hundred feet of assigned altitude. Advise if unable."

All right. *All right.* I get the point. "Jeez," I want to say, "I was just looking for Hadrian's Wall!" In the U.S., they would have understood. Probably said something like, "Well, why don' ch'all just come down and *drive* over."

And then just before the clouds close around me once again, I see the neat line of rocks snaking over the moors from coast to coast.

Perhaps the controllers are being churlish, or perhaps it is especially busy today. Whatever the reason, my vectors are continually being changed. The direct Ostende route would have been over the ocean off the east coast of England. Probably smack in nimbostratus, smooth rain clouds that would give me a nice and steady, if uninteresting, ride straight to the continent. Instead, I am all over the place. No sooner do I get established on a vector than they change it.

Now I am coming up on Manchester and the clouds open into a pillowy series revealing a drab, wet landscape below, with miles of sooty factories, tall smoke stacks, and railway yards. It occurs to me that this is the view that the German bombers had fifty years ago. Europeans have put the war behind them a long time ago, but growing up in America saturated with movies and television, I can't think of Britain without hearing the thunder of those radial engines, the screaming bombs and Churchill proclaiming, "We shall go on to the end ... We shall fight on the beaches. We shall fight on the landing grounds. We shall fight in the fields and in the streets. We shall fight in the hills. We shall *neva surrenda.*"

"Seven four five, squawk three zero one one and ident."

Now they are even changing the transponder codes on me. I twist the knobs to the new numbers and push the little ident button. The radar indicator light flashes brightly in response.

This peculiar instrument was developed for the second world war. In the 1930s, the British began to use radar to detect aircraft, but it was hard to distinguish enemy from friend with only a little phosphor blip on the screen. The Allied powers invented a cockpit radio that senses the sweep of the radar interrogation beam and returns a number. In the military, this system is still called by its original name: IFF, Identification Friend or Foe. The newer, more sophisticated transponder is now required in all but the simplest aircraft, with an assigned number that identifies not only your location and status, but your altitude as well. In the Iraqi gulf war, it was a transponder failure, or confusion, that caused the mistaken friendly fire that led to most of the American deaths. Now, the light on my unit flashes almost continuously in response to a half dozen air traffic control stations monitoring my progress on their radar screens.

Wonder if they will let me fly over London? Not a chance. After Manchester, I'm given a vector to the coast and then a starboard turn to Ostende. An hour later, I've crossed the channel and come up to the continent. The airport is pretty much as advertised: a capacious, thirty-two hundred meter runway with a large adjoining apron. There seems to be no other traffic. I'm beginning to wonder if the field is closed, but a man walks out of the fuel station as I pull up.

"*Bonjour.*" He gestures to the terminal. "*La douane, s'il vous plait.*" I walk over to the customs office.

"*Bonjour. Voudriez-vous remplir cette fiche?*" the clerk asks, handing me a form.

I try to dust off my limited knowledge of French, but it clearly isn't up to the task and I admit defeat. "*Excusez-moi. Je ne parle pas bien français. Y a-t-il quelqu'un qui parle anglais?*"

"Sure," he replies. "Could you please fill out this form? Let me know if there is something you don't understand."

To my relief, it turns out that just about everyone here speaks perfectly good English.

After a weather update and a snack at the restaurant, I am ready to go again. This time, the vectors are clear and simple, following the officially designated airways over Belgium to Luxembourg. Below, the fields are a kaleidoscope of yellow and orange flowers outlined by pretty hedges and dikes. I see windmills, with their vanes turning ponderously, like pudgy old scarecrows waving me on. Go. Go. Go on to Switzerland.

It is to Switzerland that I am going, as the sun sets. Back to Switzerland, even though I did not come from there. It is my parents' homeland, not mine. And yet, there is something from my heritage that I lost there. Something that I am now on my way to retrieve.

$\perp$

When I returned from Asia, I was a year older but felt a decade more mature. I began a Master's degree in anthropology, this time not for knowledge but for a more practical goal. To work as an anthropologist, I needed the academic credentials. After the Master's, I started the doctoral program, and looked forward to being a university professor.

As I got close to completing the Ph.D., I began to have doubts. From the outside, the life of an anthropologist was all exotic adventures and ivory tower academia. As a graduate student, I taught introductory archaeology and anthropology courses and my friends kidded me about looking like Indiana Jones. I admit I played it up and enjoyed the fantasy myself. But from the inside, the life of an anthropologist is quite different. There was an endless struggle for research funds and intense competition for the few teaching positions, even at the community college level. The field of anthropology did not rank high in the National Science Foundation's disbursement of grants. Even as my colleagues and I bitterly complained about this, I began to wonder if it didn't make sense. What benefit, after all, did we provide to society? With the exception of an occasional interesting pre-historic or cultural study, the vast majority of the journal papers were obscure investigations that no one, not even other anthropologists, cared much about.

I wanted to do something more meaningful and turned my attention to public health. The core science of public health is epidemiology, the study of the cause and distribution of diseases in populations. With its heavy emphasis on logic and population dynamics, my background in philosophy and anthropology gave me an instant advantage over those who had come into the field from medicine.

The University of California, Berkeley, is one of the world centers of knowledge. I was thrilled to be a student there. My advisor in the epidemiology program was an elderly scientist, Dr. William Reeves, whose work on malaria during the second world war had him declared a national treasure. He guided my work on mosquito-borne encephalitis and the resulting journal publications gave me a bit of academic respect. I would have been happy to continue on that level, but Dr. Reeves encouraged me to focus on mathematical statistics. Most students treat this subject as a necessary evil, a dull and tedious number-crunching exercise that hopefully supports your hypothesis. I felt the same way, and preferred to tramp around the desert collecting mosquitoes rather than sitting in front of a computer. But Dr. Reeves persisted and I reluctantly followed his suggestion.

The more I learned, the more intrigued I became. To my surprise, I discovered that there is a remarkable beauty to statistical techniques. At its essence is the concept of randomness, which underlies not only every formula, but the entirety of human thought and existence.

What does it mean when something is *random?* At first, this seems very simple: random means without order. In fact, randomness is not simple at all, since it is possible to find some sort of order in almost everything. The concept has plagued philosophers, mathematicians, and every type of scientist since the beginning of modern thought. It has frustrated computer programmers to no end. The problem is that it is virtually impossible to design a system that will generate a truly random number. Companies like the Rand Corporation have gone to great lengths to publish a book of simply random digits. It is not just a modern problem, either. The ancient Greeks were disturbed by apparent randomness in nature and decided that there must be an underlying order to everything. The medieval philosophers argued that the *lack* of randomness in itself was proof for the existence of God. Great figures from Pythagoras to Einstein found randomness intolerable. "God," as Einstein famously declared, "does not play dice with the universe."

It seems to me that the universe is at the same time both marvelously orderly and completely random. How can that be? I think that natural order does not exist. My guess is that the universe is, in fact, made up of completely random processes. Whatever order we see is just something we read into our world. So we can read into it as much or as little as we like. Take the night sky, for example. You can gaze in poetic mystification at the beauty of the stars strewn randomly in the sky. Or you can organize the stars into groups, make up constellations and single out the planets and nebulae. It doesn't really matter how you group the stars into constellations. There is no "natural" order. The ancient Arabs, Chinese, Polynesians, and native Americans all had their own systems of astronomy. One method is just as good as the other. The point is, order helps make sense out of things.

I personally find it very practical to live in a world of order. It is comforting as well. No matter where I am on the planet, I look up and see my favorite constellations—in the northern skies, Cassiopeia or Pegasus, and in the southern hemisphere, Crux or Centaurus—and feel like I am on familiar territory. Every little kid delights in recognizing the big dipper. Order gives us a feeling of comfort and control.

And that is the beauty I found in statistics. It creates order out of chaos. With statistical techniques, you can distill simple answers from an otherwise unwieldy flow of data. You can make sense out of nonsense.

I completed the Ph.D. in 1983, followed by a Master of Public Health degree in 1984. It was difficult to leave Berkeley, so I looked for a job in the San Francisco Bay area. Against the advice of my advisor and colleagues, I took a tenure-track position as Assistant Professor at San Jose State University.

"You should be at a research university," they said. "How are you going to get funding for your projects?"

I argued that my research in arbovirus mosquito vectors was well supported and would continue. But the truth is, I just wanted the status of being a professor. To stay at a research university would have meant years more as a postdoctoral fellow, barely a step up from a student. As predicted, though, my research funds began to dry up when I was no longer affiliated with a renowned university. I couldn't do field research without money, so I turned to theoretical work, for which I only needed a computer account.

I got absorbed in Monte Carlo methods, so called because each scenario is like a spin of the roulette wheel. If you repeat the spin enough times, you will know *exactly* what the probability is of the little ball landing on each of the numbers. You will also understand why Monte Carlo and Las Vegas are rich and the gamblers leave town penniless.

Mathematicians are always looking for formulas, but there are complex real-life situations where formulas simply do not exist, or would be much too complex. The weather is one example. Even with a global network of monitors and high-speed computing, it is not possible predict the weather with accuracy beyond about two days. Human beings are another problem. One of the reasons that the social sciences are so ridiculed is because people just don't always behave the way they are supposed to according to the scientific models.

There is a solution to this. Rather than use a grand formula, you can simply map out a statistical distribution, called a probability density function, by repeating a scenario a high number of times. For example, suppose you don't know what is going to happen when the AIDS epidemic hits a place like San Francisco. No mathematical formula will come close to the truth. There are just too many variables. Instead, you make up a simulation on the computer, run it, and look at the outcome. That is one possibility. Then you do it again, under ever so slightly different circumstances. That outcome is another possibility. What if you do this, say, ten thousand times? Eventually a picture will emerge. You notice that no matter how things are altered, a pattern comes up. Now that is a powerful technique. You can turn the unknown into the known. As it happened, my colleagues at Berkeley were able to predict with remarkable accuracy how many AIDS cases would show up, before the unfortunate patients even knew they were sick.

With computers, you can do these simulations easily. But the more complex the problem, the more computing power is needed to run each spin of the wheel. San Jose State University is in the heart of Silicon Valley and although it is not a highly ranked academic center, it benefits from the local support of some of the most sophisticated companies in the world: Lockheed, IBM, Intel, and about four thousand other computer firms. I was lucky to get time on a Lockheed supercomputer. The jobs were submitted as batch Fortran code for the computer to crunch at night, taking seconds or minutes to do a job that would have tied up our university machine. Because my routines were recursive, the code looked deceptively small, often just a few hundred lines. A recursive function is like a loop, going back on itself thousands or millions of times, each time slightly altered.

On one occasion, the university computer system operator looked at me dubiously when I presented my program. "Why don't you just use our mainframe?" she said. "You don't really need supercomputing for this, do you?"

"You'd be surprised," I answered.

The next day there was an urgent call at my department. "What was that program?! We couldn't figure out what happened. The Lockheed sys-op had to come in. It took over *three hours!*"

But I got the answers I needed.

⊥

It has become dark out. A quarter moon lights up a few streaks of cloud and the ground is twinkling with lights. I passed over Brussels just a little while ago, with a pretty view of the grand European parliament buildings, but now I no longer recognize the cities. There are dense clusters of lights becoming more brilliant as the night deepens. I follow the vectors and occasionally look at the charts, but there are too many towns and cities to try to compare with those on the map. At some point, I cross into France and guess that Strasbourg is off to the left. It starts raining again and gradually I am in and out of thin cloud layers. A couple of hours pass.

Not far ahead is the Basel-Mulhouse airport, in France near the Swiss border, where I have arranged to land. Down to five thousand, then three thousand, then finally intercept the glideslope localizer on the airport instrument landing system. In smooth, clear air, this is child's play and feels like a computer video game. At night, in clouds, it is your lifeline. The crossed needles of the glideslope dance like a crucifix. You focus, very carefully, to move them to the center as you precisely position the aircraft on an invisible approach trajectory. The cockpit marker beacons light up, blue for the outer marker, and out of nowhere a loud crow-like *caw, caw, caw* sounds to mark the outer threshold of the instrument landing system. Then suddenly the clouds part to reveal the massive runway right there before you, sweeping parallel dotted lines of red and white lights on a sea of black ink, with piercingly brilliant white strobes zippering up to the threshold. You feel like a starship entering a space dock. It is an incredible sight and I love it every time.

The red lights flash by as I gently flare and let the main wheels crease the surface. A slight tugging as the rubber takes the weight. I slowly drop the nosewheel, then gently apply the brakes as I roll to a maze of blue and green lights that outline the taxiways. The engine idles as I taxi over to the terminal on the glistening wet surface, lightly splashing through little puddles. I park and tie down for the night. I'll take care of the details in the morning.

My eyes are used to the soft red glow inside the cockpit and now the terminal lights seem harsh and bright. I go through customs once again. A perfunctory look at my passport and a stamp. I walk on through the terminal, past tired passengers and closed shops, to the underground metro station. The train comes in with an echoing sea-gull cry. It is almost empty. I get on and study my guide book and a city map. There is no indication when we cross the border, but when I walk out of the station, I am in Switzerland. I have to economize, so I walk along the medieval streets and find the youth hostel in an old building near the river.

"Good evening. Please fill out this form. All questions must be answered," the young woman behind the counter tells me in heavily accented English. She has short, razor-cut brown hair with peacock-blue sides and a black leather jacket with chrome studs. Euro-punk, I figure. She is probably a mild-mannered high-school girl, but this is the contemporary look. She doesn't know I speak the Swiss dialect.

I am exhausted and my eyes blur as I look at the form. ROUTE OF ARRIVAL, it says, with boxes for TRAIN, BUS, AUTO, and BICYCLE.

"I came into the Basel airport, flying my own airplane." I ask, "Which box should I check?"

She gives me a sarcastic smile, as if to say I am not being funny, just irritating, and takes the paper away. "Your room is upstairs," she says and hands me a key.

I notice that she has checked TRAIN.

Chapter 14

COMMUNICATION RADIOS

SEPTEMBER 1: BASEL, SWITZERLAND

There is a point in every journey where the plan breaks down. The vision gets slippery. One day, all the long thought-out plans and preparations just don't seem to fit anymore and you look around and wonder why you are here.

I have reached that point. I have been so focused on the Atlantic crossing that I haven't given much thought to what I am going to do once I get to Switzerland. My overall goal has been to fly to South Africa. But now that venture seems far too ambitious. I have risked my life enough already; I was lucky to get this far. There is a strange sense of having achieved part of my goal even though I have only the vaguest idea of what that goal entails. Today, I am in Switzerland with an airplane, a ballooning credit card debt and rapidly dwindling resources and options. I feel that I have simultaneously lost my way even as I have arrived.

The morning is gloomy with a low overcast as I step out of the youth hostel. The building is next to the Rhine river and I walk along the ancient streets, climbing cracked stairways and admiring the stone balustrades. Basel was founded by the Romans in 44 BC and has played a significant although unpretentious role in European history. The city somehow always kept its autonomy through shifting alliances with the French, Germans, and Swiss. It is hard to believe that the Emperor Henry II walked these same streets over a thousand years ago. I pass the Drei Könige hotel, built in the year 1026. The guide book says that it hosted Dickens, Voltaire, Napoleon, and Queen Victoria. This city seems redolent with history.

My immediate objective is the airport. I take the metro back to the terminal and then spend a half hour completing paperwork for the various fees. From a distance, I can see that there is something odd about the Cardinal and, when I walk over, I find that the right main tire is flat. Without removing the wheel fairing, it is difficult to determine the problem. The airport maintenance office offers to tow the airplane into the hangar for repair. I can't afford their mechanics and ask instead to borrow some support blocks. Maybe I can fix it with my own basic tools. A couple of men amble over and offer to help. We support the fuselage to free the landing gear, remove the fairing with its eighteen screws, and disassemble the wheel. I examine it closely and see some sharp rock fragments in the rubber, probably causing a slow leak.

As I work, the men at the maintenance facility have been looking over in curiosity. They are used to corporate or airline pilots, who rarely get their hands dirty. Now when I come over to them with the wheel, they offer to patch the tire sometime today for a minimal fee.

There is a flying school nearby. I walk over and chat with a couple of student pilots. In Switzerland, flying is a sport of the wealthy. Landing fees in the United States tend to be non-existent for small airplanes and even where they officially exist, such as San Francisco International, the airport will often let you go without payment. In Basel, on the other hand, every touchdown costs the equivalent of sixty dollars, and the Swiss are very meticulous in keeping records. Every airport in Switzerland, even small grass strips in the mountains, have landing and parking fees, often with an attendant with a pair of binoculars sitting on a lawn chair near the approach zone to jot down the registration number of arriving aircraft. One student pilot I talk to has already spent over a thousand dollars today practicing landings.

I have to move my airplane; I can't afford to stay here. By mid-afternoon, the tire is patched and tested. I replace the wheel and fly to Birrfeld, a local airfield for sport aircraft and gliders in the interior of the country. Switzerland is so small, the flight takes no more than fifteen minutes. The parking fee is much cheaper and I can afford to leave it here for a few days while I decide what to do. I walk out of the airport into the countryside. The Cardinal has been my home, my ship, and my companion—but now it is a burden.

As I walk along the narrow country lane in the cornfields, a car pulls up alongside. A Lexus. The man rolls down the window and I see a woman beside him. The relationship between Switzerland and Germany is a bit like that between Canada and the United States. Germans tend to be more forward, and their media and culture easily overwhelms their much smaller neighbor. With the border less than twenty miles away, it is quite likely that these people are German, but it might be rude to make this assumption.

"*Grüezi mit d'anand,*" I tell them, in the usual greeting. If they are German, they won't know what I'm saying; the Swiss dialect is considered impenetrable.

"*Grüezi,*" they reply and we are both a little surprised that the other is Swiss. "Would you like a lift?" The man, Jurg, introduces himself as a lawyer and student pilot, in a humorous, self-deprecating way as if to hint that neither role is very prestigious. "I'm a blood sucker," he says, and in protest the woman gives him a playful jab in the ribs, "but it pays for the lessons." He saw me come in and noticed the American registration. He has never seen one before and can hardly restrain his curiosity about how I have come to be here.

But first things first. "I don't suppose we could stop at a little cafe, somewhere?" I ask.

We park by a pretty outdoor restaurant and order a glass of amber ale, shrimp cocktail, quiche and pastries. We talk about flying and then, in response to their questions, I explain. By birth, I am an American and have a United States passport, but by ancestry I was registered by my parents as a Swiss and I also carry a Swiss passport. (I was naturalized as a Canadian citizen and also have a Canadian passport, though I don't often carry it.) I admit that I haven't quite figured out my transportation within the country. Jurg immediately lays out the options. Between him and his wife, they seem to know the price of everything from car rental to the various train packages.

"With your U.S. passport, you can get a tourist discount on a two-week rail pass. These are only available within Switzerland, but just for visitors—and you must go to the station in Brugg to get it." He shrugs, laughing, and his wife says, "You just have to know the tricks. Otherwise it is very expensive."

They refuse to let me pay for my share of the lunch and take me to the Brugg station, saying it is on their way.

So. The girl in the youth hostel was right. I am traveling by train.

After my father's death, my family lost touch with relatives on his side. In my previous visit to Switzerland, I hadn't bothered to look up any of them. Now, it is important to me to do so. One of the reasons I have come on this trip, I realize, is to re-establish this connection to my father. My mother gave me the phone number of my father's younger brother, who inherited the family farm. I have it in my pocket, but it is afternoon already and it seems too late in the day to go there.

With a shrill whistle, the express train pulls into the station and I get on. First to Zürich, then Winterthur. It is evening by the time I arrive and walk out into the chilly autumn air.

There is some kind of folk festival in the town square, medieval music with mandolins and lutes and piccolos, and I see people dressed as minstrels. I wander around and listen for a while, then make my way up to the youth hostel, a converted fifteenth-century castle, the Hegischloss, a short hike past the outskirts of the town.

I feel tired, not so much from the work and all the walking around today, but from the weight of my indecision and mounting debt. This castle is maybe not a good choice to buoy my spirits. The stone walls are three feet thick and the low ceilings of heavy wooden beams make the interior dark but not cozy. I wrap myself in heavy woolen blankets and drift off to sleep.

A dream. I am walking along a forested road where there are many dangerous bears about. The local villagers sometimes shoot them. I feel bad about that, but then I am charged by a bear. I raise my rifle and shoot it as it comes close. The dying bear changes into a pretty young woman. She begs me to finish her off, to take her out of her agony. I am filled with sorrow. She reverts back to a wild beast, threatening me again, and I shoot her in the throat. Then she dies, a beautiful girl once more, with a helpless, pitiable look on her face.

SEPTEMBER 2: WINTERTHUR, SWITZERLAND

I wake up late to the sound of pouring rain outside. The other bunks are empty. I hurry to the dining room, where they are putting away the dishes from breakfast. Since I had already paid for the food, I scramble to get a tray of leftover bread, yogurt and salami just in time. The dream was disturbing. I have no idea what it means, but I sense it has to do with my purpose in Switzerland. Why am I here, really?

I call my uncle, Jakob, my father's brother whom I have never met. His wife, Benedicta, answers the phone. Jakob is out in the fields. They had heard from my mother that I would be coming and she talks excitedly about my visit. She does not know how to drive and will send a daughter to pick me up at the nearby town of Wil.

I take the local train to Wil and amble out onto the almost deserted platform. A long-legged, pretty girl strides up and shyly introduces herself as Michaela, my cousin. She drives to a huge old stone farmhouse on a hill, the shuttered windows draped with hanging ivy and flowers. Jakob and his wife are waiting outside. As I step out, he comes forward with tears in his eyes. I am overwhelmed. His face, his muscular build and thick farmer hands, and most of all his deep, resonant voice, are exactly those of my father.

The three of us go into the large farm kitchen. Benedicta, called Benita by the family, is a strong and plump farmwife, but as she bustles about the kitchen, she begins to sob in happiness. Jakob and I can hardly take our eyes off each other. He tells her, "Oh stop it, now!" but we are both pretty emotional ourselves. Benita pours a tumbler of red wine for each of us and we sit and talk. Jakob and Benita have ten children. A few of them are grown and have children of their own. I learn everyone's name, ten younger cousins whom I knew nothing about. Jakob was very close to my father, but when my father died so far away the connection to my family faded. Now, he tells me, he feels as if his own long-lost son has returned.

Three hours later, we are still talking and empty bottles litter the table. The sentimental emotions have been replaced by a drunken satisfaction and I feel like a shadow of me has been there all my life and has finally been re-connected with the rest of my body.

"Ohmigod," Benita says, "I forgot about dinner!"

One by one the other children come in, all of them tall and radiantly healthy. They are curious and polite with their new cousin. They don't quite know what to make of me and the story about the airplane sounds like I arrived by UFO. In remarkable short order, Benita rustles up platters of ham, *spätzli* (a type of stuffed croquette), homemade applesauce, and roasted potatoes. I can see why all the children are so big. These people eat well.

In the evening, Benita shows me around the five hundred year old house and leads me to my room. It was my father's room. She pulls out boxes of old black-and-white photos and even older, sepia-toned pictures of my father as a child, a young man, a farm worker, an army officer. I look out through the open shutters to the valley below. The tinkling of bells drifts up from goats walking back to the barn. And then a louder tonkling sound of the brass cow bells as they plod to the milking machine and the stable.

I settle on the creaky wooden bed. There is a black bear skin on the floor. Probably quite old. The claws are still on it, but there are ragged holes where the eyes would have been. The memory of my dream comes back.

SEPTEMBER 3: WIL, SWITZERLAND

By the time I wake up, the house is empty and quiet. No one is around, so I go down to the kitchen and find a piece of bread to chew on. I don't see anything else readily edible. The cupboards have bulk grains and flour and spices and the refrigerator has large blocks of cheese in oiled brown paper. After a while, Benita comes in, lugging a metal milking pail.

"Oh, I'm glad you slept well. You know, as farmers we're up early, before daybreak, but it's better for you to sleep. You need your rest after that long trip! How about some milk? Here, let me pour you a bowl." And she pours almost a quart of the milk she is carrying into a deep bowl which she sets in front of me. The milk is warm and vaguely fragrant, with tiny flecks of floating yellow fat. "It is sheep's milk, very good for you!" In a twinkling, there are slices of pumpernickel and a hard, dry sausage beside the bowl. "We won't have lunch for another two hours," she says.

The practical thing for me to do is to sell the airplane here and take an airline flight to South Africa. I make some phone calls. There is a Cessna dealer in Buttwil, an airport used for aerobatics and glider training. The dealer's name is Herr Eigenberger, and I call him up. When I describe my airplane, he is quite hopeful about its sale potential. "Bring it over," he says. "I'll be happy to look at it and perhaps I can help you."

It would really be ideal to sell the airplane, but I know this may not be possible and I can't count on it. If I have to, I'll continue with my original plans. I make a few other calls. The Swiss pilots association office doesn't have any more information on flying to Africa than I was able to get in the United States. I try a few embassies in Geneva: Egypt, Saudi Arabia, Malawi, and Zimbabwe. Their responses range from an abrupt "Impossible" to a long series of hand-offs to other counsels and, in the end, the answers are the same: "We have never had this request." "Perhaps you should try the civil aviation authority ... no, we do not have that number." "Which airline are you?" "Please prepare a proposal for your route. We should be able to give you an answer within six months."

Surely other small aircraft have flown to Africa. Is this really so unusual? In California, I flew the Cardinal on a half dozen trips down to Mexico, and once to Guatemala. How much different is that? Switzerland is no farther from Morocco or Algeria than Santa Cruz is from Baja California. Tunisia looks to be no more than a three or four hour flight away. Don't European pilots get bored with just cruising around their own countryside?

Back to the Swiss pilots association. "Yes ... there is someone who has flown to Africa," the director said. "Bruno Keppeler. In Geneva. You know, last year he won the turboprop category in the *Arc en Ciel* around-the-world race." I'd read about that race in the flying magazines, but hadn't paid much attention to it. Entrants ponied up $150,000 apiece to compete for a little trophy. Definitely out of my league.

I reach the secretary of Mr. Keppeler, a high-powered

lawyer, and I am relieved when she tells me that he speaks English. This might be complicated and I prefer to switch from the Swiss dialect to English for any kind of technical discussion. She patches me through and I introduce myself. Mr. Keppeler is encouraging and happy to talk for a few minutes, no doubt an interesting diversion from his work. "It will be very difficult to get the flight permits," he says in well-articulated English, "but it is possible."

"The biggest problem," he goes on, "is the political instability throughout the whole continent. Forget West Africa, it will take you years for the permits. Your only chance is an eastern route. But there are civil wars in the Sudan, in the Eritrea region of Ethiopia and in Somalia. Stay out of Zaire and Mozambique.

"Let's see," he pauses, clearly enjoying making up the flight. "About the only way is to Egypt. Fly past Saudi—they will never give you permission to land, but you might be able to get overflight permission for Jeddah—stay *right on* the airspace division between Yemen and Eritrea, they won't shoot unless you really come into their airspace. Then Djibouti. It has a good airport. From Djibouti to Addis Ababa in Ethiopia. Nairobi, Kenya. Don't land in Tanzania, but continue to Harare in Zimbabwe, and then South Africa."

"Do you think I can do that with my range? I can't really count on more than about eight hundred miles."

"If you have a good tailwind," he chuckles. "But if you are forced to land without permission, you will certainly lose the airplane and perhaps much more."

My only practical option is to sell the airplane here, for whatever I can get.

SEPTEMBER 4: WIL, SWITZERLAND
I take the trains to Birrfeld and it is midday by the time I have walked back along the cornfields to the airport. The Cardinal looks a little lonely parked among the European sport aircraft.

I get a peculiar sensation when I see it, like seeing your dog in a municipal kennel. We have been through so much together.

The flight to Buttwil takes me close to the Alps and this time the sun is shining. The scenery is breathtaking. On my right are the Eiger and the Jungfrau, rising at an almost vertiginous angle from the deep valley floor of Interlaken. Banking the airplane, I follow the contours of the ridges, looking down on the net of ski lifts and cable cars hanging like tinsel on a Christmas tree. Another carving turn and the brilliant glacier of the Aletsch slips behind me to reveal the craggy beauty of the Matterhorn. Now I feel like James Bond, heading toward a little mountain airfield for a clandestine rendezvous.

Threading my way through the mountains, I remember that there was an airport near the hospital where I worked as an eighteen year old. I have a sudden temptation to fly there. The thought of seeing the hospital again, the mountains where Trix and I skied together, and to walk once more along the old streets of the town brings a jolt of melancholy. The chart is clipped on to the control column and I find the airfield. It is a jointly operated military and civilian field and I wonder if I could get permission to land.

No. I have to be practical. I have an appointment today with Herr Eigenberger, and a lot depends on his impression.

The Buttwil airfield is a grass strip on a ridge in the alpine foothills. There are quite a few aircraft stationed along the forested edge to the runway: a few Cessnas and Pipers, an old Stearman, and a Polish Warszawa Wilga. There are not many Wilgas in the world and I have never seen one, but recognize it immediately. It has a boxy taildragger stance, like a horned lizard standing on its forelegs. A real air tractor.

I taxi over to the far end of the grass tie-down area. No point in acting like I own the place. The dealer office is beneath the small air traffic control room. Herr Eigenberger is on the phone when I come in and he motions me to sit down. When he is done, we talk for a while and then we go out to look at the airplane.

"Yes," he says, "it seems to be in satisfactory condition. The main concern is the noise of the engine. European countries have stringent noise regulations. It is very difficult to retrofit the aircraft for noise reduction." If mine is too loud, it will not be salable.

"What about those?" I point to the Wilga. Compared to that, my airplane probably sounds like a sewing machine. As for the Stearman, its powerful radial engine will rattle your teeth. In the United States, it is an air show favorite partly just because it is so deafeningly loud.

"*Ja*," he smiles knowingly. "We have an exemption to use them for glider tows, and only on Saturday morning."

The noise testing involves special instrumentation and is quite expensive. Herr Eigenberger sympathizes with me and says he will do it free. We both know that if he can sell it, he will get a good commission.

I leave the keys with him and take the trains back to Wil.

SEPTEMBER 5: WIL, SWITZERLAND
I call Herr Eigenberger. Bad news.

"The noise level was within limits. It is a good airplane. But there are some new regulations for registration of aircraft. The standard engines are no longer acceptable. The official reason is that they pollute too much. I don't think so. I think it is because of the new trainers from Aerospatiale." He suspects the regulations were passed to protect the fledgling Swiss, German, and French small-aircraft industries. I've read of a few new models of flight training aircraft, but they are highly priced and apparently not selling well. "The only way this is possible," he says, "is to replace the engine. When is your overhaul due?"

"Not for another seven hundred hours," I reply.

He whistles. "Then it will be expensive. A new engine is about twenty thousand dollars."

"Is it possible to sell it for a reduced price? Maybe the buyer can replace the engine?"

"I think it will be very difficult to sell an airplane that cannot be registered. And a lot of problems can come up when you install a new engine. No one likes to take the chance."

"If I install a new engine, will I be able to sell it for sure?"

"Oh, yes. Probably."

"Probably?"

"It is not certain. I thought that we could sell it as it is. But now, you see, this is not possible."

"What can you recommend? I can't fly it back across the ocean."

He laughs. "Yes. You really are an American. A Swiss would never have done that."

I feel a tightening net. When I went to Mexico, I had a rusted old truck to worry about. Now I am in a much worse predicament, with a forty-thousand dollar airplane and another fifteen thousand in debt, close to maxing out my credit cards.

I thought I couldn't fly to Africa. Now I can't sell the airplane.

Africa seems incredibly complicated and frightening. Back in California, it was an adventure— "Hey, let's just see what happens." At this point, I have already had my fill of danger, but the true adventure, the real step into the unknown, is just beginning. It gives me a sick feeling in my gut. But at the same time, there is a little thrill. What is the worst that can happen? I'll probably sacrifice the airplane. So what? It is just money. Maybe I'll crash. Maybe end up in a bad political situation. I'll survive. I always have.

As for heading off into the unknown—that, I realize, is the stone truth at the heart of this journey.

A little snake of adrenaline slowly begins to uncoil at my tailbone and make its way up my spine. This is my life. I am going to fly on. Eight years as a university professor has turned me into a putz. A spineless wimp. I remember the summer I taught a public health course in Nairobi, Kenya. Naturally, I took the opportunity to go out on guided safaris. One early morning we pulled up to a freshly killed wildebeest. Three lions glowered at us and one walked up to me, blood dripping from her jaws, and stared at me with yellow eyes. I boldly stared back, no more than four feet away inside the vehicle, but we both knew that if I was out there alone, I would have pissed my pants in fear. I felt like a slab of lunchmeat in a can.

Now my life as a professor is over. It is time to put this piece of meat to the test.

SEPTEMBER 7: WIL, SWITZERLAND

On the second underground level of the vast Zürich train station are the central offices of the national postal, telephone, and telegraph system, the PTT. There are banks of international telephone and telex directories and soundproof booths to make the calls. I spend a couple of hours finding numbers for the African countries. Most of their aviation offices do not have telephone numbers, just telex. In the PTT, there is only one person, a surly older woman, who knows how to use the telex machine. I thought these noisy, slow, clacking contraptions had about disappeared along with Morse code. In this day of fax machines, it seems incredibly antiquated to punch in the telex code. The woman reluctantly shows me how to use it. Letter by letter, I key in the codes, starting again from the beginning with each mistake. The machine is cantankerous and I often have to go find her. To continue her assistance, I shower her with compliments while trying to avoid sounding too insincerely flattering. It takes me the entire afternoon, but I manage to send off the requests to Egypt, Saudi Arabia, Djibouti, Tanzania, and Zimbabwe.

There are no numbers for telephone or telex for Ethiopia or for Kenya. But, as luck would have it, the Kenya consulate is just a twenty minute walk down the promenade of the Limmat.

I make my way down there. It is closed.

There is nothing to do but wait.

SEPTEMBER 8: WIL, SWITZERLAND

Back to the Zürich train station. There are no responses.

Well, what can I do? I am in Switzerland, waiting. But I have the rail pass. I decide I might as well see some of the country and spend the rest of the day jumping trains to any place that looks interesting. The impression is so different from what I remember as an eighteen year old. Much of the charm is lost. There are far more people and everyone seems a little worried or depressed. Europe has changed. While there is a forward-looking mood in Germany, France, Italy and the other countries to the great economic union, the "United States of Europe" with its talk of a common currency and removal of borders—there is a sense that Switzerland is being left behind. Whenever the subject comes up with the people I talk to, they say the same things: "We had it too good." "Now we must either be swallowed up in Europe or become an economic backwater." There is a pervasive gloom about the future of the country.

It is not just economic. I am sitting across from a woman with tight lines in her face. I gaze out as we pass a nuclear reactor and then look back at her. She looks as if she has had her share of troubles.

"Switzerland sure has changed, don't you think?" I try as an opener.

She looks at me, startled. People don't talk much on trains nowadays. In fact, most people don't even use the trains anymore, preferring to drive.

"Yes ... my God, yes," and suddenly she is eager to talk to this odd stranger. "Last year, I was robbed in Zürich. On the street. In the daytime. This is something I could never imagine. Now, I am afraid even to walk by myself. When I was a girl, you could leave a suitcase on the platform at the train station and it would still be there two days later. Now I don't feel safe in my own city. It's terrible."

"It's the *drögler* " ['druggies' or 'dopers'], an old woman near us chimes in, hearing our conversation. "They are everywhere, especially in Zürich. Sticking needles in their arms. In the park, right in the open! *Ugghh!*"

Somehow, the needle parks of Zürich and Lucerne don't bother me so much. They are an expression of a deeper malaise that has seized the whole country—just the visible canker sores of a syphilitic nation now suffering from its past indulgence.

As I speed past the high-rise apartment blocks and industrial parks, it is hard to connect with my first visit to Switzerland. The geography may be the same, but time and modernity have created a chasm I'll never be able to bridge to the youth I once was. Somewhere out there, Trix is probably living with her husband and family. Knowing her, she could be anywhere in Europe or the world. Or she could be just minutes from me, in one of those stately chateaux overlooking the valley. It hardly matters; our lives had long ago drifted too far apart.

SEPTEMBER 9: WIL, SWITZERLAND

There are telex messages from Egypt and Saudi Arabia. The office has kindly transcribed the rolls of tape onto a printed page. The punched telexes would have been difficult to read otherwise. The messages request more information: A description of the aircraft, its avionics and contents. A brief biography of the pilot. My entire route, beginning in Europe. Times to the minute of landings and airspace penetration and all radio frequencies to be used en route. I can hardly believe it. Many of the radio frequencies are not even on the charts and change erratically in third world countries. Times *to the minute?* I'll be lucky to be within days of my estimate.

Back at my uncle's farm, I spread out the charts and go to work with the plotters and calculator. The whole thing is an absurd exercise, a complete fantasy, and I just make up the numbers. Jakob is looking on, fascinated.

"How does it work with the radio? How do you know who to talk to?" he asks.

"I'll be using VHF, Very High Frequency, radio. Its signals go in a straight line and are of high quality for voice transmission. There are special frequencies for air traffic control at every airport. Even if the airport is unattended, there are published frequencies to be used. This is called Unicom. You make the transmission to anyone who wants to listen."

"How are you going to do that? Don't they speak Arabic, or African languages?"

"Throughout the world," I explain, "there is a standard aviation language, and—lucky for me!—it is based on English. Even here they use it." And I mimic, "Chess-na fife vahn Rrromeo Foxtrrrot, rrreport down-veend," rolling my Rs. He bursts into laughter and I laugh along with him.

"You mean all Swiss pilots have to know English?"

"Just enough for the air traffic control. There are standard phrases. It is only maybe one hundred words altogether." The airline pilots are pretty good about this, I think, but it is hilarious when you hear the local pilots struggling with the phraseology and then abruptly lapse into a stream of the local language, only to be chastised by the air traffic controllers, who, of course, understand them perfectly.

"I remember when I did my military service," he says, "we used Morse code."

"Yes, VHF was only invented in the 1940s and the modern system was not accepted internationally until the 1960s."

"Don't they use Morse code anymore?"

"Actually they still do, for vague signals like navigation identifiers that are too far away to hear clearly. But most pilots don't even learn Morse code, anymore." My uncle likes to know the history of things, so I continue. "An Italian, Guglielmo Marconi, developed the first practical radio in 1896, but he could not yet modulate the radio wave. So he just switched it on and off, to send Morse code signals. But it only took a few years for others to figure out how to modulate the wave to turn it into a transmission for voice and music. First the amplitude of the wave—that's AM, for amplitude modulation—then the frequency of the wave, which is FM."

"What are you going to do when you are too far away from the radio station? In Africa, they won't have this in just every village, like we do here."

"I'm going to use HF. High Frequency radio." I'm thinking of how unreliable it was over the Atlantic, but my money may have been well invested after all. "VHF radio signals are straight, so they go in line of sight, right out into space. So they are only good for about a couple hundred kilometers at best. But the HF radio uses a lower frequency that bounces off the ionosphere, high above the earth's atmosphere. So I can use it to talk directly—these are called ground waves—or in the bounced back sky waves," I wave my hand in a porpoising motion, "reaching thousands of kilometers. As long as I can talk to them, I should be all right."

SEPTEMBER 10: WIL, SWITZERLAND

The telexes are sent. I have provided all the information to not only the requesting countries, but the others as well. Tediously punching in the numbers has taken hours. I am getting pretty good with this machine. The staff now recognize me and nod as I enter the telegraph office, and even the surly telex woman throws me a glance of approval. But there are no new messages.

I enjoy the evenings on the farm. Jakob and I go for long walks. I tell him about passing the Drei Könige hotel in Basel and how interesting it is to see something so old.

"Oh, that is nothing," he says. "You see the church in our village? It was built in the 700s, but the exact year is not known. And over in that village," he points to the next valley, "are the ruins of a church built in the third century of Our Lord."

We tromp across an old wood and stone bridge. "You see, Napoleon was superstitious and marked every bridge he rode across. Look here." There are some weathered gouges in the wood in the end beam. "This is Napoleon's mark," he says, as if the emperor had just passed through last week.

SEPTEMBER 11: WIL, SWITZERLAND

No messages.

But the Kenya embassy is open, finally. I go in to state my request. They clearly have no experience in this. They take my information. The consul smiles, perfect white teeth in an ebony face, with a pleasant British accent. "Yes, you must visit. No, you do not need to check here. We will make sure to contact you when we have the permission. There is no need to call this office. Why not take the airline? It is much better. I think you will enjoy Kenya very much."

I walk down the Limmat to the Zürich See in a despondent mood. This is really going nowhere. There are some benches along the old seawall and nearby is a kiosk with beer and sausages. There must be some sort of opening here, I think, some opportunity I haven't seen. I've got to think this through. A tall glass of beer and hot white sausage with sharp mustard makes me feel a little better as I sit on the bench gazing out over the water. I remember a Swiss man I met a few years ago, about my age. Rudolph. A social worker in Lucerne. I should give him a call. Maybe get together. He always had a good, if slightly cynical, attitude, and it would be nice to see him again.

After a couple of tries, leaving messages on his answering machine, I reach him at home in the evening. He is really delighted that I am in Switzerland and would come to visit him. "Come any time," he says, "and if you want, you can come with me at work, too. I'll show you some things about Switzerland that you've never seen."

SEPTEMBER 12: WIL, SWITZERLAND

A response arrives from Zimbabwe. Permission to land! This is the first good news.

There is nothing else.

I go back to the farm and help shovel out the barn. It feels good to be doing some physical work and it keeps my mind off my problems.

Jakob and I talk about women. He is amazed that I am without a wife or children. It is a difficult thing for me to explain and, I suppose, I don't really know what the reason is, since I would love to have a family. As always, his expressions crack me up, like when he talks about the fuel consumption of his tractor, *Er sufft 'n hufe Most*—"He drinks a lot of cider."

"*Ja*," he now says knowingly, "American girls are *Mollchästeli*,"—little paint boxes. The allusion is delightful.

SEPTEMBER 13: WIL, SWITZERLAND

No telex messages. But there is a call from Herr Eigenberger. He wants to know what I intend to do with the airplane. Parking charges are accumulating.

I talk to Jakob about the problem. He knows of a farmer at Lommis, just north of Wil, with a small grass strip next to some hog barns. He makes a call and then hands the phone to me.

"This is a four hundred meter field," says the man on the other end. "Can you land in that?"

Hey, wasn't I trained as a bush pilot? "No problem," I answer.

"OK then. If you will be so kind to refuel from me, you can park the airplane as long as you like."

Understandable. Filling my tanks costs about five hundred dollars.

With that little problem solved and the rest of the day free, I call Rudolph. We meet in the late afternoon and walk around the old town. The stonework of the ornate buildings, the towers and ramparts, and the famous long bridge are really beautiful, and Rudi is an excellent guide. He is a "street worker," a social worker who gets out into the streets to connect with the drug addicts, prostitutes, and runaways to help them in whatever they need to get back to a normal life. His specialty is the heroin addicts. Tonight, he will run a needle-exchange program. Do I want to come along, he asks?

At ten P.M., we pick up a large white van and then drive to a pharmacy warehouse to get twenty cases of insulin syringes, each holding a hundred syringes, and boxes of sterile wipes, bleach packets, large plastic sharps containers, and some pamphlets. We drive to a location under a street lamp adjacent to the city park. By the time the back door is open, addicts have already drifted over. Some stop by as if on impulse, as if they were just going down the street and happened to see us. Others come straight toward us in a nervous walk, hold out a hand with a dozen used syringes, ask for new ones, and leave as quickly. They don't talk to each other, or hang around. They just ask for syringes and, when we offer bleach and the cleansing wipes, they sometimes say thanks. Hearing them speak Swiss provokes a baffling dissonance in me. I always think of the Swiss as so orderly. So hard-working and educated. I carry the stereotypic view as much as anyone. These people—scrawny, homeless, frightened teenagers; women with needle tracks and dark, vacant eyes; filthy men stinking of smoke and body odor—these are not the Swiss I ever thought existed. And there are hundreds of them. Rudi seems to know quite a few. He murmurs some words to each. "Hey, Hans, you don't look good, man. Come and see me tomorrow." "Regla, you don't have to go back to your mom. Your sister said you can stay with her." Rudi is never critical, never seems judgmental, but just gives them a pamphlet or a card and lets each one know that if and when he or she is ready, Rudi will be there.

By one A.M., we close the van and head home. The boxes

are empty. In this picture-perfect Swiss city, we have handed out two thousand syringes.

SEPTEMBER 14: LUCERNE, SWITZERLAND

Rudi and I sleep late and it is almost ten by the time we go out for breakfast. He laughs off my worried impressions about what I saw last night. "Don't think you can do anything about it," he says. "If you think you can change them, you'll just burn out eventually—and then you'll be bitter and just as messed up as they are. Don't even try too hard to figure it out. Everyone has his own reasons for doing what he does. My job is to be there if they want to make their lives better. If they don't, well, I'm not responsible for that."

He listens with interest to my story, but doesn't seem as concerned as I thought he might be about my predicament. I guess when you have found fifteen-year-old kids dead from an overdose—kids you have known and helped and who might have considered you their only true friend—then a problem with an airplane might seem pretty trivial. He shrugs and says, "There must be a reason you came on the trip. Don't run away from it. Just do what you have to do."

He's right, of course.

"You know," he says brightly, going on to another subject, "I've been thinking a lot about love and hate. The power of love. 'Love thy enemy.' All that sort of thing."

"*What?*" I exclaim. "That doesn't sound like you at all. Are getting religious? That'll be the day!"

"No, really," he says. "Just think. What is the most powerful force in the world?"

"... love?" I reply and burst into laughter.

"No," he answers in a matter-of-fact manner, "the most powerful force is confusion."

"So what are you saying? That love is confusion? Now that sounds to me more like the Rudi I know."

"Here's how it works," he explains. "You can hate your enemy. So what? He hates you, and unless you are stronger, you won't win. But say you respond with love instead. Do some deliberate kindness. Something truly in appreciation. Now your enemy is totally confused. He is working on the assumption that there must be a benefit to you. If that's not true, he can't figure out your motive. He is confused and the confusion messes him up. How can you hate someone who loves you? You see, it is not the love he is responding to, but the destruction of his logic."

"Hold on here. I'm not sure most people are all that logical. If they hated someone, they would probably just give only a little attention to any act of kindness. Or *love*." I have to laugh when I say it—it just sounds so maudlin. "Most people are too caught up with their own purpose."

"Yeah," he says, "it is a little more subtle than that. You see, hate is something outside of a person. In fact, the weirdest thing about a lot of evil people is how normal they seem and how friendly they can be. They just totally externalize their hate, so it doesn't affect them. But love gets inside a person. I tell you, a person who loves his enemy will get close to his enemy. He will eventually undermine his enemy. His enemy is acting out a role. It's like a business strategy. He expects that his action will bring a certain response. But if you are genuinely kind, the expectation is wrong and the role doesn't fit. It is not an action anymore, but a personal connection. You can't hate something that is close to you, or you will destroy yourself. Believe me," he says on a more personal note, "I've seen that too many times."

Rudi looks at his watch and ponders a bit. "Paul, if you could stay another night, I'd like you to join me this evening. It is a meeting at the city hall. A bunch of stuffed shirts talking about the drug problem. I have to go and it would be a lot less boring if you came along. And by the way, at these meetings, they usually serve some really good wines."

He has some business, so we arrange to meet for dinner

and then go to the meeting. I walk on alone to the Glacier Garden, a park with an exquisite stone sculpture carved out of the natural rock wall. Near the park there is a museum with a maze of mirrors. It is the most incredibly disorienting place I've ever been. The mirrors are full length and arranged so that once you have stepped into the maze, you see your reflection on all sides—it is almost impossible to tell which way is out. Each reflection is reflected itself by the mirror on the opposite side, again and again, so that you see hundreds of images of yourself, fading into the distance. Even more oddly, you see the entrance to the maze, and the flower stand in the center, but you can't tell where they are because they are all just reflections. As soon as you take a step forward to the expected opening, you bump into a mirror. I finally hit on a strategy to find my way out: I look down at my feet. If there are no reflected feet, the way ahead is clear.

When I call Rudi at our meeting place, he apologizes for running late. An unexpected problem came up. He finally arrives, breathless, and says we should just go directly to the city hall.

The meeting is upstairs in the council chambers. A broad staircase leads up along stone walls with carved hardwood moldings. The high-ceiling rooms are appointed in sixteenth-century furnishings. There is a very formal reception service and I feel a bit underdressed. As promised, there are side tables laden with a variety of cheeses and a selection of local wines. Rudi makes his rounds, networking with ease among the politicians and the wealthy burghers of the city. I make my way over to the table and accept a glass of Dôle. It is a full-bodied red, not one I've ever had before. I try the Humagne next. The hostess smiles sweetly and assures me that it has a slightly more robust flavor, although I can't really tell the difference. It wouldn't be fair not to try the whites, so I have a glass of Fendant, a glass of Muscat, and another of the Ermitage, which the very pleasant hostess tells me is good with cheese. I haven't eaten much cheese, nor anything else since breakfast, and I slur the words when I tell the hostess how pretty she is.

Rudi comes over, grabs me by the elbow and steers me to our seats. The meeting is about to begin. Even at the best of times, I have difficulty with formal German speech, but now I can barely understand half of what they are saying. It seems that everyone is concerned about the drug problem and tonight is a debate about the effectiveness of strategies to solve it. The needle exchange program is mentioned. Someone argues for a police crackdown as a hardline measure. Others recommend more social workers. America is mentioned occasionally, in reference to different strategies that have been applied. At one point, the moderator says, "We are fortunate to have someone from America here tonight. A professor of public health. Dr. Gahlinger, perhaps you could say a few words about your impressions of the drug problem in our city."

Everyone claps politely. I shoot a horrified look at Rudi, who is trying his best to suppress a grin. There is no way out. I get up unsteadily and walk to the front of the room, turn and face the audience of about eighty people. I'm having a little difficulty focusing and desperately hope that I can speak coherently.

"Thank you for the invitation to be here tonight, and I appreciate your interest in my impressions. My visit to Lucerne has been very enjoyable. It has also been a good opportunity to compare the drug problem in America and Switzerland." Just as I am starting to get warmed up, I shift my left leg, which seems to have gone asleep, and stumble a bit, catching myself just before falling over. I hope to God no one noticed. "The main problem with drugs in America is somewhat different," I say, and launch into a comparison between crack cocaine and heroin use. Since they asked me to speak, I feel that I at least ought to say something useful. So I go on to talk about some ethical issues. About prescription drug abuse and the *real* drug problem in our society: tobacco and ... uh-oh, ... I don't like where this is going. I better wrap this up quick before I get into trouble.

"In summary," I abruptly conclude, "the drug problem is extremely complex and has no easy solutions. Thank you." I walked stiffly back to my seat, with my face burning, followed by the same polite applause.

When we get out into the street, a merciful half hour later, I'm ready to strangle Rudi. He throws up his arms, laughing, "I swear I didn't know they were going to call on you. But you did okay, I must say. Everyone was just waiting for you to fall over."

September 15: Lucerne, Switzerland

There are no messages at the Zürich PTT when I call.

Rudi drives me to Buttwil. We say goodbye and I fly the airplane to Lommis. When I see that I am high over the approach of the tiny field, I abort the first landing and go around. I must be getting rusty. The second time, I nail it, touching the wheels just past the little hummocks at the button of the runway and rolling to a stop halfway down the strip. The friction of the grass helps. But taking off with full fuel will be another story.

September 16: Wil, Switzerland

No messages.

I am starting to get desperate. I call Mr. Keppeler again. This time he is a bit brusque and I am afraid that I have become tiresome in my pestering requests for information. Or perhaps he is just busy.

Nevertheless, he is a consummate professional and gives me some crisp advice. "You telex'ed the requests? Forget it. You will never get a response. Get an Airline Pilot Crew Card. Then go through Swissair."

"But how can I do that? I am not a Swiss airline pilot."

"You are Swiss and you are a pilot. That is all that matters. Go get the card. It will open many doors. And don't worry about that 'to the minute' nonsense. Just put down your estimate, then add at the bottom, 'All times plus or minus forty-eight hours.' Remember, they are just a bunch of bureaucrats. Work with them. Play the game."

I thank him profusely, but he cuts me off and hangs up. This guy's help is invaluable, but I think I have about used it up.

SEPTEMBER 17: WIL, SWITZERLAND

The Swiss pilots association office is located in Glattbrugg, near the Zürich international airport at Kloten. I decide to spare them the details of my little airplane and act as if I am an independent corporate pilot. They look at my commercial pilot's license and documents and then refer me to a notary. The whole thing costs a few hundred dollars, but at the end of the day, I have a shiny plastic card with Swiss insignia and the large words AIR CREW, with an imbedded photograph underneath of which is my name.

It is evening when I reach the Operations Control building of the airport. Heavily tinted plate glass and two enclosed security gates prevent visitors from passing beyond the foyer. I show them the airline crew card and the guards wave me through. The gates open into a busy scene that reminds me of a stock market. There are airline pilots everywhere. Paper flight plans and teletype strips litter the floor, while attendants call out messages and scurry around with portable phones. Overhead, electronic monitors give a continual readout of the weather conditions around the world. Stacks of rice-paper Jeppesen charts lie on the large plotting tables and there are wall-sized maps of Europe, Asia, and Africa, imprinted with the international airways.

Feeling a little sheepish, I bring my telexes to the counter. I figure they are going to laugh me out of this place. A pert young woman in a crisp, black Swissair uniform takes them from me, smiles, and says, "Thank you. We'll get these sent off tonight. Please come back tomorrow."

I wander around for a few minutes to take in the place, but find that I really don't have anything to say to the other pilots. Their world and mine are just too different.

SEPTEMBER 18: WIL, SWITZERLAND
I enter through the security gates of the Operations Control as if it is routine, flashing the crew card, half expecting to be stopped and told, "*Halt.* You may not enter. Please leave." Instead, I am waved through once more. I walk up to the counter. A young man takes my name and disappears. A few minutes pass and I am ready to face another frustrating exercise.

"Sorry about the delay. Here you go," he says cheerily.

To my astonishment, he hands me a packet of permissions for the landings or airspace penetration of every requested country.

Chapter 15

AUDIO PANEL

The arrival of the landing permissions has suddenly put my journey back on track. I spend the morning calling for weather updates and planning my flight to Egypt. Getting out of Europe is more complex than I expected. The winter storms are coming in and already the high alpine mountains are white. These storms can shut down general aviation in Switzerland for as long as a month.

My plan is to fly over the Alps to Italy. There, I face another problem. The most direct route to Egypt is over the Adriatic Sea down to Crete and then south to Alexandria. But the fighting in Bosnia and Croatia has turned the Adriatic into a war zone. I call an advisor at Operations Control to ask about flying along the Italian east coast.

"We don't know what type of anti-aircraft weapons are being used in the Yugoslavian conflict. There are reports from Ancona that civil aircraft have been fired upon with short-range missiles." In a more personal tone, he continues, "Their armies are undisciplined. It is complete anarchy. Our position is that flights in this region are not recommended."

That gives me something to ponder. I spend the rest of the morning helping Benita and Michaela bring in a harvest of plums and preserve them in large glass jars with rubber rings. Almost everything we eat has been grown on this farm.

Last night I had another bothersome dream, one that I've had often. I am visiting Switzerland, but have somehow by-passed the country. I end up in Austria, but when I try to take the train to Switzerland, I get lost, or the train speeds past. I am overcome with an indescribable homesickness; I have lost something here.

As I stir a huge vat of cooking plums, I realize what it is that I lost. I didn't come to Switzerland just to meet my other family, although that has been a great experience. I also came to find Trix.

All at once, an undercurrent of anxiety seems to dissipate with this realization. I wonder how I can find her. It has been twenty years since I last heard from her. She would certainly have married and likely taken her husband's name. Perhaps it will be very awkward even if I could find her. Certainly, her husband will not be enthusiastic about the two of us meeting again. But I just have to follow through, whatever the outcome, so that I can lay this dream to rest.

I remember her father. I call the telephone company of his former home town, but they have no listing. When I explain the problem, they suggest a central, countrywide information service in Bern. Yes, it turns out that the Bern registry has a number for that name.

When I dial the number, a pleasant, elderly male voice answers. It is him.

"Sorry to bother you," I say. "I am visiting here from the United States. I was a friend of your daughter Beatrix about twenty years ago. In fact, I met you once in Pontresina. I was wondering if you could help me get in touch with her. I would like to call to say 'Hi.'"

He is not the slightest bit hesitant. "Beatrix would be delighted to see you. She has three wonderful children; she has been divorced about eight years now. I know she would be happy to see an old friend. Give her a call." And he gives me her number in St. Gallen, about an hour's drive away.

I am too nervous to call and pace around the house in agitation. I borrow some running shoes from my youngest cousin Damien, whose big feet are exactly my own size twelve, and head off into the forest. The air is cool and I can hear only a rustling of the trees and the crunch of the gravel underfoot. When you get away from the cities, the highways and ski lifts, it seems that Switzerland hasn't changed in a thousand years. I slip into a rhythmic loping gait in the sheltering embrace of the forest, feeling like an ancient hunter. Only now there is nothing to worry about, for the wolves and bears are long gone.

When I return, the house is empty. The others are probably out for the evening milking. I dial the number and the moment she hears my voice, she explodes in delight. "I don't believe it! I never thought I would hear from you again!" She gives me her address and we arrange to meet tomorrow, Sunday.

In the evening I sit with my uncle's family around the supper table and they tease me a little. There are no secrets in this house. Somehow, the talk shifts to the mines. They are endlessly curious about my experiences and I have come to realize that my hospitality at this house, for which I am so grateful, is not entirely one-sided. I am a source of entertainment, an oddball from another planet. It reminds me of when someone came to visit our house when I was a child. It was a window into a different world and we pestered the stranger endlessly to tell us stories.

Now, I tell them a few stories about the mines.

"I can't imagine how dark it must be down there, utterly pitch black," says Benita.

"Like the darkest night," says Michaela.

"Like the inside of a cow," says Jakob. And I almost choke on a bite of potatoes, convulsing in laughter.

Another cousin, Phillip, drives me to St. Gallen. We are delayed along the way by herds of cows and goats trundling along the road. The animals have garlands of flowers around their necks and the herders are dressed in Lederhosen and vividly embroidered vests emblematic of their villages. It is the *Alpabfahrt*, the ritual return of the herds from the high alpine summer pastures to the lowlands for the winter. There is a sweet, earthy odor of dung and the air rings with brass bells, the lowing and neighing of the animals, and the yips and hoots of the young herders.

I stop at a flower stand to buy a bouquet of lilies, and then Phillip drops me off at the house.

Trix opens the door. Her cropped, blond hair, fine lines in her face and slightly more voluptuous body have only enhanced her beauty. She gives a little gasp. "You look so much the same ... I didn't know what to expect."

We move gingerly around each other, afraid to get too close. She has prepared a light lunch of bread and sliced tomatoes with basil and cucumbers out on the patio, and uncorks a bottle of Riesling.

"So," she says, "I want to hear everything. And don't," she squints at me and moves her pointed finger back and forth, "leave anything out."

We talk for hours and I recount my erratic attempts to find a meaningful career, and end up with my flight, which now seems a little preposterous. She listens and then tells me of her own difficult times. There was so much promise back then, yet life has been hard.

I meet her children: Franziska, fourteen, Katalina, "Lina", eleven, and a boy Lukas, nine. They are polite, deferential, but interested when their mother tells them I am from America.

"From Las Vegas?" Franziska asks.

"No," I laugh, "California." And immediately they think of Hollywood. It is amazing what people know of the United

States. Our movies and advertising present a strange picture to the world.

I ask Trix about her mother.

"She had a stroke a few years ago when she was up at the cabin, walking outside. They found her face down in the snow; she had already been dead for hours."

"I'm sorry to hear that. She was a good woman."

"No she wasn't," Trix says quietly. "You don't need to say that."

In the afternoon, Trix asks me if I want to go for a stroll to the park overlooking the city. She promised Lukas she would take him there so that he can fly his model airplane. We sit on the knoll and I yell out encouragement to Lukas as he runs back and forth, the paper airplane carving circles in the air above him. I am struck by what Trix tells me. I had always assumed that she embodied success and everything desirable, while my own life was the one that was lacking. Now I discover that she had been as devastated by my departure as I had. She married only after many years and then not for love, but because he was persistent and she wanted to have children. When the marriage broke up, he married again and now has another baby.

"It's hard on the children," she says. "When we divorced, he still came to visit. But now he is busy with his new family and the children feel abandoned."

Night has settled. It is time for me to go.

"Why don't you stay a little longer?" She puts the children to bed and we relax in a silent home. Without quite realizing what I am doing, I lean forward toward her and our lips touch. I feel her cool fingers on my neck, her breasts against my chest. A familiar streaming warmth washes over my body. There is no thought, no purposeful intention, my arms just so naturally find their way around her. At this moment, I feel so close to her that I have the oddest sense that we have never, actually, been apart.

SEPTEMBER 21: ST. GALLEN, SWITZERLAND

This morning, Trix works a half day as a physical therapist at a clinic, while the children are at summer programs of horse riding. I laze around the house, feeling like a pampered Tabby cat. I remember a dream I had last night. Airports around the world were mouse holes with chunks of cheese and airplanes were flying around, looking for the *Käsen*.

I am more confused than ever. It would be so easy to stay here. I feel as if I have stepped into a parallel world. One of me is a lone wolf, prowling around airports. The other is a contented papa with his wife and children.

The family regroups for lunch. The afternoon is free. I should go to Lommis to check on some preparations. "Would you like to see my airplane?" I ask the kids.

"Yes! Yes! Yes!" they clamor and Lukas's eyes light up like flash bulbs. "That would be *awesome!*"

We pile into the car and drive to Lommis. As I unscrew the cowling to examine the engine, the children wriggle around the interior. "Do you think we could go flying?" Lukas asks breathlessly. There is only one seat free. I am not inclined to make four flights.

What the hell. It may not be legal, but there is no one around. "OK. Trix will sit in the front. You kids, you can squirm your way into the back, behind the fuel tank. Don't grab *anything*. It will be very noisy, and scary. Maybe it would be better if you stay on the ground."

"We promise! We'll be good!" They jump up and down.

I take care to ensure that everyone is secure. All three kids squat in the baggage compartment and fit remarkably well into the small space, their faces peering out the plexiglass windows. Trix is settled into the co-pilot seat. I give her a headset.

"With these, it will be quiet and we can talk calmly. The microphone will automatically activate with your voice."

"How will I know when to talk? Won't you be talking on the radio, too?"

"We are hooked into the intercom. You see this line of buttons? It is the audio panel. Each switch is an instrument: two VHF navigation radios, two VHF communication radios, HF radio, ADF receiver, the marker beacon, like so." I point to each switch in turn. "We can communicate with each other. To the outside. Or any combination."

"It looks complicated," she says, "to talk in so many different ways."

I am curious to see just how much of this runway I'll need, lightly loaded, but take no chances. I taxi into the tall grass off the downwind end of the runway, lower the flaps to fifteen degrees and stand on the brakes while I push in the throttle to full power. The engine roars, flattening the grass with the propwash and the aircraft shudders in the strain. I dump the brakes and our heads are pushed back with the force of acceleration. We power down the soft airstrip like a speedboat in seaweed. The airspeed picks up and there is a sudden release as I pull it off the grass. For a moment we float in ground effect, picking up more speed. Then I lower the nose, raise the flaps, climbing steadily, and soon we are cruising over the Swiss countryside.

Here I am. Family man. Taking the kids on an afternoon flight. It just feels so natural. With Trix beside me, I would give anything to have shown this image to that tortured eighteen-year-old boy. It would have been a wonderful fantasy for him. And yet, I feel that this is no less a fantasy today. This is just a pretense. I've stepped into someone else's role. Who am I kidding? I don't really belong here.

After we land, we stop off at the farm. The kids go to play with the sheep and goats, while I gather my things and say good-bye to Jakob and Benita. I have to leave soon. The rest of my journey is waiting.

It is night and the girls have already gone to bed, but Lukas comes to me in his pajamas.

"How can I become a pilot?" he asks me.

"The first thing," his mother says, "is you have to do

better in school. You can easily do the work, but you just don't apply yourself." And to me, "Last year they threatened to hold him back to repeat the class."

"But it's so boring," he says. "I don't want to be in school. I want to be outside. I'd rather learn how to fly than anything."

"Come here." I put him on my lap. "To learn how to fly, you have to know many things. Mechanics, navigation, weather and all the rules and regulations. It is all very interesting. But first you have to know the basics. Especially arithmetic and writing. It is like reading a book. First you have to learn the letters of the alphabet. They are not so interesting, but once you learn them, you can read everything! Now, your job is to do well in school. Pay attention. Learn your lessons well and then you can be a pilot."

Lukas listens thoughtfully, then he changes the subject. "I have always been afraid of skeletons." He uses the term *Knochenrichten*, "set of bones." I'm puzzled; it is not an expression I know. Trix senses my confusion and softly translates to English for me. Lukas continues, "But then today, I realized that I am a skeleton myself." He touches his eyebrows and jaws and looks at his hands.

Trix immediately holds up her arms and says, "And I'm a skeleton too!" We all laugh and poke our bony elbows and knuckles at each other. Then, in a soft voice, Trix says to me, in English, "He has never talked this way to anyone."

SEPTEMBER 23: ST. GALLEN, SWITZERLAND

Today is the day I had planned to leave. The date corresponding to my flight arrangements. I had left open my journal last night and when I pack it up this morning, I see Franziska and Lina have written notes in it thanking me for the flight, for coming to Switzerland, and wishing me luck.

Trix and I drive alone to Lommis. The sky is an angry billowing mass of gray and white. The weather report said it should open up by late morning. I talk to the airfield owner as we fill up the tanks, about my chances of flying through the mountains in this weather. He gets on the telephone to Zürich.

"It doesn't look good today. Icing, with variable ceilings. I doubt you will make it over the Alps." He pauses. "Maybe tomorrow. But this weather is typical. The winter is coming, that is for sure."

We drive back to St. Gallen in silence.

My two worlds are splitting, each grabbing on to me as they pull in opposite ways.

At night, we lie together in deep relaxation.

"Why don't you stay here?" Trix asks. "With your credentials, you could find a job. At the university, they put a high value on professors that can teach in English. What is it that you would miss? What is it that you cannot have here that you have in California?"

It is a question that has been on my mind as well. I can act and look and speak the language like a Swiss, but I am an American in the most fundamental sense. I don't think I could ever live in a country with borders a few miles in any direction, where everything is so carefully controlled and nurtured into a stilted beauty like a Japanese *bonzai* potted tree.

And it is not just the country, and the culture, that I would be at odds with. I've spent half my life dreaming of Trix. She was my first love, and she became the ideal that no other girlfriend quite measured up to, at least none that would actually go out with me. I always thought that my life would be right if I could be together with her again. Well, here she is, beside me, and I find that I can hardly wait to leave. Why shouldn't I stay with her? When I lost her twenty years ago, the loss created a hole. A hole that I tried to fill with degrees and books and other achievements. Now I have the creeping realization that I nurtured that hole. No wonder no other girlfriend measured up. I wouldn't let her. Instead, I've pushed every away every possibility of marriage by carrying around this image of the ideal woman. But now that my ideal is actually lying next to me, I see that she is not an ideal at all. She is simply, like me, a person at the edge of middle-age, struggling with the choices and demands of modern life. We shared a teenage love and have now, quite serendipitously, come together again. But our lives have taken entirely different paths and we live in separate worlds.

She is breathing softly, waiting patiently with her question. I struggle for an answer, but come up with nothing and finally just say the first thing that comes to mind.

"Ben & Jerry's."

"Huh?"

"I can't live in a country without Ben & Jerry's ice cream. Chunky Monkey. Cherry Garcia. And especially New York Super Fudge Chunk."

She knows, as always, exactly what I mean. "Yeah," she agrees in resignation, "and I could never survive in California without *Biberfladen.*"

SEPTEMBER 24: ST. GALLEN, SWITZERLAND

Today, the weather is even worse. Everyone is gone from the house during the day. I walk downtown for a while, but the historic old center holds no charm for me and the sidewalk cafes are empty in the blustery wind. As I climb the steep side streets to go back, I pass by sex shops and pornographic video stores where there once were bakeries and cheese markets. A further reminder of how Switzerland has changed. I feel a sense of gloom everywhere.

SEPTEMBER 25: ST. GALLEN, SWITZERLAND

This morning, the day breaks gusty with rain squalls and I feel anxious. I have already said my goodbyes and this limbo state is enervating. We drive out to the airport again. This time, the clouds open to show brief patches of blue.

At nine forty-five, I am off the ground. The gusts have actually been of benefit. Without the burst of a twenty-knot headwind, I doubt if I could have lifted the fully fueled aircraft off the short strip and it would not have done the airplane or my reputation any good to mush back to earth on a nearby pasture.

I had hoped to break out into blue skies, but the clouds close around me. By the time I get Zürich Center on the radio, I am in solid instrument conditions. They give me vectors to the Alps, but the heavy airplane can't climb fast enough. I have to request repeated amendments to the flight plan to gain the necessary altitude. I zigzag across the lowlands of northern Switzerland, struggling to get to fifteen thousand feet. A half inch of rime ice has built up on the wings. I am no longer intimidated by it, but it affects the Cardinal's performance. I can't climb and the airplane slips helplessly back to thirteen thousand. The airspeed falls to sixty knots, then fifty-five. It is hopeless. There is no alternative but to divert to Basel and land.

I stand on the tarmac in disgust as dripping chunks of crusted ice fall off the wings. This attempt has cost me another hundred and fifty dollars in fuel and fees, and got me nowhere. Or maybe I am just too anxious to leave Switzerland. I just want to get out of here and move on to whatever fate has in store for me. Some people are staring at me from the flight school, wondering who would be stupid enough to fly in weather like this. I ignore them and walk into the terminal.

The meteorology office is a hive of activity. Without stopping to talk, the attendants hand me a stack of teletype printouts. I take them to the terminal coffee shop and study them over a mug of Ovaltine and, when I spot it on the pastry counter, a helping of *Biberfladen*.

I won't be able to make it over the Alps and the war in Yugoslavia won't allow me to go further east. But why not a western route? By skirting the French Alps, it wouldn't be too far out of my way. I outline a flight over Geneva, Grenoble, St.

Auban, to St. Tropez on the Mediterranean. From there, I should be able to make it to Sardinia, which would give me a nice start on the long leg to Crete.

I return to the weather office and file a flight plan for Olbia, Sardinia.

The ceiling is still low at about eight hundred feet above ground, but it has stopped raining and the airplane is clean and dry. A man at the flight school shakes his head slowly in disapproval as I climb in and start the engine. I give him a little sarcastic wave and taxi to the departure ramp.

Shortly after lift-off, I plunge back into cloud. It is surprisingly smooth and I have no problem climbing to ten thousand feet. Soon, the instruments tell me I am over Geneva. The air traffic control announcements from France come through clearly in heavily accented phrases. It must really burn them up to have to speak English, I chuckle to myself.

Ice is forming on the wings again and once more it is rime ice. *No problemo.* I feel relaxed enough to take a picture of the corn-like crust on the wheel fairing and wing. With a gentle descent down to eight thousand feet the ice begins to trickle away. Grenoble passes, and I skirt the western edges of the *Hautes-Alpes*, as it says on the chart. It is all theory; I can't see a damned thing out there but cloud.

The sky gets lighter and then the clouds separate into gray layers. The layers thin out into tapering wedges and then gradually disappear. Unfolding below is a pretty landscape of tile-roofed villages and a mosaic of vineyards. It is twilight when I reach the coast. Just as I pass St. Tropez, the last tiny kernels of ice flick away from the wings.

I am over water once again, the deep mazarine blue of the Mediterranean. Up front, the sky is darkening into a hazy cobalt. It feels like night over the ocean. I no longer have the survival suit or life raft, but I don't really care. I guess I'll just have to tread water if I go down. I've stepped off the edge now. This is no longer the carefully engineered crossing of the Atlantic. It is an improvisation. I don't even have any charts for this region, just some photocopies I made of my route in Basel. Like my parents before me, I am leaving Switzerland with no map, no survival gear, no clear plans, and just a hope of what lies ahead.

Night comes with the pitch black of a moonless sky over the sea. The air is a smooth bedding of satin. Another hour goes by.

"Novembore sevena foura fife, Olbia Radio."

"Olbia, November seven four five is with you five zero out at nine thousand."

"Rogerra. sevena foura fife. Reportta longga final."

There is a vague silhouette below, black on black, and I see that I am crossing over land. The Olbia approach is a long final all right: pass a flashing marker high on a craggy mountain and then a twenty-mile straight-in to a runway lit in harsh orange lights.

It is almost midnight when I land. The airport is all but abandoned. I take care of some perfunctory paperwork and get a cab into the city. The driver speaks a good tourist English. At my request for cheap lodging, he takes me to the Hotel Minerva. It looks seedy inside, but I am exhausted—too exhausted to bother reacting when, in the cramped box of the metal elevator, the manager slides his hand on my genitals. When I get to my room, I close the door in his face, latch it and fall asleep just as I hit the old mattress.

SEPTEMBER 26: OLBIA, ITALY

Back at the airport, it takes three hours to complete the paperwork, refuel the airplane, and file a flight plan over the Mediterranean to Crete. I feel like I am back in the third world: documents and more documents, each of which must be hand-written, pressing hard for triplicate copies, with the need for rubber stamps and signatures of bureaucrats in different offices half-way across the airport. The Italian flight plan is titled PIANO DI VOLO. I laugh to myself—yeah, that's what I am doing. Just playing a jazz riff. Who knows where it will go.

The airport fees are mercifully small, but the fuel costs are exorbitant. I am stunned when they decline credit cards—cash only. After I pay them, I have just thirty dollars left.

By the time this is done, a heavy downpour has started. The rain is relentless and I realize that I cannot leave today. It looks like another night at the Minerva.

Back in town, I walk the old cobble-stone streets. Olbia is a dreary city on a depressing island. Relatively few tourists come to Sardinia and most of them avoid Olbia. Rough-hewn men with meaty, sunburned faces are loading trucks, and women in lacy black shawls over ankle-length dresses scurry along the streets, looking at no one. I stop in a small restaurant and order *zuppa di pesca* with some *pane carasau*, fish soup and a local bread sprinkled with olive oil and salt. It cheers me up immediately.

It occurs to me that I have been traveling back in time, beginning with my flight in California, retracing my life to my childhood in Canada and then to my father's childhood in Switzerland. Now I have stepped even further back in time. From the medieval redolence of Switzerland, I find myself in the Roman era. Sardinia was populated centuries before Christ. In 285 BC, a band of sailors founded Olbia on a good harborage. It means "Happy" in Greek. When I look at it now, I see that it is a city that has known hardship and poverty, but is indeed not an unhappy place. I am thankful for the absence of tourists. It makes it easier to feel the Roman presence. With a small guidebook, I find the viaducts and ruins. Some of the old streets have grooves from the chariots.

There is a comfortable chair for me in a piazza and I while away the afternoon with a book. *Love in the Time of Cholera*, by Gabriel Garcia Marquez. The story's similarity to my relationship with Trix is uncanny. A few weeks ago, I saw everything as random events, dismissing order as a human invention. Now, it seems, nothing is random. There are no coincidences. Events are taking place in an eerie reflection of each other. Everything I do seems guided somehow. I feel like an actor in a play who hasn't read the script. There must be a reason why I am here, but if there is, I sure as hell don't know it.

I love Trix and I love her children, but is that what I want? I realize that what I really, truly, want is Trix as she was when we first met. Maybe that has been my illusion: everyone has gotten older, but I stayed the same. That is why I never got married, never had children, never bought a house or settled down, and why I now find myself in this ancient backwater with a ratty canvas backpack and an aging airplane.

I stop off at the Mercato Civico in the Via Acquedotto for some provisions for tomorrow's flight, then have a nice dinner of taglioníni with a sharp pecorino sheep's milk cheese. I know Trix will always be part of me. And what do I have that is so valuable that I couldn't give it up for her? On the other hand, what do I really have to offer her? It would be wrong for me to just play another role, to try on another suit of clothes and pretend to be that person. Farmboy, miner, logger, student, professor—they were just roles I had fun with for a while. How long would a life with Trix last? I couldn't bear to put her and her children through another loss of husband and father. In my core, I am addicted to adventure. I long ago fell into that crack in the world between dream and reality. Yes, I am just a pilot flitting from mousehole to mousehole. The only thing real is me and this pecorino cheese.

SEPTEMBER 27: OLBIA, ITALY

The warm front has passed and the skies are clear with a brisk, northwesterly wind. Luck is with me. It will be a good tailwind. With yesterday's paperwork out of the way, I get an early start.

After lift-off, I make a slow sweep to the north and east,

getting an eagle's view of the interior of Sardinia. Dry, almost desert, the hills are necklaced with stone walls. And then I am over the Costa Smeralda heading out to the sea.

It is time to call in my position report. "Rome Control, November three zero seven four five is level on Victor three five foxtrot."

Rome. Far away from me here, yet it controls the airspace almost the whole length of the Mediterranean. So little has changed in two thousand years.

I am lost in thought on a steady cruise at eleven thousand feet when I see a black rope of smoke in the distance. The air traffic control assigned airways don't allow you to motor off wherever you like and I fight the temptation to bank over for a closer look. It is Mt. Etna, a graceful volcano on Sicily, emitting gigantic coils of smoke and ash. I unbuckle and climb into the co-pilot's seat to snap off a few pictures as it passes on my right.

A coast is up ahead. I pass over the terraced fields of the narrow Calabrian peninsula of Italy and then to the Ionian Sea. For this region, my chart is sprinkled with the alert advisories:

WARNING

Aircraft may be fired upon

without advance notice.

I am quite a distance south of the Adriatic and this is one problem I hopefully won't have to worry about.

The hours pass as I continue on toward Crete, taking notes, munching on cold pizza and *dolci*, assorted cakes and sweets, and drinking bottles of mineral water. I urinate into a sturdy snap-lid plastic bottle that I use for that purpose. I've done it so often, I can perform the maneuver easily even in busy flight conditions.

After almost eight hours, I pass the west coast of Crete and continue on the airway to Nikos Kazantzakis International

Airport at Iraklion. I chuckle at the name. Who would have thought of naming an airport after the author of *Zorba the Greek*?

"But don't you believe in anything?"
"No, I don't believe in anything. How many times must I tell you that? I don't believe in anything or anyone; only in Zorba. Not because Zorba is better than the others; not at all, not a little bit! He's a brute like the rest! But I believe in Zorba because he's the only being I have in my power, the only one I know. All the rest are ghosts. I see with these eyes, I hear with these ears, I digest with these guts. All the rest are ghosts, I tell you. When I die, everything'll die. The whole Zorbatic world will go to the bottom!"

I gaze down on the central spine of mountains and the long sandy beaches. I am still at eleven thousand feet and it is time to descend. But I have not yet received permission for the descent and I can already see Iraklion in the distance. There is other airline traffic. Maybe the controllers are busy. When I sense a break, I remind them that I am waiting for landing clearance.
"Seven four five maintain eleven thousand and standby."
Now I am almost to the airport. This is ridiculous. If I don't descend, I'll have to do another approach, which means I will have to return to an airway intersection at the west end of the island. This will take another half hour and waste a lot of expensive fuel. I am tired and in no mood for this lazy inefficiency. I request clearance again, pointedly reminding them that I am ready to land, *now*. There is no other traffic on approach.
"Seven four five, standby," and then, when I am almost over the runway numbers, "seven four five cleared to land."
Ah ha. So this is their little game. You can't go from two miles high to sea level when you are already over the runway. Of course, now I'll have to decline and do another approach.
But they haven't expected a former bush pilot.
"Roger, seven four five is on final," I reply tersely.
I drop a wing and slip the airplane into an almost perpen-

dicular crab, carving a tight spiral straight down. The vertical speed indicator unwinds backward, one thousand, two thousand, twenty-five hundred feet per minute. The airplane falls like an autumn leaf, twirling gently as it plunges toward the ground. I pull out at three hundred feet above the runway, almost stall the airplane, lower full flaps and easily land at mid-field.

"Seven four five," a hesitant voice comes over the radio, "... taxi to the transit ramp ... at your discretion."

It is a short cab ride into town and the driver takes me to an old, stucco building just off the main street. The Hotel Rea is comfortable and accepts credit cards. I take a long, hot shower and then wander into the evening. I've gone from the Roman to the ancient Greek era. On the hill to the right is the palace of Knossos—I had plenty of time to study it at eleven thousand feet when I was waiting for my landing clearance. The palace was built by King Minos sometime between 2100 and 1500 B.C. Daedalus was its architect, and it is from there that he made his flight.

There are tourists everywhere. Except for the shopkeepers and the wait staff at the outdoor restaurants, everyone is white and dressed in the casual summer fashion of Benetton or Banana Republic. I take a seat at a busy restaurant. The fish soup was so good yesterday, I order a bowl of *prarosoupa argolemna*, along with a saucer of *tzatziki* (yogurt, cucumber and garlic), *dolmades* (stuffed grape leaves) and *spanakopitta* (spinach pie). I wish I could eat like this every day.

There are young couples everywhere. Nuzzling, taking pictures, joking with other couples. Groups of four, six, eight. No one seems to be alone. And no one, I am sure, is worried about how to pay for four hundred liters of aviation fuel tomorrow.

SEPTEMBER 28: IRAKLION, GREECE
It is time to take stock of my finances. I walk into a large bank. After a few forms and phone calls, a manager informs me that

my credit card has reached its maximum. I pull together everything I have, a couple of other credit cards with high interest rates that I use less often, but they are almost tapped out as well. I manage to get a cash advance to their limits. Altogether, it comes to about six hundred dollars. I could call my friends or family, but no one I know has much money—not the kind of money I need, anyhow. Some way, I've got to make this last until I can sell the airplane. So long as I can use the maxed out credit cards, I'll be okay.

Back at the airport, I have come to expect the ritual of forms and stamps. Landing and departure fees are cash. The fuel facility takes the credit card. Aviation refuellers rarely check a credit limit. Like the man said in Iqaluit, "Everyone knows aircraft owners are rich." Now I just need to look rich and I'll get by.

I want to get out of here before someone comes after me for more cash. Taxi to run-up, hold, then departure, climbing out into the serene, porcelain sky. I bank left, to the south, and gaze down on the ruins of Knossos. Maybe some day, I'll come back to have a closer look at them. But for now, they fade back into history.

I am heading due south. The sun is bright and the peaceful sea below sparkles in reflection. Its moiré pattern of waves and currents looks as smooth as a silk cloth. After three hours, the haze on the horizon is severed into sea and sky and a coastline emerges. Ahead on the right is a vast delta and the coarse accretion of Alexandria, like a barnacle on an old ship.

It is the shore of Africa.

Chapter 16

GLIDESLOPE

Egypt has always had a fascination for me, as it has for most people of the Western world. As the cradle of civilization, ancient Egypt was an obsession for the British, French, and Germans. Americans were equally mesmerized by the land of the pharaohs. The pyramids have been symbols of power and mysticism for everyone from the founding fathers to contemporary pop artists.

As a child, I was entranced by photographs of camel caravans on the desert horizon, towns dating back to biblical times, and the great temples and monuments. Now, I have a chance to see this land as the ancient prophets had seen it. Away from the highways and power lines. I drift down to two thousand feet. Low and slow. I want feel the texture of these stony ridges and arid plains fought over by bygone empires.

The delta of the Nile is splayed out like a palm frond, holding villages in tight honeycomb clusters of stone buildings. From my perspective, it looks just as it might have looked thousands of years ago. I follow the great river upstream. The delta narrows and now I can see the sand dunes of the Sahara on either side of the irrigated corridor. An hour later, Cairo comes into view. I can hardly take in the size of this metropolis. The controllers give me vectors to fly and I zigzag over the western part of the city, gazing down on the congested streets. There are date palm plantations to the north and south, but everywhere else the urban concrete reaches all the way to the dunes. The core of the city is enshrouded in a dense haze. Visibility is down to a mile or two. I can see the jumbled high-rise buildings in sharp relief close below, but all around me is a brown-tinted cloak of smoke and dust. The vectors turn. They have routed me around the city and are bringing me in from the south. I catch a glimpse—yes!—of the pyramids through the haze. Then they are gone.

I'm on final approach for the right of the two vast, four thousand meter parallel runways. The buff-colored landing surfaces blend with the desert and I can't make them out, even though I must be within a couple of miles. Visibility is down to zero. The airplane bumps and rocks in turbulence and a sprinkle of sand comes through the cabin air intake vent. God almighty, I am in a *sand*storm! I've got to make an instrument approach. The crossed glideslope and localizer needles swing to life and the abrupt caw of the outer marker beacon indicator gives me a fix. The sky has turned to a sesame brown. Sand is blasting at the wings and windshield with a raspy hissing noise. It is time to lower the flaps. There is a stuttering buzz. One of the flaps halts at five degrees and the airplane yaws to the opposite side. I retract them hurriedly. In this turbulence, I'd better come in fast, anyway. The two crossed needles dance coquettishly with each bump and thrust. I've got a firm grip on the control column and guide that crucifix to the center. The airplane squirms and yields under the strain and buffeting of each gust. Baby, we're coming in. With a final whoosh of gritty wind, the runway slides underneath and I touch down in spent momentum.

With sighs of relief, I taxi the long, sweaty miles toward the terminal.

"Seven four five, Cairo Ground. Turn left next intersection. Park and await transport bus."

I turn at the designated area. There is a row of about a dozen parked airliners. DC-9s, Boeing 707s and 727s, an Ilyushin, a Yakovlev, a six-engined Antonov transport. There are no smaller aircraft and I pick an open spot between two jets. Climbing out, I feel like a rat in a stable of camels.

Presently, a large city bus arrives, evidently to transport me and my little backpack to the terminal a quarter mile away. The bus is otherwise empty.

"I can just walk, it's no problem." I know there is a fee for everything.

"Please. You must not walk. Please. I will take you," the driver insists.

A minute later, we arrive at the huge terminal. Everyone seems no less confused than I am, and it becomes clear that Cairo International does not have much experience with small aircraft. I have to walk back outside the building, then come again in through an arrival gate. Then to the ground transportation office for the expected fee.

"One hundred and sixty dollars, please."

"One hundred and sixty dollars! Just for that little ride?!"

"Pardon me. Maybe you have come in the small crew bus. That is only one hundred and eighteen dollars." There is a sharp exchange in Arabic between the ground transportation manager and the others. One of them runs out, someone else comes back, with further excited conversation with the manager.

"He says you arrived in the passenger bus. That will be one hundred and sixty United States dollars."

It is obviously one or the other.

"Now why would I, by myself, come in a *passenger* bus? Surely, it was the crew bus?" I argue.

This goes on for a full hour and tempers are rising. The manager finally concedes that the crew bus fee will suffice. I count out a single hundred dollar bill and eighteen ones. Each of these is examined by an assistant functionary, whose job, it seems, is to hold the note up for inspection, flick it lightly, smooth out the creases and place it neatly in a pile. I am asked to write the serial number of each bill on a triplicate form. I have never paid much attention to the serial numbers on U.S. currency. Now I am learning more than I have ever wanted to know. It is a letter followed by eight numbers and another letter. After I am done, the functionary confirms my printed numbers against the bills, has me make a few clarifications and corrections where the ball-point pen didn't penetrate to the third copy, and pronounces himself satisfied.

Next is passport control. Ahead of me are perhaps a hundred people waiting in line before a turnstyle. They move at a glacial pace. I can't bear it and walk over to another customs official, whose gate is closed. I show him my aircrew card and hand him my passport. He languidly stamps it and waves me through.

A final office. The airport landing and parking fees. The Cairo terminal is huge; it has recently been doubled to accommodate a hoped-for surge in tourism. I am almost lost in the vastness and wander around for a half hour before I discover that the airport director is located in yet another building. In my wanderings, I exchange some currency to Egyptian pounds. Then I find some black-market hustlers who give a much higher rate, and change some more. Now I walk across the outside apron to a hangar-like structure a couple of hundred yards away, moving quickly lest someone should kindly think to send a bus for me.

This building, like the hangars, is unpainted concrete with open doors. Desert sand blows in freely, rounding out the base of the walls and giving the place an abandoned look. I find the office of the airport director. He is a middle-aged, portly Egyptian man in a dark business suit, slightly shiny from wear. As I walk across the carpet, he rises from his desk and greets me warmly in good English. He inquires pleasantly about my flight from the United States. I respond casually as if it were no big deal. He wants to put the immediate concern of the landing fee out of the way and says a hundred dollars will suffice. Cash, only. The daily parking fee is also one hundred dollars, but he will wave that for tonight. I sense that this man is not terribly busy and might have a little latitude in his business operations.

"Would you like some tea?" he asks.

"Yes. That would be very kind."

It is now late afternoon and I am tired from the flight, the haggling and the uncertainty of everything. A cup of tea would be welcome.

His office is amazingly shabby. The desk and the other furniture look as if they came from a thrift-shop. There is a chipped glass coffee table with a dainty tea set on a dinted brass tray, an old couch with tufts of stuffing herniating through the fabric, and his desk, over which hangs a large framed picture of President Mubarak. The carpet on the floor is grainy with sand and has worn through in frazzled strands where the furniture has pinched it. There are also thinner carpets hanging on the walls. With each rumble of a departing jet, they give off a tiny shower of sand.

He steps out and comes back a moment later with an electric kettle. The plug is missing from the cord, which ends in two naked wires. Jiggling them just so, there is a spark as the wires are properly placed in the outlet. He smiles as the kettle begins to whistle. It is all I can do to keep from bursting into laughter.

"There is no general aviation fuel here," he is saying, "only jet fuel. But there is an airport nearby, at Imbaba, where you can get fuel. It used to be a military training field. Now there are a few small airplanes there and a flying club. Maybe there is no landing fee; you will see. Parking will be much cheaper."

He steps to the door and barks a few Arabic phrases to a young man waiting outside, then comes back to the couch. "He will make a photocopy of the airport pattern for you and help you file the flight plan. In Egypt, all flight plans must be filed at least twenty-four hours before the flight."

By the time the flight plan is completed it is almost five o'clock and the director hints that it is time to go home.

"I will arrange a taxi for you into the city. It will be much cheaper this way. But first," he asks, "could you make a purchase for me?"

We walk to the new terminal and go into the duty-free shop. I am not surprised by what I guess to be his request. As a Muslim he is prohibited from buying liquor. The duty-free shops are there to accommodate foreign tourists. Many Muslims, however, like to keep a bottle for private celebrations and to impress their friends with the forbidden liquid.

The director seems unexpectedly well-acquainted with the supplies. He immediately selects two bottles of Johnny Walker Red for me to take to the cashier on his behalf. When I place the bottles on the counter, he reaches over and pays for them with a distinctly familiar one hundred dollar bill.

Outside the building, he waves down a taxi. An ancient black Datsun with rusted floor boards. There is no window on the door and a crumpled coat hanger serves as the handle. After some quick conversation with the driver, he turns to me: "Pay him twenty Egyptian pounds, no more." It is about one tenth of the tourist rate.

We speed toward the city in descending darkness. I have taken cabs all over the world—New York, Tangiers, Bangkok, Calcutta—but I have never seen such manic driving. We hurtle right into a maelstrom of vehicles, the drivers yelling, waving and pounding the outside of their doors. It seems that there are no traffic rules whatsoever. He cuts into the other side of the road and we dodge oncoming cars and donkey carts, then back again. I should be nervous, but I am running on fumes. I've given myself over to fate.

When I ask for a cheap, emphasizing *very* cheap, hotel, he drops me in front of a tall edifice near Tahrir Square in the heart of Cairo. I climb past the broken concrete entrance to the foyer. A dour old man is behind the desk. Four pounds for the night. About thirty cents. He waves at the stairs, littered with garbage; the elevator is broken. I walk up to the fifth floor and enter the room. There is quick skitter of rats, surprised by my arrival. Evidently part of the plaster ceiling has collapsed, leaving a heap of rubble on the floor. No matter, this will do.

SEPTEMBER 29: CAIRO, EGYPT

I get back to the airport late in the morning and spend a couple of hours sitting in various offices while my flight plan is checked, stamped, and checked again. When I am ready to leave, I feign the need for a breath of fresh air and step outside the terminal, then sprint to the airplane, hoping no one sees me. Either they haven't noticed, or they are too lazy to bother sending the bus.

The Cardinal is in sad shape. There is a pale curve of naked aluminum along the leading edges of the wings where the sand has stripped off the white paint. I flip on the Master switch and cycle the flaps, up and down. There is that same stuttering whir. The starboard flap grinds weakly into position, but the port flap is quietly immobile. It is not just sand. The port flap motor is ruined.

I radio to ground control and get a clearance to taxi to run-up. The tower clears me for departure and I take off on the short flight to Imbaba. Almost before I climb to the pattern altitude of fifteen hundred feet, I can see the airfield. It is, in fact, hard to miss, as it is the only clear open space in western Cairo. At one time, the Imbaba airport must have been a nice country field, conveniently located next to the world's largest camel market. Now, high rise tenements crowd right up to the retaining wall around the airport. The camel market still exists. Each Friday, some seven thousand camels, goats, and horses trade hands.

When I radio in, there is a single response: "Cleared to land." I hear nothing else.

Without flaps, I have to make a shallower approach and land far down the runway. I spin the airplane in a one-eighty and taxi back on the narrow, cracked and weathered surface to what appears to be the terminal building. Alongside, there are a number of Russian helicopters in obvious disuse, with heavy burlap wrapping around the rotor assembly. They hunker in mute repose, relics of the former Soviet superpower influence in Africa. There are only a few other aircraft outside. Most of them are Sperber motor-gliders, Austrian-made balsa wood aircraft that were to be used by Egypt in a crack-pot scheme to invade Israel.

The tower is at the top of a white concrete terminal building. I walk over to it, see that the bottom floor is empty and continue up the worn stone stairs to the lookout. Three men are sitting up there, smoking and drinking tea. The only radio in evidence is a large, cubic metal box of second world war vintage. A bulky hand microphone is attached to it with a long, fabric-covered cord. This, evidently, is not a busy airport.

No one makes mention of any fees. I chat with the men for a while and casually ask, "I don't suppose anyone here might be interested in buying my airplane?"

"As a matter of fact," one of the men observes, "here is someone who might be," and points to a cream-colored Mercedes that has pulled up. "It's Hakim," another man says to me and, when he sees I don't understand, "Hakim Nasser. The son of President Nasser."

I walk down to the car and introduce myself. Hakim is a soft-spoken and pleasant man in his forties. He walks with me over to see the Cardinal and we talk a bit about flying. He recently got his private pilot license and is quite enthusiastic about the value of aviation in Egypt, a Texas-sized country with very few roads. There is a look of slight disbelief when he learns that I flew it from America. He recently bought a Cessna Skylane, a substantially larger but similar aircraft to mine, and spent a great deal of money to have it ferried from the United States. It is now in a hangar he had constructed for it. "Why don't you come back tomorrow morning?" he says. "I'd like to show you the area."

The center of Cairo is a tumult of daytime activity. I walk around, pick up some snacks from a street vendor and buy an Arabic phrase book.

Back at the hotel, I lie on the lumpy mattress and stare at the broken plaster ceiling. I've reached the end of my options. I feel like a rock climber who has come to an impassable overhang. I can't go down. I can't go up. I'm hanging on by my fingertips, slowly tiring. Soon, I will either fall ... or I will find another tiny hold and keep climbing.

SEPTEMBER 30: CAIRO, EGYPT

I meet Hakim at Imbaba and we examine his Skylane. It has a very clean appearance. The hangar helps, especially since it seems furnished with several full-time servants who hand-polish his airplane after every trip. We roar off over the city. Each flight in Egypt is on a rigid flight plan, I have learned, but this evidently does not apply to everyone. A few phrases in Arabic to air traffic control from Hakim and suddenly we carom off on our own.

"Have you seen the pyramids?" he asks me.

"Not really. Just a glimpse."

We carve a sharp bank toward Giza. "Now don't try this on your own," Hakim warns.

He pulls back the power and we drop down, right to the ground, no more than fifty feet above the crowds and tour buses, and *whar-ooom*, we buzz right between the two larger pyramids, scattering camels and stunned tourists. He yanks the control wheel back and we bank to avoid hitting the Sphinx.

I'm laughing helplessly. "That was ... *incredible!*"

He grins. "Let's go out into the country." We head off into the desert. At Dahshur, he points out the more ancient pyramids of Snefru, built 4,600 years ago. There are other, even older and more primitive structures far from the city and roads. Step-sided pyramids and smaller, rectangular mausoleums called mastabas. We have an ideal perspective. Faint, dotted lines in the sand indicate patterns that would have been impossible to discern on the ground. I can make out the vague remnants of the birth of human civilization.

Back at Imbaba, chairs and a table are set out next to the runway. Formally dressed waiters bring us tea and pastries. Several other men come over to join us. Ahmed and Ayman Mufti, chubby and jovial middle-aged twins, who own Avis rental cars of Egypt. There is Captain Wahid, a polite former Egyptian military officer. And Colonel Monem, whose military background is less clear. He in an elderly man of perhaps seventy and is clearly held with special respect by the others. He is considered to be the most knowledgeable aviator of the group. Among his many pilot certifications, he was also an aircraft and powerplant mechanic. For almost twenty years, he tells me, he lived in Los Angeles and worked for the United States Air Force.

Together, they form the Egypt Flying Club. Occasionally, one of them will take up a Sperber, or perhaps a Quicksilver ultralight. But the principal club activity appears to be what we are doing right now: drinking tea and talking about aviation for hours at a time. If there is one thing I am good at, it is endless chitchat about flying. I am determined to become a member of this club. It is my only handhold.

Evening descends over Cairo. The skyline is bathed in shades of rose and lavender. A warm, dry breeze comes from the desert. The moment is magical and time seems suspended.

OCTOBER 3: CAIRO, EGYPT

A little routine is developing. Get up, have a quick breakfast on the street, grab a cab to the Imbaba airport and spend the day drinking tea and socializing. I consider it my job.

Ayman Mufti shows up and asks if I would like to take up a Sperber.

I've never flown one before, I tell him.

"No matter. I'll fly in the front seat and you can take it when we get to the practice area."

The glider has a small engine to avoid the need for a tow up to altitude. We climb into the narrow plywood cylinder that makes up the fuselage and latch the plexiglass canopy over our heads.

Normally, glider practice areas are over unpopulated districts. No doubt the Imbaba practice area was once countryside, probably date-palm orchards, but now all I see underneath are high-rise tenements. I am skeptical when Ayman shuts off the engine and gives the controls over to me. Perhaps this isn't such a good idea. I find a few weak thermals, but the uninterrupted terrain of concrete below doesn't provide much lift potential. We gradually drift down. The variometer (a sensitive vertical speed indicator in gliders) shows us losing a hundred feet a minute. It is time to go back.

But Ayman can't restart the engine. The propeller cranks a half turn, stops, cranks, and stops. A few quick calculations: we are miles south of the airport with a ten-knot north wind, and less than a thousand feet above the crowded high-rises. I can see laundry hanging from the rooftops and children playing in the canyon-like streets. This is bad. Really bad.

Ayman continues to crank the engine. "Don't worry. This has happened before," he says, but his voice is tense. The battery is getting weak and the propeller barely turns over. He cranks the engine one last time, bringing the propeller to a stop at a horizontal rather than vertical position, so that it won't catch the ground when we hit. Then he focuses on a gentle slalom toward the airport, picking up a tiny lift here and there. I have a grim vision of ourselves slamming into a building like a winged torpedo. But Ayman has an expert touch. We silently glide within a couple of hundred feet of the rooftops and he eases it right up to the brick airport retaining wall, pulling back at the last second so that we hop over the wall and bounce to a stop on the other side.

For a minute, neither of us says anything. We both know that we've been incredibly lucky. A difference of a few feet, a tiny shift in the wind or temperature, and we would have been dead. Ayman forces a weak smile—"Maybe you want to take it up alone next time?"

"Sure."

But I'd rather crawl through a cartload of camel shit than get inside that thing again.

Naturally, this little episode is good for more than an hour of today's runway tea party discussions, with a lot of hand waving mimicking the performance of the glider. Two months from now, Captain Wahid will find himself in the same predicament, but without our luck. The result will be the loss of both the Sperber and his life.

OCTOBER 4: CAIRO, EGYPT

"We are flying to the Sinai. Why don't you join us?"

That seems like fun and it is a chance to show off my airplane. I hope to impress the flying club that the Cardinal's performance is almost equal to Hakim's much more expensive Skylane. There are still a few hours of fuel left in the tanks and the thought of flying to the Sinai is irresistible. I know that a foreigner would never get permission to fly there.

"We are going to Ras Sudr. The airstrip was built secretly by Israel when they occupied the Sinai. It is not on the charts. But you will see, it is very pretty, next to the Red Sea."

I'm all for it and then find out that I will have another passenger. Gamal Sadat, the son of the late president. Gamal is a dashing young man in his thirties, also smitten with the aviation bug. With Hakim and the others, they form a sort of royal family of Egypt, the privileged offspring of the country's rulers.

He divides his time between his yacht and some business inter-
ests in the United States and Egypt. But in the past year, all of
them have become interested in flying and there is clearly a bit
of one-upmanship going on. Now that Hakim has his own
airplane, Gamal, I suspect, is interested in buying one as well—
and I have just the machine for him.

I can fly the plane from the co-pilot seat, so I encourage
Gamal to take the controls, leading him carefully through each
step. We take off and form a formation with the Skylane. I contact Cairo Tower and then turn the transmission over to Gamal.
There is some discussion in Arabic, then what sounds like a bit of
an argument. Gamal banks to a heading out toward the eastern
desert. "You don't need to talk to them anymore," he says to me.

With Gamal flying, I turn my attention to the land below. The view of the rugged terrain is spectacular in the bright,
clear morning. This is the country of Moses and the Israelites.
We come up to the Red Sea, etched in the purest ultramarine
against the beige and topaz dunes of the shore. Black crescents
flit on the water below. We glide down to a hundred feet above
the surface to see schools of dolphins scattering diamonds of
sparkling water with every leap.

The airstrip at Ras Sudr is simply a length of smooth white
concrete on the sand. We land and then Colonel Monem asks
to take a spin in my airplane. It is all done as a playful gesture,
but I sense that everyone is curious about his impression. He
treats it like a fighter jet, powers up to a few thousand feet, a
half loop, an Immelmann, and then a snap hammerhead. After
landing, he pronounces himself pleased and everyone murmurs
admiration.

Back to Imbaba. As we come in for the steep approach,
Gamal reaches for the flaps lever. I stop him. "Oh, there is no
need for that. It is good practice to land without them. They
need to be adjusted, anyway."

The afternoon tea party talk has started to drift to the sale
of my airplane. I never bring up the issue and act as nonchalant

as possible, pretending that I have no particular need to sell it, but might do so if the price is right. These guys are inveterate traders, far more crafty than I am. Ahmed Mufti begins negotiations, saying he is interested in buying it for himself. I am sure that he is a front man for someone else. He shows me a fax from an American aircraft dealer with a blue-book estimate, and offers me $13,700. I am infuriated. I am hoping for fifty thousand and expect a low starting offer, but this figure is a joke. I let him know it. The fax, I point out, refers to an older, cheap training airplane, not at all like the Cardinal.

In the evening, we all go out to dinner at a high-class restaurant. The Egypt Flying Club has its core members, but there are also a few less active participants who show up now and then for a ride or a lesson, or just to walk around the airport with their children. Now one of them is holding forth on his failing investments in the United States.

"I put three and a half million dollars into Los Angeles commercial real estate," he whines, "and it is losing money."

I have become a sort of de facto ambassador from the United States and the complaint is directed at me as much as it is to let the others know how much money he has to toss around.

"Who told you to do that?" I say. "Everyone knows L.A. is a bad investment. The defense industry is winding down and it doesn't look like it is going to get better anytime soon. That doesn't sound like a good place to put your money. From what I've heard, there are much better investments."

They listen attentively. They seem to like this guy who came from nowhere, who has plenty of time for them and who asks for nothing. They are especially interested in how Americans perceive Egypt. I am aware that no matter how powerful and wealthy these men are, they carry, somewhere deep inside, a bit of the colonial inferiority complex of being a third-world country. The British may no longer rule Egypt, but there is still a tiny fear that the world's industrial nations look down on these men. I do my best to dispel this notion.

"We are entering the space age. Astronomy was developed by the Egyptians. Think of the stars in the belt of Orion: Al-nilam, Al-nitak, Mintaka. Almost every bright star has an Arabic name." The majority of northern hemisphere bright stars have traditional Arabic names, although professional astronomers prefer to use their standardized Yale number series designations. I mention a dozen other stars and the men repeat the names in amusement when they figure out my poor pronunciation.

I go on to a closer example. "America has always had a tremendous respect for Egypt. You know, we even put the pyramid on our money."

"No! That can't be true!" They look at each other. These men have contempt for the soft Egyptian currency and carry on their multinational dealings with U.S. dollars, British pounds, or Deutschmarks. But evidently they have never looked closely at a one dollar bill. They search their pockets and somebody finds one, holding it up for the others to see. Everyone lets out a chuckle or exclamation in surprise and delight.

My own star has just risen a bit.

OCTOBER 5: CAIRO, EGYPT

The negotiations are underway in earnest this afternoon. I regret my lack of composure yesterday. That was really dumb. I need to do what they do: say, "Yes, yes of course," to everything in obsequious agreement, while committing to nothing and just letting everything flow. I am learning a few phrases. *Bokran* means tomorrow. Like *mañana* in Latin America, it is a frequent answer to every significant request. *Malesh* is another handy term, meaning, "It can't be helped." It is often followed by *Inshallah*, "If God wills it." Together, this is the most basic vocabulary needed to survive in Cairo.

There is a new man at the airport today. I can tell immediately by his accent that he is Swiss and strike up a conversation with him.

"Mike," he says by way of introduction, "but that is not my real name."

Mike was Brother Michele, a monk for seven years in the Benedictine monastery in Rome. He was a classical scholar, studying Latin, Hebrew, and Aramaic, the language of Christ. Mike has a headstrong personality and, after some long-running disputes with the abbot, it was mutually agreed that Mike should leave the monastery. He traveled a bit, ended up in Cairo and fell in love with the city. One day he walked into Radio Cairo, the respected radio station that broadcasts in half a dozen languages each day. Mike is fluent in English, German, French, and Italian and with his smooth voice and classical diction, he was soon given a job as an announcer. Now, a few years later, he is the voice of Radio Cairo, with a daily news and culture program in those four languages. And he is also fluent in Arabic.

"Don't you know?" Mike asks me. "Egypt is run by IBM."

"IBM? Really?"

"Yes, *Inshallah, Bokran, Malesh!*"

Mike is here for a flight in the Sperber. He enjoys gliding but has never been in a small powered airplane. After the flight, we talk a bit more and he invites me to come and stay with him in his penthouse apartment in a nicer section of Cairo. I am not sorry to leave the hotel.

OCTOBER 6: CAIRO, EGYPT

Today, I have to go to the dreaded Mugama. The transit stamp in my passport has expired. The only way to get an extended visa is a visit to this labyrinthine, fourteen-story administration building on Tahrir Square. It is said that twenty thousand people pass through the Mugama every day. It is also said that its administrative routines are so antiquated, many of them actually date from the time of the pharaohs. My guidebook notes: "It is a Kafka building. If you enter there, you can get the same job done in five minutes, five days, five months, or five years.

There is no prediction." I go in equipped with a supply of Egyptian pounds for payment, and U.S. one dollar bills for *baksheesh*. Bribes. On my third try, I find the right office. A photograph is needed. Not one that I have with me. It must be one taken today. In the grand foyer of the building, there are photographers for this purpose and I marvel at the sight. These men have enormous, antique, wooden box cameras on tripods. I am told to stand still in front of one of them, while the man drapes a black cloth over himself, hand-flips the shutter and flash bulb, then develops a print from the plate.

A couple of hours and a few dollar bills later, I have my stamp.

This evening, Colonel Monem invites me out to dinner, with him alone. He enjoys reminiscing about his time in Los Angeles. We talk about a wide range of subjects. When he touches on the matter of the airplane sale, I tell him that negotiations are going slowly.

"Don't trust them," he warns. "Be careful and don't believe anything they say. It is Gamal who wants the airplane. But he is mindful of his public image. He doesn't want to look like a rich playboy. Ahmed will probably buy it for the club, with Gamal's money."

"By the way," he asks, "how did you ship the airplane to Europe?" He doesn't believe that it could have been flown from the United States. I describe some of the flight to him and offer to show him the log books, but he listens dubiously and changes the subject.

OCTOBER 7: CAIRO, EGYPT

Once more, hours of tea and chat produce a few small steps toward the sale of the airplane. I'm desperate to get out of here and continue to South Africa. But I have to be careful. One by one, as I find myself alone with someone, he warns me about the others.

"You know, Colonel Monem. Don't trust him. He really wants your airplane for his son. Just you wait and see. He is using Ahmed to break the ice. Then he will step in."

In late afternoon, Ahmed comes to me with an offer for $29,000. This is much better. It is getting into an acceptable range. Now I feel that, with a little luck, I just might pull this off. I calculate all my debts and expenses. I'd like to get fifty thousand for the airplane, its proper value in Africa, but to break even I would need thirty-five.

I am basking in the feeling of imminent success when a messenger runs to our table. He breathlessly explains something in Arabic and their faces fall. I wait respectfully until someone can explain. Colonel Monem's son, a promising young air force officer, has been killed in an automobile accident.

Everyone is in shock. The funeral will be tonight. To my surprise, I am invited to come to the mosque.

Khalid, one of the airport mechanics, was a friend of the dead man. He now takes me under his wing and explains how I should dress and act. At dusk, he picks me up at Mike's apartment.

In the late sunset glow, the grand mosque of Cairo dominates the sky. I take my place in line and covertly look around. The top echelons of the government and the military are here. A muezzin begins a low chant, gradually building into a powerful wail. There is no other sound. His voice cuts a rasping echo of sadness and grief. The voice steps to a higher pitch and repeats the wail, ringing out now. Again a higher, and higher, and even higher pitch, until the amplified cry is a screeching, blistering torment of agony and loss. No funeral has ever brought to me so much the pain of the death of a child.

OCTOBER 8: CAIRO, EGYPT

There is no point in going to the airport today. I take the opportunity to play tourist, visiting the Egyptian museum and the pyramids. In the evening Mike shows me around old Cairo. It was built around 500 BC and expanded by the Persians into the fortress of Babylon. We go to the bazaar, the souq Khan al-Khalili, and sit at smoke shops where I nibble on mysterious snacks and he smokes *shisha* from a large water pipe.

OCTOBER 9: CAIRO, EGYPT

I mosey on over to the airport. Not to conduct business—it is too soon after the funeral for that—but just to socialize. Colonel Monem shows up.

"I am so sorry," I say. There is really nothing I can think of adding. I don't want to patronize his grief. He wants to talk about flying and I sense it will be a release for him. So we chat, for hours, about aviation in America and Egypt.

OCTOBER 10: CAIRO, EGYPT

Life is returning to normal. This morning, Colonel Monem is busy at the airport, ordering parts for aircraft and speculating about plans for the flying club. Everyone is happy to see him active and talkative. In the afternoon, we sit drinking tea. He tells the group flatly, in front of me, that I could not have flown the airplane from America. It is just not possible.

"Then how did he get here?" someone asks.

I feel like a piece of furniture. If it wasn't for Khalid and others interpreting for me, I would feel completely invisible.

But Monem is not about to call me a liar. "It was the will of Allah," he says to them.

And then to me, in English, "It is not possible to fly over the ocean in that small airplane. And yet you are here. Allah has brought you to us. Why, I do not know."

Everyone looks at me. Whatever the old man says, it must be true.

I feel like saying, "Well I'll be damned if I know, either!" But I hold my tongue.

Later in the evening, Mike laughs uproariously when he hears my story. He is really enjoying the whole spectacle and has his own calculations on who is behind the negotiations. It is all a big soap opera to him. So typical of life in Egypt, he says.

OCTOBER 11: CAIRO, EGYPT

I spend some time cleaning up the airplane, working with Khalid to see what can be done about the flaps. He believes a new motor can be installed without difficulty. Otherwise, the airplane is in functional shape.

Against my better judgment, I push the negotiations and arrange for an actual transaction the following day, telling them I am expected in Southern Africa and can no longer delay.

OCTOBER 12: CAIRO, EGYPT

Today is the day. It has got to be. All the pieces are in place. And yet, there are many small meetings to which I am not invited. I sense that they are talking about me. Nevertheless, I sneak a look and see that some documents have been brought. This looks promising.

In the afternoon it is hot outside and we all sit around a table in the cool interior of Hakim's hangar, drinking tea as usual.

Suddenly, a tremendous vibration seizes the aluminum walls and the building shudders as if it is about to rip apart. It sounds like a jet is making a low pass right over our heads, but the deafening racket does not let up. The walls are rattling with a ferocious clamor, ready to snap apart. We jump up and run outside. The ground is shaking and a Mercedes is rocking up and down on its suspension.

There is only one thing I can think of to cause this. An earthquake. Trying to act unalarmed, I put on a false show of confidence. "Feels like about a six," I say.

Living in California, you get used to earthquakes. On the Richter scale, each increase of the number is ten times an increase in the force. An earthquake of level four sounds like a car back-firing down the street, enough to rattle your windows a bit. A five is a heavy truck rumbling past on the road, shaking the whole house. A six makes the ground heave like you are next to a freight train. The highest I've experienced, the Loma Prieta earthquake of October, 1989, was a seven point one. This one, I would guess, is about a six.

The rumbling has stopped. The others look at me in horror as if I have gone completely insane.

"It's an earthquake!" one of them shouts.

"Of course it's an earthquake," I say, "and it feels like about a level six force. It will cause some minor damage, should not be too much."

They look at me seriously now, with panic on their faces.

"We have never had an earthquake here!" Ahmed gasps.

In the distance, there is smoke rising from the city and we hear the faint wailing of sirens over the usual traffic horns. Each of the men rushes to his car and gets his cell phone. The switchboard is overwhelmed and they cannot get through. They jump in to go home to check on their families and I ride with one of them.

There are traffic jams everywhere so that progress is exasperatingly slow. I climb out and walk instead. The streets are filled with scenes of desperation. Some of the shoddy buildings have collapsed and people are shouting and tearing at the rubble. A woman is on her knees, weeping hysterically, rubbing dirt into her hair. I hurry on to Mike's apartment block. It hadn't looked like the sturdiest building.

My whole journey seems increasingly bizarre. As I rush along, threading my way through the pandemonium in the streets, I feel that my trip has become completely irrational. My only escape from this ridiculous venture is to sell the airplane and do something sensible with my life. But at each step, some unexpected obstacle has come up. I was so close to actually getting rid of the airplane. And now there is an *earthquake!* What the hell is going on?!

October 13: Cairo, Egypt

Mike's place was fine. So were the surrounding apartment blocks. The earthquake is described in the newspaper today as a five point nine. Some eight hundred buildings have collapsed and another ten thousand are damaged in the poorer districts of the city. Maybe five hundred people have died. But the upper-class district of Heliopolis has escaped damage and the families of the flying club are unaffected. In this hive of eighteen million souls, life goes on.

October 14: Cairo, Egypt

There is a different mood at the airport today. Ahmed says the earthquake caused a disruption in his business and he can no longer afford the airplane. I don't believe him. There is something else going on. Maybe people are spooked by this strange event. Maybe now I'm not the saint sent by Allah, but the devil. After all, since my arrival, there has been a death and a natural disaster.

Whatever. There is a strange mood at the airport and the negotiations are dead in the water.

Mike disagrees. "Nah, it is just games. You don't know these Egyptians. They are buying time. They know you want to leave. They can see right through you. They are playing for time, until you have to *give* them the airplane."

Then he startles me. "Actually, I want to buy your airplane."

"*You?*" I laugh, "What would you do with the airplane? You've never even flown in a small airplane!"

Mike is a bit annoyed and defensive. "Why not? You said it isn't so difficult to learn to fly."

Now I feel a little guilty. In the evenings, I have told Mike a lot of stories of flying in Canada, in the United States and Mexico and, of course, my flight over the ocean, around Switzerland and along the Mediterranean. I naturally extolled the beauty and wonder of flight. Now I see that I may have overdone it.

"But look, Mike. Seriously. It is expensive. I need at least thirty-five thousand for it. You don't have that kind of money. And it has mechanical problems that will cost money for repairs. It's really not in very good shape. How are you going to learn to fly it, anyway? The Cardinal is not a training airplane. You don't know what a headache it can be to own something like this. Let me sell it to the Egyptians. Then it will be their problem."

But now Mike is offended and I feel bad. "When I was a little boy," he says, "I dreamed of flying my own airplane. It is a dream I've forgotten until these past few days."

"Oh, *Jesus*. Mike, *every* kid in the world dreams of flying. Maybe you can rent it from the Egyptians after I sell it."

"You don't understand. I'm a stubborn asshole. When I decide to do something, I do it. And besides," he smirks, "it would really bug the hell out of the Egyptians if I buy it from under their nose!"

We decide to leave it unresolved. I don't want to dump my problems on to Mike and have a horrible feeling that I have somehow tricked him into this.

OCTOBER 15: CAIRO, EGYPT

I tell the people at the airport that I am leaving the country within days. If they want the airplane, this is their last chance. Ahmed tells me to wait, he may be able to sort out some cash-flow problems. A couple of other names are mentioned and suddenly it seems that three or four people are actually interested in the purchase, though none of them are available today.

Mike approaches me again in the evening. "I've talked to my father. He has kept a trust fund for me in Switzerland. He can transfer thirty-five thousand from it to your bank in California." A pause. "I'm serious about this. I don't want to spend the rest of my life here as a radio announcer. Let me buy it."

Okay. We sit down and work out some arrangements. When I get back to California, Mike will come and stay with me to get his pilot's license. I will do anything I can to help him achieve his goal.

OCTOBER 16: CAIRO, EGYPT

I go to the airport one last time to retrieve documents and review every detail of the airplane with Mike. He can barely conceal his glee when he tells the others that he has bought it.

Ahmed pulls me aside. "I thought you were going to sell it to me." He thinks this might be an elaborate bluff from Mike and me.

"You're too late," I say, and we both know he has lost this little game.

I arrange a ticket to Cape Town. Because there are still sanctions restricting commercial traffic to South Africa, I have to go through Israel and Athens. I have done enough flying for a while, so I buy a bus ticket to Tel Aviv. Besides, I am interested in the drive to the Suez Canal and Gaza. It would be really interesting to see some of this land, the cause of so many political problems. I pack up my logbook, my journals and notes, and take off the amulet I have worn around my neck since my sister gave it to me. It has served me well. Mike accompanies me to the post office, where I send off the package, and then we go to a tiny, floating restaurant on the Nile to celebrate.

OCTOBER 17: CAIRO, EGYPT

Mike takes me to the bus station at four o'clock in the morning. There is already a line of people waiting and I patiently take my place at the end, chatting with a couple of highschool girls from Hong Kong. But the bus is full and they have oversold the number of tickets by one. When I come to the front, the ticket handler, a muscular young man, says, "Sorry. Come back tomorrow." I am furious. These past weeks have been a tremendous emotional strain. I just want to get out of Cairo, out of Egypt. Today.

I argue with the ticket handler and hold up the bus for twenty minutes while I force him to make another count of the seventy passengers. Finally, he says, "Yes, go on," and points out a seat about five rows from the front. To accommodate me, I guess he has put someone else in his front seat so he has to stand at the back. It is his problem, not mine.

We roll out and head to the outskirts of the city. The wide roads are almost empty in the gray light of morning. I can hardly believe everything I have lived through these past few weeks, and there is still a feeling of unreality in the fact that I have succeeded in my goal. After all, I flew to Africa, and I sold the airplane. The others on the bus are dozing, but I am too emotional to sleep and gaze at the industrial zones as we pick up speed to about fifty miles an hour.

Finally, I say to myself, I am done with Cairo.

But Cairo is not yet done with me.

Ahead, a train has slowly rolled across the highway. Maybe our driver has not yet noticed it, a gray train in the gray light. Or perhaps he has fallen asleep. Or maybe had a stroke. Whatever it is, we don't slow down. I wait for the sudden brake as we get close. Closer. Then in an instant I see that we are not going to stop and I reflexively lean forward onto the seatback in front of me, with my face cradled in my bent arms, bracing for the impact. At the last second, I can't bear not to look and open my arms a crack to see us hurtling toward the train. There is an earsplitting crash of metal and glass as we slam into it. The front of the bus has crumpled like an accordion. My seat is now just behind a great gaping hole of twisted metal.

There is silence for a moment. Then the bus begins to fill with moans and cries. I take a quick survey of myself. My elbows have punched through the flimsy vinyl covering of the seatback and are jammed in the metal frame and springs. I ease them out. There are jagged lacerations on my arms and knees and my shirt sleeves and pants are seeping with blood. But no broken bones and I feel otherwise unhurt. I get up, shakily. The ticket handler had been standing at the back and was flung clear. Now he jumps up, remarkably uninjured, and yells out, "Everybody off the bus!"

I move toward him and say, "I have some medical training. I can help." He immediately shouts, "This man is a doctor!"

Triage, I tell myself. Sort the wounded into categories. I help the handler direct or carry people out of the wreckage and sort them on the roadside into groups. Most of the passengers seem unhurt, especially those who had been sitting at the back. It isn't easy to tell. Some are doubled over and crying uncontrollably. A couple of dozen have minor injuries. I tell them to sit by the embankment, I will come later. The Hong Kong girls have taken the blow in the face. One has only a bloody hole where her mouth was; the other has a shattered nose and broken jaw. They are in shock, staring in a wide-eyed drifting gaze. I lead them to the embankment and they sit quietly in detached numbness.

Everyone who can move is out. I climb in with the handler. I feel like I am bumbling, stiff and awkward, moving in a dream. He is abruptly efficient. We find the driver, his head contorted in a gruesome twist. He is obviously dead. Another man is trapped in the front wreckage and has been yowling in pain. We try to free him, but from his chest down his body is completely embedded, crunched in the metal. Blood is oozing out of his mouth in jellied, purplish-red globs. His choking yells become moans. Then he stops breathing. And then he is still.

A young man rushes up to me. "I'm Andy, from Colorado." He points to another young guy standing nearby in a daze. "We were sleeping in the back. We're not hurt. Tell us what to do."

The bus has struck the train near the end of one of the railway cars, knocking it and the following one off the tracks. Now vehicles on the road are slowing down to drive around the wreckage, the drivers gawking at the people on the embankment.

"Get out on the road and stop the cars," I say. "Put these people in first. Just yell HOSPITAL and load 'em in."

I can't think. From all sides, people are clawing at me, asking me to help them, to see their friend. I can hardly remember anything I learned. I'm rushing from one person to another, but I don't really know what to do.

There is an Egyptian man lying on the ground. He looks to be about thirty. There is no obvious injury. When I draw close, he turns his head to me with a fearful gaze and begins talking excitedly in Arabic. Maybe he is just in a panic. I run my hands over his hips and there is a crunchy feel of bone against bone. He probably has a pelvic fracture with internal bleeding and is in shock. He needs intravenous fluids. He needs a hospital. I try to feel his pulse at his neck and his hand grabs my shoulder. He looks at me in wide-eyed terror, jabbering to me, again and again. I bend over to his ear and say ENGLISH but he keeps insisting, pinning me with his eyes. His hand relaxes and then falls away. He looks at me imploring, his mouth twitching wordlessly. Then he stops. His pupils are dilated, still staring at me in an open-eyed expression of fear and confusion. His body is limp. There is no pulse.

I can't believe this is happening. The man is still. His eyes stare at me, in question, in fright, in frozen astonishment. I edge away in horror. There is a sensation of ice water on the back of my neck, seeping down and chilling my whole body. I stand up jerkily and stare dumbfounded at the people tugging at my arm. They pull me from body to body, but I am just going through the motions. If only this were a dream. I just want it to be over.

The handler is marching around, telling people where to sit, to be quiet, or to bring their question to me. It has a strangely calming influence and I am filled with respect for him.

It has been almost an hour since the accident. The ambulances finally start arriving. I go into the wreckage to where the Hong Kong girls were sitting and search the area for her teeth. When I find them, they are longer than I expected, probably broken right out of the jaw. I wrap them in a scrap of cloth, take them to the girl and explain that they might be re-implanted. She nods, whimpering. The ambulances take away the remaining wounded. Then a minibus comes and takes some others. A tow-truck arrives and they cut out the driver and the other man. When only the unhurt are left, a last ambulance waits. The handler goes over to talk to the paramedic and suddenly breaks down, sobbing in his embrace.

I sit on the embankment in a stupefied daze.

An hour later, another bus comes. The driver says the company will put us in a nice hotel tonight and give us air tickets to Israel tomorrow, or we can take this bus to Israel now. Everyone wants to leave now.

As we drive to the Suez, no one sleeps.

Chapter 17

Automatic Direction Finder

"Welcome to South Africa. I suppose you've come here to get away from racism in America?"

Professor Veldman spoke with a twinkle in his eye and shook my hand firmly. Tall and ruddy-faced, with an Oxford tweed suit and polished brown shoes, he leads me into his spacious office at the Department of Communicable Disease, Faculty of Medicine, University of Cape Town.

"We called California to check on your arrival, but they said you had left a couple of months ago, that you were somewhere in North Africa."

"Yes. I was delayed a bit."

"Well, we are delighted to have you here. Professor Benatar has already scheduled two lectures for next week—I hope you don't mind. We had to set the curriculum last month for printing. I understand you are also interested in volunteering at Groote Schuur?"

That was the plan. I arrived here last Thursday and have been staying at a charming bed and breakfast, the Koornhoop

239

Guest House in Mowbray, not far from the university. I was to present a couple of lectures here as a visiting professor and then volunteer at the famous university hospital, Groote Schuur, where the world's first heart transplant had been done. With two thousand beds, it dwarfs its American counterparts, and is renowned as a facility that treats all patients—white, mixed-race coloured, black, or bushman—and the more difficult or exotic the disease, the better. It is a place where a wealthy industrialist might be treated next to a tribal herdsman, like a combination of the Mayo Clinic and Cook County General Hospital. Seeing it from the inside, in the role of a medical student assistant, would be a great way to learn about South Africa.

A few more introductions. There are not many visiting professors here, especially from the United States, and I am treated with far more respect than I deserve. Someone mentions a journal article I had written. Another tells me some computer programs I had published are being used here. I am flattered with their familiarity with my work, even though it is probably just a polite gesture of appreciation.

There are a few black faces among the medical students and faculty and I am surprised when one of them, an intern, repeats Professor Veldman's little joke.

"So," he says in a lilting accent, "you have come to escape the racial problems in your country?"

South Africans, I learn, do not believe they have a "racial" problem. Even this man, who until last year could not enter most of Cape Town without a special passbook, who had to use only bathrooms for non-whites, take a designated non-white coach on the train, and had to enter the post office by a separate door—and still now does not have the right to vote. Even this man, incredibly, does not believe that there is a racial problem in his country.

"Don't you think you have it a little more difficult here than the blacks in America?" I ask him.

"My name is Grushan," the young doctor in the starched

white lab coat replies in the most pleasant way, ignoring my question. "Why don't you come to my home for dinner sometime? My family would like to meet you. Perhaps you will see a different side of South Africa." And with that, he jots down his phone number on a slip of paper, hands it to me, and disappears down the hall.

Back at the Koornhoop, I relax on wicker furniture and look out the open window to the pretty flower gardens. I'll read some magazines, and maybe a South African history book or two that I picked up at the bookshop today. I'll read until late tonight, waiting for sleep to come. Although I know that sleep will not come. Since the accident, fatigue arrives intertwined with anxiety. And eventually, despite every distraction, eventually I lie in the darkness and hear again the jabbering Arabic, I see his face beseeching me and then that look of fear and astonishment.

OCTOBER 27: CAPE TOWN, SOUTH AFRICA

Cape Town is one of the most beautiful cities on earth. In fact, its setting against the backdrop of the cape peninsula, ringed with white sand beaches and the blue waters of the confluence of the Atlantic, Southern, and Indian oceans, may well be the most photogenic on earth. Neighborhoods of colonial British mansions and Dutch cottages cling to the skirts of Table Mountain, shaded by enormous trees and blossoming hedges. The cape region is a botanist's delight. There are thousands of species of indigenous plants. Window boxes the world over are filled with flowers that originated from here. If South Africa can ever sort out its political problems, I am convinced it will become one of the greatest tourist destinations.

But now, at the end of apartheid and before the first truly national election, there are few tourists. An uncertainty grips the country. It is clear that the majority government will be dominated by non-whites, but no one knows how this will work out. In every African country where this post-colonial change has taken place, the result has been corruption, dictatorship and civil war, as old tribal enmities suddenly take the national stage. Nelson Mandela promises to be a wise leader, acceptable to the Cape Town liberal white population. He survived imprisonment for twenty-seven years on an Alcatraz-like island just off this shore. That alone commands respect. But he is an old man and no one is sure how firm his grip will be, or whether he will even survive long enough to lead.

On the other hand, the Inkatha Freedom Party and Zulu forces of Chief Mangosuthu Buthelezi threaten to Balkanize the country into a collection of feuding tribes. The only thing helping Buthelezi is the even worse specter of the Pan-African Movement. Those militant radicals have terrorized the country with their spray-painted slogan ONE SETTLER, ONE BULLET, and promise a bloodbath civil war.

I walk along the streets of Observatory, the neighborhood next to the Groote Schuur complex. There is a Room To Let sign on a small Dutch cottage just a block from the main hospital. The owner is a tall, muscular and handsome young man whose shoulder-length blond hair makes him look like a comic-book Tarzan. Andrew is his name. We negotiate a couple months' rent and I move in. Andrew tells me that he flunked out of business school, but is very eager to get in on the ground floor of a new economic order.

"You'll see," he tells me, "after the election, the economy is going to boom. The sanctions are coming off already. This is the time to start a business. *Any* business. I've started a used-car rental company—by the way, do you want to rent one?—and I am going to buy another house in Observatory as soon as I can get a loan."

Andrew is one of the new generation in Cape Town. He doesn't care about politics or social class. In addition to English, he speaks Afrikaans, a smattering of the Xhosa and Sotho tribal languages, and he is studying German. His friends include blacks and coloureds and Indians. They all share a common interest, and that interest is money.

NOVEMBER 5: CAPE TOWN, SOUTH AFRICA

The lectures go well. After years of teaching at a state university, I have learned to simplify mathematical concepts and spice the theories with plenty of historical anecdotes or comical examples. All too often, I had seen the eyes of my students glaze over, or had them in my office the next day saying, "Just tell me what I need to do to pass the course." It was a constant challenge to keep them interested. So I gradually developed a style that was quite informal, more like a talk-show host than a traditional professor. I don't know how well this came off today, but the small audience of students and faculty seemed to enjoy my talk. If they were a bit mystified by my approach, or just being polite, I couldn't tell. In any case, I am glad to have that task out of the way.

In the evening I wander around the neighborhood and then head downtown, to the waterfront. Andrew is surprised when I walk in the door.

"You shouldn't be out at night. Take a cab if you must—or why don't you rent one of my cars?—but it isn't wise to walk after dark, especially outside of Observatory."

"I thought you said that there was no racial resentment, that everyone is looking forward to the elections?"

"It's not a political thing. Cape Town is surrounded by townships. Khayelitsha alone has over a million people. The people there live in total poverty, cardboard or plywood shacks without electricity or running water. Under apartheid, they had to have a work permit to come into town, like Malis."

It is the first time that I realize that Malis, the shy, plump Xhosa maid who cleans Andrew's house, had to have an official permit until recently to enter the city from her shanty-town of Guguletu.

"Now they are everywhere," he continues, "and they just see you as someone with money."

"Have you ever been in Guguletu or Khayelitsha?"

"Actually, no. In fact, I don't know of any whites who

have gone in there. In the townships, it *is* a political thing. The Pan-African Movement is quite active in those areas. You would be dead in an hour if you wandered around there."

NOVEMBER 9: CAPE TOWN, SOUTH AFRICA

Six o'clock. Morning rounds on the internal medicine service. I follow the registrar, the resident physician, as he examines each of the thirty patients on his service. This is quite different from an American hospital. There are twenty or more patients to a room, with very little nursing attention. While this arrangement makes it easier for the physician to keep an eye on so many patients, there is virtually no privacy, even for deathly ill patients.

Unlike the U.S., there are no phlebotomists here and it is the doctor's job to draw the blood samples for the day. I push a little cart as we go. He shows me how to puncture the veins and I am happy to make myself useful. I try on the cheap South African-made surgical gloves, but they shred in my hands. The sanctions have reached everywhere. "Don't bother with them," the registrar says. He uses his bare hands, despite the fact that many of the patients are HIV-positive. I am pleased with a successful stick and discard the used needle assembly into the sharps waste basket. "Hey, don't throw that away!" he yells at me. Then he softens. "Groote Schuur may be famous, but it is not rich. You can throw away the needle, but put the plastic barrel in your pocket. It can be reused."

He stands with his clipboard and asks me to give a preliminary impression of each patient as we come to the bed. We make our way along and I try to make as thorough a presentation as I can with my limited knowledge. I nudge one that appears asleep. But there is no sign of breath or heartbeat and when I press on her flesh it is cold and doughy.

"This one is ... ah ... I think she is dead."

"Okay." He glances down and crosses a line through her name on the clipboard. "Next."

One of the patients is a black construction worker, with skin the color of coal. He looks up fearfully, breathing in jerky gasps. His face has a remarkable appearance: one side is sweating profusely and the other side is completely dry, with a border between them precisely down the middle from the top of his forehead to the tip of his chin.

The registrar takes the man's hand tenderly. "This doctor has come all the way from America just to see you," he says to him. The man looks up at me while I examine him and gives me a weak smile of relief and gratitude. For a moment, there is no pain and his breath is gentle.

"Did you notice his face?" the registrar asks me later. "It is Horner's syndrome. He has a Pancoast tumor, an advanced lung cancer. I doubt if he will be alive by this evening."

"Isn't there anything we can do?"

"No."

After we complete the rounds, I spend some time learning the fine points of blood draws on obese or elderly patients who have difficult veins to find or puncture, then graduate to learning about arterial punctures, paracentesis, drawing excess fluid from the abdomen, and pleuracentesis, from the lining of the lungs. This is so different from my academic work. I like the immediacy, the feeling that something is happening to make the patient better, right now. Most of all, I like the human touch. But the sickness frightens me. I am afraid to get too close, to feel their suffering. I don't have the emotional reserve. Now and then I retreat to the windows and look out on the slope of Table Mountain next to the hospital. There is a herd of wildebeest on the grass and I half expect to see zebras and giraffes. Out there, so much beauty, and in here, there is so much pain.

Just after two o'clock in the afternoon, the Pancoast man dies.

NOVEMBER 17: CAPE TOWN, SOUTH AFRICA

Professor Veldman looks up as I knock on the open door of his office.

"Dr. Gahlinger. How nice to see you. How is your experience at the hospital?"

"Good. It is very interesting."

"What can I do for you, then?"

"Do you think that I could visit the townships, Khayelitsha or Guguletu?"

He looks thoughtful. "It is not a safe area. Especially Khayelitsha, which is rather the worse of the two. I, myself, have never been there. I would not recommend it." He notes the disappointment on my face. "But I can see you are not easily dissuaded. There is a doctor who goes out there once a week, God bless him. Mark Bletcher. Why don't you give him a call? Maybe he can take you along."

As it turns out, Dr. Bletcher is in the hospital today.

"Just call me Mark," he insists when I find him. "I work with SACLA, the South African Christian Leadership Association. We get donated medicines and supplies from the drug companies. I'm going to Khayelitsha this Friday. You're welcome to come along—I could use an extra hand. And by the way, make sure you wear a white lab coat."

NOVEMBER 18: CAPE TOWN, SOUTH AFRICA

Another sleepless night, and the thought of going in to the sight of blood and pus and the smell of death is too much. This morning, I made it clear that I had other work and that my attendance would be irregular. I feel a little guilty about being so lax in my duties. But after all, I am really here only as a volunteer and they can get by just as well without me. The work is interesting and I try to convince myself to stick with it, to focus on learning what I can and be of some use to these good people. The problem is, I am not quite sure anymore about what it is I am trying to learn, or where this is supposed to lead. The country is on the verge of cracking up and I had been looking forward to a self-righteous ringside seat at this national drama. Instead, it is me that is cracking up.

In the afternoon, I leave the hospital and take the train to the beach at Muizenberg.

The railway is wonderfully quaint. In fact, the whole city seems like a nostalgic image of Britain in the nineteen fifties. The barber waving from his shop. The grocer on the corner with his green visor. The city train, with its leather upholstered seats and wood-shuttered windows, that stops every couple of blocks to pick up men in knickers and ladies with Easter bonnets. Everyone sits primly, reading a newspaper or chatting quietly as the carriages trundle slowly through the picturesque white neighborhoods of Rosebank, Rondebosch, Plumstead, and Simon's Town, and then much faster through the Indian and coloured districts. So very civilized. At the station, they always automatically give me a first-class ticket, which is quite inexpensive, in any case. There is no second class. And the third class window is always closed.

Out of curiosity, when the train comes in today I walk down the platform past the first-class coaches and enter the third class. There are only narrow, hardwood benches along the walls. A sea of black faces looks over in mild surprise. "Hi," I say, holding up my ticket. And to the young man beside me, "I'm visiting from America."

He chuckles at my ticket. "You don't need that here."

"How come?"

The people in the coach relax when they see that I am a foreigner.

"Last year they stopped making the trains segregated. They painted over the NON-WHITE sign, and just called it third-class. But no white conductor will come back here. So we ride free!" He laughs.

As we pull out of the station, someone plays a harmonica,

another throws dice on the floor and a deck of cards material-izes. Some women start to sing. And suddenly there is a party. This is a lot more fun than first class.

November 19: Cape Town, South Africa

Tonight is my dinner date with Grushan. When I called him last week, he had begged off, saying he was too busy at the hospital. That seemed true enough—as an intern, he was there virtually twenty-four hours a day. I wondered if I hadn't mis-taken his invitation for mere politeness. But when I saw him in the hall today, he apologized and insisted that I come over this evening.

Grushan is of the Shangaan tribe, near Zimbabwe. His family moved from the northeast part of South Africa to find work. They now live in the formerly coloured district of Cape Town. He introduces me to his mother, uncle, grandmother and a couple of teenage siblings who seem almost painfully shy. His father is away, working in the mines, and can only visit his family once a year. They look at me incredulously when I tell them that I also worked as an underground laborer in the mines. A hearty meal is prepared of corn mash, squash, beans, and some gristly pork, which I politely nibble on. Grushan and the elders howl with laughter when I tell them about taking the third-class train. They are delighted by my impressions and the chance to look at their home through my eyes.

We spend the evening talking about race relations and the coming election. They see the present problems as "history," and are quite optimistic about the future. "You cannot change the world overnight," Grushan's uncle says. "We will get the vote. There will be gradual improvement. We do the best we can, with what we have."

What they can't understand is why America should have ethnic problems. In South Africa, the television has constant news clips and special reports on racism in the United States.

Some of the reporting is actually quite good and very insightful. But the slightest incident—a black boy in Alabama is expelled from school, or a black fireman in San Francisco claims discrimination—is played up on the evening news. It is a small wonder that South Africans see the United States as a cauldron of racial tensions.

The hypocritical nature of this is quite obvious: You got problems? Show that the other side has more problems. By the constant reports of racial problems around the world, especially in America, white South Africans can tell themselves that ethnic conflicts are the natural order of society and that discrimination in South Africa is neither unique nor excessive. Of course, most non-white South Africans don't share this view. They are very aware of the inequalities of apartheid, and don't see racial problems in America as comparable in any way. In fact, Grushan's family cannot understand why American blacks have anything to complain about. I try to explain—the history of slavery, the open discrimination until the civil rights movement, the continuing isolation in ghetto cultures, poor schools, etc.—but I am hardly a suitable representative of American black culture. They listen carefully, but they still don't quite get it. I realize that, at least in this group of black South Africans, there is no sense of entitlement. No belief that there must be restitution. No belief that the whites must taste some of the centuries of suffering they have caused for their countrymen. And the very absence of that belief may well save the country.

NOVEMBER 20: CAPE TOWN, SOUTH AFRICA
Seven o'clock in the morning. Dr. Bletcher comes to my house in a battered, yellow pickup truck. In the back there are a few boxes of medicines, dressings, needles, sponges, and cleaning solutions. We drive out on the freeway, then on to pot-holed roads, then dirt tracks, and finally navigate through a maze of crowded shacks, tethered goats, squalling naked children, and

piles of garbage. Without Table Mountain in the distance, I could never find my way out of here.

"We trained a community health worker in each district," he is explaining. "Usually an older woman with local respect. She arranges for people to be seen in order of need. The clinic will be at her house."

We pull up at a well-swept shack with a tree in front. There are about twenty people sitting on benches in its shade, some moaning softly, others cradling limp babies. A matronly woman comes out and helps us carry our supplies inside. Then we take our place with the group and all of us join hands—the sick, the wounded, the mothers—and they begin a church hymn in thanks that Mark and I have come. Everyone sings, even the lame man lying on a board beside me. The sound lifts us together. It lifts away the sickness and despair. The melody is so joyous and the voices so very beautiful. It is too much for me. I have to lower my head in embarrassment as tears roll down my cheeks and drop into the dust at my feet.

The clinic begins. Mark and I are inside and the matron brings in one patient after another. Wounds are cleaned and dressed. Medications are dispensed. Intravenous fluids are given. I help when I can and take notes for those whom Mark will send to the hospital. We work efficiently and I am surprised to see that it is one o'clock when the matron brings in some gruel for us to eat. At three, the patients begin to thin out.

"I'll take care of the rest," Mark tells me. "Why don't you wander around a bit? Don't go far. And I suggest you keep your lab coat on. That way, people will know you're with this clinic."

The coat is filthy from this morning's work and it is uncomfortably hot outside, but I take his advice. It is interesting to get a close hand look at this place. I marvel that people can survive with so little. Some bony young men begin to follow me about ten feet behind, stopping when I stop, gradually moving in. They remind me of wild dogs. Silent, with a cold look in their eyes. Now that lab coat feels like a protective shield. A gaggle of children in rags overcome their shyness and draw close. I formally introduce myself and shake hands with each one. They don't understand a word I'm saying, but they giggle at this gesture and put their little hands into my empty coat pockets. I dearly wish I had something to give them.

NOVEMBER 23: CAPE TOWN, SOUTH AFRICA
Another sleepless night and I am exhausted. In the guise of academic interest, I leave the medicine ward and wander down to the emergency room to talk to the doctors there. At a private moment, I try to briefly describe the bus accident to one of them, and ask what I could have done better.

He shrugs. "There isn't anything you could have done. On the road? Forget it. There isn't a damned thing you can do."

An older doctor, the director of the emergency department, seems sympathetic. I tell him a little more, not just the accident, but my problem sleeping.

"Remember this," he admonishes me. "You did the right thing. You triaged them and then arranged for transport. That's really all one can do. The most important thing that you did was simply to be there. The outcome would have been no different, but you gave them hope and comfort."

Then he adds, "It is not an easy thing to see people die, or to see people badly hurt. You get better at it. Why don't you work with us here? It just might help you."

NOVEMBER 24: CAPE TOWN, SOUTH AFRICA
On the train this afternoon, I'm reading the *Argus*, the main newspaper of Cape Town. Yesterday, there was a clash between the police and some militants not far from here. Over thirty people were killed. This story is not even on page one, but buried away in the second section. Instead, today's big headline is about the latest evidence in the investigation of a murder in a love triangle.

A white murder, of course. It seems that the husband was unfortunately shot by a crossbow soon after he discovered that his wife was romantically involved with her church minister. The urgent news today is that the murder weapon was purchased by someone whose description is a lot like the minister.

NOVEMBER 25: CAPE TOWN, SOUTH AFRICA

Earlier today, I hiked to the top of Table Mountain. The rugged trail was a good workout. Maybe the physical exertion will help clear my head. As I got to the level plain of the summit, a cold wind and fog abruptly enveloped me. The guidebook says this is a common weather pattern. It warns that many people get in trouble from disorientation or hypothermia from hiking there and suggests going only in a well-prepared group. I am not worried about the cold or being out alone, and disregard the warnings. On some level, I am aware that I have become detached from the environment. It just doesn't seem that real, so it is hard for me to take the guidebook seriously. The strenuous hike has left me feeling invigorated and stronger emotionally.

Now it is night and I am at the ER. "Come at dusk," the director told me. "That is when the real action starts." I learn a few useful phrases. *Ipi indau ebu shungu* is Xhosa for "Where is the pain?"

Sure enough, the injuries intensify with the night. Stabbings. *Panga* wounds from fights with machete-like bush knives. Later, a tribal man is brought in with a spear through his thigh. I help staunch the bleeding and assist in the surgery. The patients are remarkably stoic. None of them cries out. The men, especially, make no sound at all, just a tightening of the throat even during an excruciating procedure.

As long as I am doing something technical, I try to focus on the task and do it as well as I can. But when I am with vacant, feverish patients, or children crying from unending hurt, I feel an overwhelming helplessness.

NOVEMBER 30: CAPE TOWN, SOUTH AFRICA

Hiking again. With each step, I feel like I am going somewhere. Although, of course, I know I am going nowhere. I can't bear to go back to the suffering at the hospital. Already, everything seems too illusory, like being trapped in an annoying dream that doesn't really hurt you but won't go away.

It is hard enough to get a handle on what I am doing in Cape Town, but the work in the ER seems even more unreal. Suffering patients are actors in some drama that I stumbled into and don't understand. Those who die no longer affect me. They are just corpses. Cadavers. They once were alive. Now they're dead. So what?

I have lost sight of what I am doing here.

When I try to sleep, the trauma at the ER seems to be in another world, forgotten, but the jabbering Arabic is always there. Always inside me.

DECEMBER 11: CAPE TOWN, SOUTH AFRICA

All I have left is to walk. My legs feel like spring leaf steel, and walking is almost effortless. I walk day and night now. It doesn't matter where or for what reason or for no reason at all. I walk in a rapid, nervous, striding clip as if an electrical current is being discharged through my limbs. Sometimes I hear gun shots. I pass new cars with the windows smashed in. The elections have been delayed and tensions are increasing. Even the *Argus* is reporting the violence that has spread into the city. I don't care. Maybe it would be better if I was beaten up or killed. I doubt if I would resist.

Andrew invites me to party in Clifton, a pretty beach town on the other side of the peninsula. The only way is to drive around Devil's Peak, Table Mountain, and Signal Hill. But why not walk straight across? Four hours later, well after dark, I show up at the party. There was no trail for the last couple of miles, so I tramped straight through the thornbush. I'm dressed in shorts and my legs are badly scratched and bleeding. Andrew is aghast that I hiked over the mountains at night. The others at the party are not just impressed; they think I am a lunatic.

DECEMBER 14: CAPE TOWN, SOUTH AFRICA

I feel totally lost today. The sky is threatening thunderstorms. I've got to push something to the limit. Something has to got to give. In mounting wind and freezing rain, I climb to the top of Devil's Peak. The clouds roll in, it begins to hail and then the air is screaming and ripping at my clothes. I cower at the base of the stone marker at the summit, staring into the storm. I have come so far. So far, for nothing. It is the end of the road and all I have found is my own emptiness. I would do anything, accept anything, if there was a purpose to my being here, or at least a sign. Anything. But there is nothing here except the freezing wind.

DECEMBER 16: CAPE TOWN, SOUTH AFRICA

The Zulu Chief Buthelezi announces that he will not be subservient to the African National Council headed by Nelson Mandela, who is from the Xhosa tribe. He wants KwaZulu, his region of the country, to be an independent state. I watch him on television, strutting around pompously in his leopard-skin robe. He claims to be a peacemaker and, to demonstrate his beneficent diplomacy, he adds a teenage Xhosa girl to his many wives. The National party of the white government, everyone suspects, is supporting Buthelezi as a balance to the ANC. On the other side of the hall, the white Conservative party wants to split the country along ethnic lines, like Northern Ireland. All of the newspapers are warning of the possibility of civil war.

Somehow, I feel entirely empathetic when I study this unfolding scene. Everyone is confused, nervous, frightened and ready to fight but not sure for whom or for exactly what purpose.

I sit at home and read *The Washing of the Spears: The Rise and Fall of the Zulu Nation,* by Donald Morris. It is an engrossing account of Victorian-era global politics. South African history is incredibly complex and involved much more than a struggle between colonizing Europeans and native Africans. The great Boer wars were not even between white and black, but between the Dutch farmers and the British merchants and industrialists. Some of the most renowned literary and political figures of the century had a role in shaping this country: Kipling, Gandhi, Mark Twain, even Will Rogers started his career in South Africa. Winston Churchill fought in the Boer wars and hardened himself as a prisoner of war. Even Sir Arthur Conan Doyle was heavily influenced by his time here and wrote *The Great Boer War.* The history of South Africa is a microcosm of the history of the western world.

But today, the pieces of the puzzle lie next to each other, unmatched and unconnected. It is as if six nations occupy the same country. Everyone wants what the Afrikaners call the *lekker lewe,* the good life. But no one knows how it will be possible to satisfy each of the many factions. All the different groups of people in this country are scared. Afraid to lose what they have, and afraid of not getting what they never had.

And I float through this fear, like a journalist in a war zone. I am also afraid, but of what? I feel like six men, occupying the same body.

DECEMBER 20: CAPE TOWN, SOUTH AFRICA
I have hiked every trail now. My loneliness is making me withdrawn. I find it hard to talk to people even as I crave their company. It is easier to be alone. My life has become utterly pointless.

DECEMBER 25: CAPE TOWN, SOUTH AFRICA
Christmas Day. Andrew has gone home to his family. It is hot and the beaches are likely to be crowded. I sit inside all day and read history books.

December 26: Cape Town, South Africa

On the road near the hospital, someone yells my name. It can't be for me, so I keep walking. Then someone pulls alongside in a ratty old car. It is Grushan.

Always happy. I have never seen Grushan with any other expression, even when he has just worked thirty-six hours straight.

"Come with me," he says. "I want to hear what you have been doing!"

We sit in a coffee shop and I try to pretend that life is fine and that I am doing what I came here for. But it isn't working. So I give up and tell him about the bus accident and my depression, and that I believe I have lost my way. He looks at me closely.

"No," he says. "You were lost long, long ago. There is too much sorrow in you."

"Grushan. How do you do it? How do you keep happy when you see so much suffering? How do you know which direction to go? How do you find your way?"

"I have an automatic direction finder."

"You have an Automatic Direction Finder? An ADF?? *What!!!*" This is absolutely absurd. Now I feel like my worlds have collided. I've totally lost my grip on reality. There is a faint buzzing in the room and I am aware of every tiny sound of the click of silverware and rustling of clothes and breathing of the other customers. I stare at Grushan incredulously, uncomfortably, dumbfounded by my confusion.

Grushan is startled by my reaction.

"Yes," he continues and points his finger to the ceiling.

He goes on, "There is something that automatically shows me the right direction. It is not really from up there," he laughs, "and it is not in here either," and taps his finger to his chest, "and it is not out there," and waves his arms to the room. "I just know. I listen, and I just know."

He looks at me in a fatherly manner, even though I must be a decade his senior.

"Paul. You have so much energy and a good heart. But you don't listen. The Lord has given you strength. If you listen, He will also point the way."

"Grushan, you know I don't believe in God."

He laughs, gently, as if I was kidding him, and clasps his hand on my forearm. "Keep in touch," he says softly and leaves.

DECEMBER 27: CAPE TOWN, SOUTH AFRICA
The thought of another day of aimless pacing makes me anxious. Maybe I should get out of town. I stride over to a Back Packer youth hostel on the other side of the city, where there are sometimes interesting travel notices. Among the guests from England and Australia are a couple of young men from Germany. They work for an international relief organization and have a semi-truck with sixty tons of milk powder and dried foods for the famine in Angola. But that country is in a civil war, so they have been waiting in Cape Town for over a month. They are ready to go up at least to Namibia in the chance that they can unload the food near the Angolan border. When they learn that I can drive the truck, they ask me to come along.

DECEMBER 28: CAPE TOWN, SOUTH AFRICA
We set off this morning to drive the thousand miles to Windhoek, the capital of Namibia. It feels great to be on the road, with an expectant feeling of going somewhere. The wine country of Stellenbosch, north of the Cape, gives way to ranch lands and desert. A hundred years ago, the Boers trekked through here on their long march to freedom, in wagon trains remarkably like those of the American pioneers. The modern highway follows the wagon route for a while and then continues north to Namibia. We drive all day and into the night through the trackless desert of the Kalahari.

December 29: Windhoek, Namibia

The German boys and I sit around outdoor cafes in Windhoek, drinking beer. They are a good-natured pair and I am happy to be in their company. Because they are from Munich, their dialect is quite similar to Swiss and talking with them makes me feel a little like I am with my brothers.

December 30: Windhoek, Namibia

The food has been delivered to the border and the Germans have taken a flight home. Suddenly I am alone again. It is too late to make any plans. The hotels are full, so I walk to the outskirts of the city at the edge of the desert, where there is a guest house for laborers. At night, this un-airconditioned, dilapidated shack is crowded with a dozen bunks to a room.

Now it is after midnight. I lie in my bunk and listen to the others snore. It is impossible to sleep. I get up and walk out into the darkness.

I wonder what that Egyptian man was saying. He was in shock. Probably delirious. It could have been anything. Most likely gibberish. Did he see anything in that last glimpse of life? Why was he astonished? Maybe it was just physical. An adrenaline surge of circulatory failure could make his pupils dilate. But why that very clear, very aware look of surprise? There is something he discovered, I'm sure. Something we will not find until it is our turn to die. Now I know why people kill themselves. They can no longer look at that closed door; they just have to step through.

But at the same time, he was looking right at me. Maybe that is what bothers me so much. He was astonished at something he saw and yet he was looking at me, trying to tell me something, maybe ... the thought gives me a slight chill. There is something the Egyptian man understood about him and me. The two of us, together on the pavement.

My life has been a mess. But is it really so unusual? I

haven't had it any harder than most people. I've really got nothing to complain about. Maybe I fought a bit more than other people. I refused to accept what was given to me by fate, but I haven't actually gained that much more. All the hard work, the loneliness, the search for some sort of integrity to my life. It has all come down to this: a sweaty sleepless night in a bunkhouse in Namibia.

These last months have just been a downward spiral to expose my emptiness. I can deal with pain. I can tolerate any hardship. If I had to, I would walk the length of Africa. But I can't deal with the emptiness.

I sit in the quiet darkness on a bank of sandstone. All my life, I have had only myself to believe in. I have depended on nothing and no one. Not family, not nature, nothing. Like Zorba, I don't believe in anything except myself.

*I believe in Zorba because he's the only being I have in
my power, the only one I know. All the rest are ghosts.*

My father had everything to believe in. He had a wife and nine children. He had a house and farm and a career that gave him a great sense of achievement. Most of all, he had his religious faith. There was never a question in his mind about his purpose in life. And he died. Now I am the age at which he died and I have nothing to believe in. But I am alive.

What my father really had, more than anything, was a sense of home. He felt connected. He *was* connected. A large family depended on him, but he also felt responsible for a much greater group of people. He loved the common effort, whether it was the war or the church or the local community. His career was his way of trying to lead a productive life, of improving life for all people. When he was dying, from what my mother told me, it was the work left undone that bothered him so much more than the coming end of his own life.

In comparison, my whole life, my journey and my worries

seem so childish. A baby thinks it is the only thing in the universe and that everything else exists just to nurture it and meet its needs. But somewhere in childhood, I realized that I had to take care of myself. Now, I'm not so sure I ever grew out of that phase. I took care of myself, all right, but that is all I did. I made my own way in life. If there was a problem, there was always a simple, defiant solution—I left. I left my family. I left my country. I can't even remember how many jobs I've left. Somewhere, sometime, I believed, I would find a home. But the only place I have ever felt at home was in an airplane cockpit.

In the faint starlight, I walk farther into the empty desert and climb up a stony outcrop. At the top, there is a patch of bare rock to sit on and I gaze out at the distant horizon. My friends are envious when they hear of my travels and adventures. I realize now that there has been a price to pay for all that freedom. I've never really committed to anything or anyone. I've succeeded in surviving, but in the process I got disconnected from anything more meaningful in life.

I have never expected anything from anyone and I never gave anything. The first rule of survival is to not trust anyone. But without trust, you are truly alone. Somewhere inside of me a well of sadness opens. I know that I've cut myself off and it is destroying me.

Half my life, I've longed for some sense of position in the world, for a father, for Trix, for a family, for a career with integrity. And yet, there was never any need for these longings. My home was always with me. All I needed to do was to look around me. To be with the people I was with, and to trust them. Everywhere I have been, I have met people, good-hearted, kind, wonderful people, who have opened their hearts to me. I don't know how I could have been so blind to them. People who trusted me, implicitly. Now I know exactly what that Egyptian man was trying to tell me. I know what he meant when his eyes caught me. He looked at me as a friend. In those few minutes, I became a brother who shared the most personal and sacred moment in his life. As he lay dying on the pavement, he knew that the only thing he had was that last glimpse of awareness before he surrendered to the oncoming rush of infinity. There, at daybreak, he clung to me. He chose to share with me what was left of his life. His message could not be more obvious. It is time for me to share mine.

An expectant glow is appearing on the east horizon. I watch as it slowly erupts and floods the sky with a brilliant silvery light. My feelings of emptiness and despair gradually lift off me. They float up and dissipate into the night. I am no longer sad, despondent, or lonely. I am just a man, watching the moon rise over the Kalahari Desert.

Chapter 18

GLOBAL POSITIONING SYSTEM

DECEMBER 31: WINDHOEK, NAMIBIA

At daybreak, I collect my things and walk the few miles into town. I have come to the end of my journey. It is time for me to go back to America.

The bus to Cape Town is a luxurious double-decker land yacht with large viewing windows on the upper level and waiters that bring refreshments. It departs Windhoek in the evening and drives through the night to escape the daytime heat of the desert. Because the Kalahari is not a good place to be stranded, these buses travel in a convoy of two, one of them towing a trailer with enough equipment and spare parts to do justice to a well-stocked service station. The dry air and absence of lights in the desert should make for superb star-gazing tonight. I am lucky to get a front row seat overhead of the driver, like being on the bridge of a ship.

The constellations of the northern hemisphere are embellished with the ancient myths of love and war. Stars of the far south, however, were not known to the civilizations of Babylon and Greece. When the European explorers began their voyages to the Americas, to Asia, and to Africa, they had to invent new constellations for the unfamiliar heavens. Today, the organization of the southern night sky is largely due to the work of one man, the French astronomer Nicolas-Louis de Lacaille. On an expedition to the Cape of Good Hope two hundred years ago, Lacaille put together a catalog of ten thousand stars. He then grouped them into constellations, whimsically named after his favorite objects: Antlia (the air pump), Fornax (furnace), Horologium (clock), Octans (octant, precursor of the sextant— Sextans had already been named) and, of course, Telescopium. He named Mensa (table) after Table Mountain. And now, with Lacaille in my thoughts, I am also on my way to the Cape.

Astronomy was the key to global navigation in that era. The colonial empires were built on accurate surveys of lands and borders and the commerce among them. The sextant became the symbol of the great voyage. After Lacaille, the earth became one world, with no place too mysterious or remote. Explorers, with their sextants in hand, raced to stand on the last remaining sites: the head of the Nile, the source of the Amazon, the North Pole, and the South Pole. It was all done by the clever art of celestial navigation. The stars became a road map to those who could read them.

Now this wonderful skill of navigation is almost obsolete. There is a new instrument available: the Global Positioning System. GPS started as an American military system to guide aircraft and missiles by signals from twenty-four orbiting satellites. With the end of the cold war, this high-precision navigational system was made available to the public. GPS receivers became smaller and cheaper. Today, with an inexpensive hand-held instrument, you can see your exact position anywhere on the planet. Celestial navigation will follow other old skills, like Morse code or using a slide rule, into the dust heap of history.

Soon GPS units will be ubiquitous. They will be built into everything from cars, telephones, and pagers, to wrist watches and clothing, and even glued onto the skin of animals and fish. The navigational men of the cockpit: the ADF, the Loran, the VOR, and even the Glideslope—they will be let go. So long, boys. Ya done a good job. GPS, the invisible global system, will replace them all.

Night has fallen and there is a gorgeous display in front of me. Beyond the shadowy plains of sand, there is an ultraviolet fringe on the horizon and then the vast dome of the heavens scintillating with countless stars. Crux, the Southern Cross, points the way.

A few hours out, the bus abruptly slows and then rolls to a stop. An announcement: our companion bus behind us has a mechanical problem. Probably a torn fan belt. We will stop here for about an hour. All hundred and fifty passengers of the two buses spill into the quiet, balmy night. The dimmed lights of the buses glow like ships on an ocean.

A couple of Dutch geologists amble over.

"Helluva way to spend New Year's Eve," one says to me, "but look at this ..." he waves his arms at the sky. "This is more beautiful than any fireworks."

He points out some stars, and we talk about their names and what we know about them. A British missionary couple draws close to hear. A few Japanese tourists politely listen to us. More people are attracted by our gesticulations and the group of heads following our waving arms and soon we have a large audience. More Europeans, a few Ovango men, a collection of Xhosa, Khoikhoi, San, and !Kung families with their melodious click languages.

Our home galaxy, the Milky Way, spills a broad creamy stream above us and a Khoikhoi woman is pointing to it and saying something. The Dutch geologist asks her teenage son to translate for us:

"This was the path of the first children of the great spirit, the path toward the rising Sun, when the rocks were only mud." Moving her finger along the irregular course, she exclaims, "See the footprints they left!"

As luck would have it, the Magellanic Clouds are centered right before us. We are seeing light that left that galaxy 160,000 years ago. Just about the time, the geologist says, that modern humans evolved from a single African woman. Earlier this century, Sir Raymond Dart discovered the bones of *Australopithecus,* the ancestors of humans, just a few miles from here.

The stillness of the night settles upon us, and people drift off into their own thoughts. I look at their silhouettes in the faint glow of the buses. We represent the great tribes of the world. On this beautiful night, we have come together to gaze on light emitted when the first humans walked on this very ground.

JANUARY 2: JOHANNESBURG, SOUTH AFRICA
Early this morning after my arrival at the bus station, I talked to a taxi driver waiting outside the terminal. Isaac Morifi, from the Sotho tribe. We worked out an arrangement: for thirty dollars, we will spend the day together, meter off, just driving around the city, the townships and anywhere that looks interesting. I just want to get a feel for this place and it seems like a nice way to spend the day.

Isaac is a slender man in his fifties, the color of weathered mahogany, with a thoughtful and gracious manner. He speaks English well, a consequence of decades of carrying fares to the whites-only suburbs. I ask him if he minds driving into the dangerous parts of the city. Isaac laughs, "There is no part of Jo'burg that is strange to me. I'll show you!"

The city sprawls over the red bluffs and craters of depleted gold mines. This is the industrial heart of South Africa. If there is going to be a civil war in this country, it is here that it will begin. We pass white stucco neighborhoods, with little parks where elderly men in spats are playing at lawn bowling. I watch for a few minutes. In between plays, young black attendants in starched shirts dart out from the sidelines to tidy up the field, and then quickly return to a discreet distance. This is the South

Africa I had heard about. But things have changed. Just a block further, there is spray-painted graffiti on the walls, "DEATH TO WHITES," and the streets are deserted.

Later in the day Isaac takes me to his home, a shed-like concrete structure in the township of Soweto. We sit next to his car and drink beer in the muggy heat. He tells me about coming from his tribal homeland as a newly wed young man, desperate for a job. He and his wife were not allowed into the city without a special pass. For years, they were forced to live in a series of makeshift squatter camps. These were occasionally bulldozed on the whim of the government, or terrorized by gangs of police, sometimes on official duty, sometimes not. In one of the raids, his wife was killed by a white policeman.

I am at a loss for words, and feel slightly uncomfortable. I wonder if he considers me to be like one of his white fares to the restricted areas of the city. To change the subject, I ask him what he thinks of the coming elections.

"I don't want majority rule. Look at what happened in Zimbabwe. Now Jo'burg is full of refugees from there. I want to vote, yes, but I want the white government to stay." He continues in his slow, measured voice with the singsong Sotho accent, "I've worked all my life for what I have. For this house. For my daughter. I never went to school, but I made sure that my daughter can go. She is a smart girl. She has taught me to read. Now she wants to be a lawyer. I think it is possible. But for that we must have a strong government. We cannot have fighting. We *must* work together."

"Isaac, how can you let it go so easily? How can you not hate the whites for what they did to you?"

"Do you know what is courage?" He fixes me with a look.

"Well … I think I do. I'm not sure. I've wondered if I had enough courage to face my fears."

"Yes," he gazes at me, "You have faced danger, I think. But that is not courage. Maybe you can call that bravery. Courage is something different."

"What is courage, then?"

"I'll tell you. It is doing what is disagreeable to you, but what must be done. Courage is living every day without giving in to your anger and your boredom and your frustration and your fears. It takes more courage to empty the shit bucket every day than it does to kill a lion. To do it every day, for years, without running away."

JANUARY 3: JOHANNESBURG, SOUTH AFRICA

Jan Smuts Airport. It is an eighteen-hour flight to New York and then San Francisco. There is a young tribal man in the next seat, a little uncomfortable in a cheap blue suit and tie that hangs stiffly on his thin frame. It is his first time in an airplane. His eyes light up when I open my backpack.

"The first thing you have to learn about the airlines," I tell him, "is that the food is not very good and they never give you enough. Here, have some of this." It is a long way to America and I have packed some *biltong*, dried strips of spiced meat, smoked snook fish, biscuits and chutney.

"I am from the Transkei," he says. "I have a scholarship to Columbia University. They say there are many black people in New York, so I will feel at home. But I know that it will be very different. It will be a new life for me."

"Yes," I agree, "we are going to a new life."

POSTSCRIPT

In the spring of 1993, Mike came to stay with me in California. Within a few months, he sailed through his basic and advanced flight training. He is now an airline pilot stationed in Sarajevo, Bosnia.

Grushan went on to be a missionary physician in his tribal homelands near Zimbabwe. We kept in touch by mail. In 1995, there was guerrilla fighting in the area and a number of missionaries were killed. I have not been able to find out what happened to Grushan. My letters to him have come back undelivered and I fear the worst.

Trix and I have kept close even as our lives have taken us down separate roads. She is busy with her creation of a successful new health practice in Switzerland, a blend of physiotherapy and Jungian psychology.

After my return, I attended medical school at the University of California, Davis, and completed the clinical training to become an M.D. Following a residency in Hawaii, I went to work in rural clinics in the Pacific Islands and in Alaska. I work as a relief physician, for a few days, a couple of weeks, or sometimes months. I never did find a home. And yet, home is every-where. Wherever I am—whether it is the Marshall Islands, putting an intravenous catheter by lamp-light into the scalp of a febrile baby, or the sterile cardiac unit of an Alaska hospital comforting an elderly native American man dying of heart failure—I have the sense that I am with the people I love. It is not the home I always imagined. And yet, I suppose it is where I belong.

My assistance is often required in a medivac flight. And sometimes, when the patient is stable, I am invited to come forward and once again take the controls in the cockpit.